INTERNATIONAL RELATIONS
BETWEEN
THE TWO WORLD WARS
1919–1939

harper 🔥 torchbooks

*A reference-list of Harper Torchbooks, classified
by subjects, is printed at the end of this volume.*

INTERNATIONAL RELATIONS
BETWEEN
THE TWO WORLD WARS
1919–1939

BY

E. H. CARR

HARPER TORCHBOOKS ❧ The Academy Library
Harper & Row, Publishers, New York

CONTENTS

INTRODUCTION

PART I—THE PERIOD OF ENFORCEMENT: THE ALLIANCES (1920–24)

CHAPTER 1

CHAPTER 2

CHAPTER 3

CONTENTS

PART II—THE PERIOD OF PACIFICATION: THE LEAGUE OF NATIONS (1924–30)

CHAPTER 4

CHAPTER 5

CHAPTER 6

PART III—THE PERIOD OF CRISIS: THE RETURN OF POWER POLITICS (1930–33)

CHAPTER 7

CONTENTS

CHAPTER 8

CHAPTER 9

PART IV—THE RE-EMERGENCE OF GERMANY: THE END OF THE TREATIES (1933-39)

CHAPTER 10

CHAPTER 11

CHAPTER 12

CONTENTS

CHAPTER 13

LIST OF MAPS

INTRODUCTION
THE PEACE SETTLEMENT

INTRODUCTION

INTRODUCTION : THE PEACE SETTLEMENT

THE duration of the first world war was rather more than four years and three months—from July 28th, 1914, when Austria-Hungary declared war on Serbia, to November 11th, 1918, when the Allies granted Germany an armistice. After the armistice, five more years were required to complete the general peace settlement. In 1919 the Allied and Associated Powers concluded the Treaty of Versailles with Germany (June 28th), the Treaty of St. Germain with Austria (September 10th) and the Treaty of Neuilly with Bulgaria (November 27th), and in 1920 the Treaty of Trianon with Hungary (June 4th). It was not until July 23rd, 1923, that the final treaty of peace with Turkey was signed at Lausanne ; and with the coming into force of this treaty on August 6th, 1924, peace was at last formally re-established throughout the world. In the meanwhile the Powers interested in the Pacific had assembled at Washington in the winter of 1921–22 and concluded a series of treaties designed to establish on a firm basis the *status quo* in the Far East. All these treaties, together with a host of minor treaties and agreements arising out of them, may be said to constitute the peace settlement. Almost every important political event of an international character in the period between the first and second world wars was the direct or indirect product of this settlement; and it is therefore necessary to begin our study with a brief survey of its most outstanding features.

THE EUROPEAN SETTLEMENT

The Treaty of Versailles had certain special characteristics which determined much of its subsequent history.

In the first place it was, in a phrase made familiar by German propaganda, a " dictated peace ". It was imposed by the victors on the vanquished, not negotiated by a process of give-and-take between them. Nearly every treaty which brings a war to an end is, in one sense, a dictated peace ; for a defeated Power seldom accepts willingly the consequences of its defeat. But in the Treaty of Versailles the element of dictation was more apparent than in any previous peace treaty of modern times. The German Delegation at Versailles were allowed to submit one set of written comments on the draft treaty presented to them. Some of those comments were taken into account ; and the revised text was then handed to them with the threat that war would be resumed if it were not signed within five days. No member of the German Delegation met the Allied delegates face to face except on the two formal occasions of the presentation of the draft and the signature of the treaty. Even on these occasions the ordinary courtesies of social intercourse were not observed. At the ceremony of signature, the two German signatories were not allowed to sit with the Allied delegates at the table, but were escorted in and out of the hall in the manner of criminals conducted to and from the dock. These unnecessary humiliations, which could only be explained by the intense bitterness of feeling still left over from the war, had far-reaching psychological consequences, both in Germany and elsewhere. They fixed in the consciousness of the German people the conception of a "dictated peace"; and they helped to create the belief, which became universal in Germany and was tacitly accepted by a large body of opinion in other countries, that the signature extorted from Germany in these conditions was not morally binding on her.

Secondly, the Treaty of Versailles, unlike any previous treaty of peace, was professedly based on a number of general principles enunciated during the war, the most famous of these, President Wilson's Fourteen Points, having been formally accepted by Germany before the armistice as the basis of the settlement. Thanks mainly to Wilson's insistence on these principles, the treaty was founded on a substructure of genuine idealism. It provided for the creation of a League of Nations, whose primary purpose was to ensure the maintenance of peace; of an International Labour Organisation for the regulation of labour conditions; and of a mandatory system of government for the colonies to be ceded by Germany. These institutions became after 1919 a regular and essential part of the new world order. Other results of the attempt of the treaty-makers to blend idealism with the exigencies of the victorious Powers were, however, less fortunate. It was not difficult for critics to discredit certain parts of the treaty by comparing them with the text of the Fourteen Points. It was perhaps open to question whether the territories ceded by Germany to Poland included only those " inhabited by indisputably Polish populations ", or whether the taking away of all Germany's overseas possessions was " a free, open-minded and absolutely impartial adjustment of all colonial claims " ; and the prohibition of a union between Germany and Austria was indefensible once the Allies had announced the self-determination of peoples as the guiding principle of the territorial settlement. These and other discrepancies between principle and practice gave an easy handle to those who wished to argue that the Versailles Treaty was a tainted document and that the Allies had violated the conditions on which the armistice was concluded.

The servitudes imposed on Germany in the Treaty of Versailles were eventually, with few exceptions, abrogated either by agreement, or by lapse of time, or by repudiation on the part of Germany. The most important of them (penalties, reparation, demilitarised zone, disarmament) will be discussed in later chapters. Here it is only necessary to summarise the European territorial provisions. In the west, Germany restored Alsace and Lorraine to France, ceded two tiny fragments of territory at Eupen and Malmédy to Belgium, and renounced her former customs union with Luxemburg. The coal-mining area of the Saar was placed under the administration of a League of Nations Commission for fifteen years, at the end of which time its fate was to be decided by a plebiscite. The mines were transferred to French ownership by way of compensation for French coal-fields devastated during the war. In the south, Germany ceded a small strip of

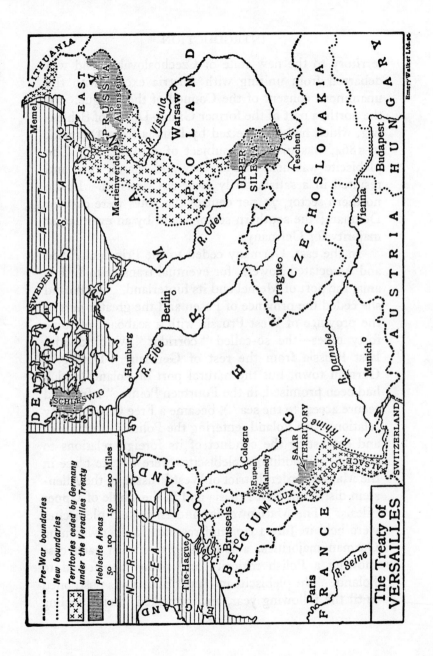

The Treaty of
VERSAILLES

Pre-War boundaries
New boundaries
Territories ceded by Germany
under the Versailles Treaty
Plebiscite Areas

0   50   100   150   200 Miles

Emery Walker Ltd. sc.

territory to the new state of Czechoslovakia, and was debarred from uniting with Austria except with the unanimous consent of the Council of the League. In the north, a part of the former Grand-Duchy of Schleswig, which had been seized by Prussia from Denmark in 1864, was made the subject of a plebiscite. The plebiscite was held in February and March 1920 and resulted in a satisfactorily clear-cut decision. In the northern sector, 75 per cent of the votes were cast for Denmark; the southern sector voted by an even larger majority for Germany.

In the east, Germany ceded to the Principal Allied and Associated Powers, for eventual transfer to Lithuania, the port of Memel and its hinterland. To Poland she ceded the province of Posen and the greater part of the province of West Prussia with a seaboard of some forty miles—the so-called " corridor " which divides East Prussia from the rest of Germany. Danzig, a German town, but the natural port of Poland (which had been promised, in the Fourteen Points, " a free and secure access to the sea "), became a Free City in treaty relations with Poland, entering the Polish customs area and entrusting the conduct of its foreign relations to Poland. In addition, plebiscites were to take place in the Marienwerder district of West Prussia, in the Allenstein district of East Prussia and in the whole of Upper Silesia. The Marienwerder and Allenstein plebiscites were held in July 1920, and resulted in overwhelming German majorities, a few villages only in each case showing a Polish majority and being transferred to Poland. The plebiscite in Upper Silesia was postponed until the following year, and provoked intense feeling and serious outbreaks of violence on both sides. Unlike the other plebiscite districts, Upper Silesia was rich in coal and iron and contained a large, densely populated industrial area. The vote proved inconclusive. About 60 per cent of the votes were cast for Germany, about 40 per cent for Poland. But apart from certain clearly defined rural areas, the result was a patchwork which rendered a decision extremely difficult. The British and Italian Commissioners on one side, and the French Commissioner on the other, submitted widely divergent recommendations. The Supreme Council of the Allied Powers failed to agree and, by an unhappy inspiration, referred the matter to the Council of the League. The Council, after another threatened deadlock, made an approximately equal compromise between the line proposed by the French Commissioner and that proposed by the British and Italian Commissioners. Since the British-Italian line had been a careful attempt to reproduce as closely as was practicable the results of the vote, whereas the French line showed a marked partiality for Polish claims, the decision of the Council was not defensible on grounds of strict equity. It was received with indignation in Germany, and did much to prejudice German opinion against the League during its early years. The territorial clauses of the Versailles Treaty involved the loss by Germany in Europe of more than 25,000 square miles of territory and nearly seven million inhabitants.

The other European peace treaties can be more briefly dealt with.

The collapse of the Austro-Hungarian Monarchy in November 1918 left German Austria an isolated and ill-proportioned remnant. Of its 7,000,000 inhabitants more than 2,000,000 were congregated in Vienna. Bohemia, Moravia and Austrian Silesia had broken away to form the nucleus of Czechoslovakia. Slovenia had joined Serbia and Croatia to form the Yugoslav state. Italy had occupied Trieste and its immediate hinterland. The Treaty of St. Germain did little but register these accomplished facts. Its only two provisions which conspicuously contradicted the principle of self-determination were the prohibition, repeated from the Treaty of Versailles, on union between Austria and Germany, and the cession to Italy of the purely German-speaking South Tyrol, which was designed to give Italy the strategic frontier of the Brenner. But Austria's economic plight was so dire (for many months Vienna was literally starving) that the political humiliations of the peace were scarcely felt. The Allies, fearing that the movement for union with Germany would assume uncontrollable dimensions, made no serious attempt to apply the non-territorial provisions of the treaty ; and the Austrian Reparation Commission transformed itself into a relief organisation.

The ancient kingdom of Hungary, of whose 17,000,000 inhabitants little more than half were Hungarian, had also dissolved into its ethnic components. The Treaty of Trianon confirmed the transfer of Slovakia to Czechoslovakia, of Croatia to Yugoslavia and of Transylvania to Roumania. In the main these decisions were just. But the frontiers of Hungary, even more markedly than the eastern frontier of Germany, bear witness to a certain eagerness on the part of the treaty-makers to stretch their principles wherever possible to the advantage of the Allied and the detriment of the enemy country. The cumulative effect of this elasticity was considerable ; and full use has been made by Hungarian propagandists of these minor injustices.

The losses of Bulgaria were almost as severe as those of Hungary. But most of them dated, not from the peace settlement of 1919, but from that of 1913 which ended the second Balkan War. In the first Balkan War of 1912, Bulgaria had combined with Serbia, Greece and Roumania to expel Turkey from the Balkans and drive her back to a line some fifty miles from Constantinople. But the victors fell out over the division of the spoil. In the second Balkan War, Bulgaria was simultaneously attacked by her three former Allies and by Turkey, and in the resulting treaty was compelled to cede territory to all four of them. The Treaty of Neuilly in 1919 confirmed Bulgaria's losses. It modified still further to her disadvantage the frontiers with Serbia and Greece, and left untouched the palpably unjust 1913 frontier with Roumania. The most keenly felt of all Bulgaria's grievances was the loss of Macedonia, which had been the price promised to her for her participation in the first Balkan War ; and here we touch on a territorial problem different in character from any hitherto discussed. It might be difficult to fix an equitable frontier between Germany and Poland, or between Hungary and Roumania ; but there was at least no doubt about the racial character of the populations involved. In Macedonia, this preliminary point was the subject of bitter controversy. The Macedonians were a people of Slav stock, whose national consciousness was weak or non-existent and whose dialect shaded off into Serbian on one side and into Bulgarian on the other. In time they could be made indifferently into good Serbs or good Bulgarians. The settlement of 1913, confirmed in 1919, had given the greater part of Macedonia to Serbia, and most of the remainder to Greece. But the Macedonians were a primitive people among whom brigandage was held in honour. The stalwart among them fled to Bulgaria and formed there a Macedonian Revolutionary Organisation, which conducted periodical raids in Yugoslav or Greek territory, terrorised the population on both sides of the frontier, and embittered relations between Bulgaria and her neighbours for more than ten years after the war. During this period, life and property were probably less secure in Macedonia than in any other part of Europe.

The only other provision of the Treaty of Neuilly which requires mention here is the clause by which the Allies undertook " to ensure the economic outlets of Bulgaria to the Aegean Sea ". The Bulgarians interpreted this to mean, as in the case of Poland, a territorial corridor. The Allies offered a free zone for Bulgaria in one of the Greek ports. The Bulgarians preferred no bread to half a loaf; and nothing was ever done to carry this disputed clause into effect.

Lastly, it should be mentioned that the newly created states—Poland and Czechoslovakia—as well as other states which had received large accessions of territory—Yugoslavia, Roumania and Greece—were required to conclude with the Principal Allied and Associated Powers treaties under which they guaranteed to the " racial, religious and linguistic minorities " residing in their territories political rights, religious freedom, the provision of schools, and the use of their language before the courts and in their dealings with the authorities. Similar provisions were included in the treaties of peace with Austria, Hungary, Bulgaria and Turkey. Germany was not asked to subscribe to any minority obligations. Ironically enough, this was almost the only respect in which the peace-makers of Versailles recognised Germany's equality of status with the other Great Powers.

THE NEAR EAST AND AFRICA

The Treaty of Lausanne, concluded with Turkey in July 1923, is the only one of the peace treaties which, for thirteen years, was accepted as valid and applicable by all its signatories and which, even in 1936 (see p. 214), was modified only by voluntary agreement and in one particular. Historically it owed this advantage to several factors which distinguished it from the other peace treaties. It came into being nearly five years after the end of hostilities when bitter passions had had time to abate ; it was not imposed, but negotiated by a long process of bargaining between the parties ; and it was signed, not in an Allied capital, but on neutral territory. It may be well to recapitulate here the long and complicated series of events by which this happy conclusion was reached.

In May 1919, while the Peace Conference, in the intervals of its more pressing preoccupation with Germany, was discussing the future of Turkey, Venizelos, the Greek Prime Minister, persuaded the Allies to allow

13

Greek troops to occupy Smyrna in Asia Minor. The Turks bitterly resented this violation of their territory, long after the armistice, by the most implacable and most despised of their enemies. From this resentment a widespread movement of national revolt was born, and found a capable and powerful leader in Mustapha Kemal. Within a year the Kemalists had swept the whole country, and only the presence of an Allied garrison kept a puppet Turkish Government in being at Constantinople. Undeterred by this warning, the Allied Powers signed at Sèvres in August 1920 a treaty of peace with the Constantinople Government. It was constructed on the Versailles model, and provided *inter alia* that Smyrna should remain in Greek occupation for five years, its fate thereafter being determined by a plebiscite.

Any faint chance which remained of the enforcement of the Treaty of Sèvres was, however, destroyed by events in Greece. In October 1920 King Alexander died of the bite of a pet monkey. In the ensuing general election Venizelos was swept from power ; and ex-King Constantine, who had been expelled from Greece during the war for his pro-German leanings, was recalled to the throne. This step alienated the sympathy of the Allies—a sympathy largely due to Venizelos' magnetic personality. In the following year, first the French, and then the Italians, made private agreements with the Kemalist Government which had now established itself in Angora. In Great Britain Lloyd George's Greek policy came in for severe criticism ; and though the Greek army had boldly advanced from Smyrna into the interior of Asia Minor, it became clear that it could no longer count on the effective support of the Allies. In these conditions, a *débâcle* was inevitable. The Greeks were slowly driven back; and in September 1922, after some particularly savage fighting, Kemal drove the last Greek troops from the soil of Asia. Flushed with victory, the Kemalists now turned their attention to Constantinople. The French and Italian Governments hurriedly withdrew their contingents. The situation was critical. A resumption of hostilities between Great Britain and Turkey seemed for a moment inevitable. But Mustapha Kemal stopped in time. An armistice was concluded, and the way paved for the peace congress of Lausanne, where the treaty was signed in the following summer.

The armistice of 1918 had found the Ottoman Empire, like the Austro-Hungarian Monarchy, in a state of dissolution, its vast Arab dominions being in the occupation of British and French forces. Fortunately, however, the Kemalist movement had from the outset rejected the ancient Islamic basis of the Ottoman Empire, and proclaimed the modern secular principle of national self-determination. The new Turkish state explicitly renounced all claim to territories containing Arab majorities; and the conclusion of peace therefore presented no insuperable difficulties. The frontier of Turkey in Europe was pushed forward beyond Adrianople at the expense of Greece; and no more was heard of a plebiscite at Smyrna. The clauses of the Sèvres Treaty regarding penalties, reparation and disarmament disappeared. But the Turkish Government rather surprisingly accepted the establishment on Turkish territory of two demilitarised zones, in Thrace and in the area of the Straits. The National Assembly at Angora, well pleased with what it had secured, proclaimed Turkey a republic with Kemal as its president, embarked on a vigorous programme of secularisation and, in the spring of 1924, abolished the office of the Ottoman Caliph, the religious head of Islam, who for four and a half centuries had had his seat at Constantinople.

The fate of the Arab provinces of the old Ottoman Empire may serve as an introduction to the mandatory system. The Covenant of the League provided that those territories, ceded by the defeated Powers, " which are inhabited by peoples not yet able to stand by themselves under the strenuous conditions of the modern world ", should be placed under the tutelage of " advanced nations ", and that " this tutelage should be exercised by them as Mandatories on behalf of the League of Nations ". The extent to which the Mandatory Powers could be said to act on behalf of the League was, indeed, doubtful. The territories in question were ceded by Germany and Turkey to the Principal Allied and Associated Powers, who were responsible for the selection of the Mandatory Powers. The League approved the terms of the mandates, and received annual reports from the Mandatories on the territories under their tutelage. But its function was limited to friendly criticism. Since it did not grant the mandates, it clearly could not revoke them. Where the sovereignty over the mandated territories resided was an insoluble legal conundrum.

The Covenant provided for three classes of mandates (commonly known as " A ", " B " and " C " mandates) graded according to the stage of development of the populations to which they are applied.

In " A " mandates, under which the ex-Turkish provinces were placed, the role of the Mandatory was defined as " the rendering of administrative advice and assistance . . . until such time as they are able to stand alone "; and it was explicitly laid down that " the wishes of these communities must be a principal consideration in the selection of the Mandatory ". It cannot be said that the last condition was fully complied with. The destination of the Arab territories had been settled during the war by a secret agreement between Great Britain and France; and though, after the war, there was much haggling over the application of this agreement, the argument did not turn on the wishes of the inhabitants. The mandate for Syria was assigned to France, the mandates for Iraq and for Palestine and Transjordania to Great Britain, the mandate for Palestine being conditioned by an undertaking given by the British Government in 1917 to establish in Palestine " a national home for the Jewish people ". The remaining Arab provinces of the Ottoman Empire secured their independence. The coastal strip of Arabia bordering on the Red Sea—an important territory in the eyes of all Moslems, since it contains the holy places of Mecca and Medina—became the independent kingdom of the Hedjaz. In the rest of Arabia Turkish sovereignty had never been more than nominal; and in so far as these regions were inhabited by settled populations, authority was exercised by a number of autonomous Sultans, Sheikhs and Imams.

In " B " mandates, which were applied to the greater

part of Germany's African possessions, the population was recognised to be unfit for any form of administrative autonomy. But the Mandatory Power was under an obligation, not only to prohibit the slave trade and arms traffic, and to refrain from recruiting natives " for other than police purposes or the defence of territory " (a somewhat equivocal phrase), but to give equal rights to the trade and commerce of other members of the League. In East Africa the whole of the former German colony of Tanganyika was mandated to Great Britain, except for the two western provinces which, adjoining the Belgian Congo, were mandated to Belgium, and the port of Kionga in the south, which was ceded outright to Portugal. In West Africa the Cameroons and Togoland were both divided between British and French mandates.

The category of " C " mandates was created for German South-West Africa, which was mandated to the Union of South Africa, and the German Pacific Islands, which were mandated to Australia, New Zealand and Japan. Territories under " C " mandates were " administered under the laws of the mandatory " ; and the essential practical difference between " B " and " C " mandates was that holders of the latter were under no obligation to grant equal rights in the mandated territory to the trade and commerce of other states.

AMERICA AND THE FAR EAST

In its attitude to the settlement made after the war, the people of the United States swayed, in a manner which appeared to be characteristic at this time of its attitude towards foreign affairs, between extreme idealism and extreme caution. At first, through the mouth of its President, it insisted on the insertion of the Covenant of the League in the Treaty of Versailles ; and then, through the mouth of Congress, it rejected the treaty on account of the obligations imposed by the Covenant. The ultimate consequences of this withdrawal of American co-operation were incalculable and far-reaching. But it had no immediate effect on the European settlement. Separate treaties, mainly of a formal character, were concluded by the United States with Germany, Austria and Hungary (the United States had not been at war with Bulgaria or Turkey) ; and peace was thus restored without involving America in unwelcome European obligations.

In the Far East the United States could not afford to preserve the same attitude of serene detachment. The close of the war had left Japan, whose own military exertions had been little more than nominal, the dominant Power in the Pacific. By the Treaty of Versailles she had acquired from Germany the " leased territory " of Kiaochow in the Shantung province of China—a decision which caused China to refuse her signature to the treaty. She had at the same time obtained the mandate for Germany's former island possessions in the Northern Pacific. By the eclipse of Russia, she had become the only Great Power on the borders of China ; and by the simultaneous destruction of the Russian and German navies, she had been left, not only the greatest naval Power in the Far East, but the third naval Power in the world. The Japanese threat to China and the Japanese bid for naval supremacy in the

Pacific were highly disquieting to American observers ; and in the latter part of 1921 the United States Government invited the other Great Powers (the British Empire, Japan, France and Italy), together with the three other Powers having territorial interests in the Pacific (China, the Netherlands and Portugal) and Belgium (whose claim to inclusion was purely sentimental), " to participate in a conference on the limitation of armaments, in connexion with which Pacific and Far Eastern questions would also be discussed ". The Conference assembled at Washington in November 1921.

The Washington Conference resulted in the signature of three treaties. The first, known as the Four-Power Treaty, was concluded between the United States, the British Empire, France and Japan, who agreed to respect each other's rights in relation to their insular possessions in the Pacific, and to consult together in the event of any controversy between them regarding these rights, or any threat to them through the aggressive action of any other Power. The importance of this simple document was twofold. It drew the United States for the first time (since their rejection of the Covenant of the League) into a limited system of consultation with other Great Powers on matters of common concern ; and it provided a decent pretext for bringing to an end the now superfluous Anglo-Japanese Alliance, which had become highly unpopular in the United States, in the Dominions, and among a large section of public opinion in Great Britain. The second, or Five-Power, Treaty provided for an extensive measure of naval disarmament, its essential features being the establishment of naval parity between the

British Empire and the United States and the fixing of the strength of Japan in capital ships at 60 per cent of the British and American figures. The French and Italian quotas were 35 per cent. No limitation was placed on light cruisers, destroyers, submarines or other auxiliary craft. The signatories further agreed to maintain the *status quo*, in respect of fortifications and naval bases, in a specified area of the Pacific. By the third, or Nine-Power, Treaty all the Powers represented at the Conference pledged themselves to respect the independence and integrity of China, and " to refrain from taking advantage of conditions in China to seek special rights or privileges which would abridge the rights of subjects and citizens of friendly states ". In addition to these treaties, yet another document was signed at Washington ; and though it formed no part of the official proceedings of the conference, agreement was certainly not reached without strong pressure from the British and American Delegations. Under this agreement, concluded between Japan and China alone, Japan undertook to return to China the Kiaochow territory which had been ceded to her by Germany in the Versailles Treaty.

The Washington Conference was hailed, not without reason, as an outstanding success. It had to all appearances restored the pre-war balance in the Pacific. Intimidated by a firm Anglo-American front and by the moral pressure of world opinion, Japan had accepted, if not an open defeat, at any rate a serious check to her ambitions. She had been persuaded to abandon her sole war gain on the mainland of China. She had not ventured to claim naval parity with the British Empire and the United States ; and her demand for 70 per cent of British and American naval tonnage had been cut down to 60 per cent. The Japanese menace to the integrity of China and to Anglo-American naval supremacy in the Pacific had been removed. Yet the situation created by the Washington treaties was insecure in so far as it depended on the unwilling renunciation by Japan of her forward policy on the Asiatic mainland. Sooner or later, Japan, conscious of her strength, would resent the loss of prestige involved in the Washington settlement. The fundamental question whether the dominant influence in the Far East was to be Anglo-Saxon or Japanese was still undecided. But thanks to the Washington Conference, it remained in abeyance for almost exactly ten years.

PART I

THE PERIOD OF ENFORCEMENT: THE ALLIANCES

(1920-1924)

THE most important and persistent single factor in European affairs in the years following 1919 was the French demand for security. In the seventeenth and eighteenth centuries France rightly regarded herself as the strongest military Power in Europe; and this tradition survived the Napoleonic wars, when she succumbed only to a general European coalition against her. In 1870 the illusion of her strength was abruptly shattered by the Franco-Prussian war. A new Power had arisen in Central Europe whose national feeling was as strong and united as that of France herself, and whose natural resources were far greater. The mineral wealth of Germany gave her an industrial development and a capacity for the production of war material which France could not hope to rival. The population of France was almost stationary at something under forty millions. The population of Germany was increasing by five millions a decade, and by 1905 had exceeded sixty millions. Moreover, the Germans displayed a genius for military organisation. The German military machine was not only better equipped and better manned, but better run than the French. In 1914 the French, as they were well aware, would once more have been a beaten nation in six weeks but for prompt British intervention ; and that intervention had hung on a

25

thread. The jubilation of 1918 was short-lived. Beneath the rejoicings a deep note of anxiety soon made itself heard. Since 1870—and still more since 1914—France had been morbidly conscious of her weakness in face of Germany. She had turned the tables on the victor of 1871. What could be contrived to prevent Germany one day turning the tables on the victor of 1918 ?

France's first answer to this question was clear and emphatic. She wanted what she called a " physical guarantee "—the possession in perpetuity of the Rhine and its bridges, across which any invader of France from the east must pass. " The danger comes ", ran a French memorandum presented to the Peace Conference in February 1919, " from the possession by Germany of the left bank and of the Rhine bridges. . . . The safety of the Western and Overseas Democracies makes it imperative, in present circumstances, for them to guard the bridges of the Rhine." To her keen disappointment, her Allies refused to give France the security of the Rhine frontier, on the ground that this arrangement would have involved the separation from Germany of more than five million Germans living on the left bank of the Rhine. After a bitter struggle, France was obliged to abandon her claim. She secured in exchange—

(1) the inclusion in the Versailles Treaty of clauses providing for the occupation of the left bank of the Rhine for fifteen years by Allied forces, and for its permanent demilitarisation (*i.e.* prohibition to maintain troops or construct fortresses west of the Rhine) ; and

(2) the conclusion, simultaneously with the Versailles Treaty, of treaties with the British Empire and the United States, under which these Powers undertook to come immediately to the assistance of France " in the event of any unprovoked movement of aggression against her being made by Germany ".

The failure of the United States to ratify the treaties signed at Versailles rendered both the British and the American undertakings void. France felt herself cheated. She had abandoned her claim on the strength of a promise which was not honoured ; and this grievance was an underlying factor throughout the subsequent discussions between France and Great Britain on the question of security.

Having thus been compelled to abandon her hope of a " physical " guarantee, France worked feverishly during the next four years to find compensation for her natural inferiority to Germany, and to allay her fear of German vengeance. She followed two separate and parallel methods : a system of treaty guarantees, and a system of alliances.

THE SYSTEM OF GUARANTEES

When it became clear, about the beginning of 1920, that the Anglo-American guarantee against unprovoked aggression would never come into force, France was left without any treaty protection against Germany other than that contained in the Covenant of the League of Nations. France had decided from the first that this was insufficient. It was true that, under Article 10 of the Covenant, members of the League undertook " to respect and preserve as against external aggression the territorial integrity and existing political independence of all members of the League ", and that Articles 16 and 17 provided for sanctions or penalties against any state which resorted to war in disregard of its obligations. But Article 10 had been accepted by Great Britain (the Power which counted for most) with reluctance; and the French proposal to create an international army, which alone could make sanctions effective, had been emphatically negatived by Great Britain and the United States. Under Article 16 members of the League were bound to break off financial and economic relations with an aggressor. But military action (and nothing less would stop Germany) depended on a " recommendation " of the Council, which required a unanimous vote, and which, when voted, could be accepted or rejected by individual states as they pleased; and the American defection cast serious doubts on the efficacy, or even the possibility, of a financial and economic blockade.

French scepticism about the efficacy of the Covenant was enhanced when the League actually came into being. When the first Assembly met in Geneva in December 1920, Articles 10 and 16 were the subject of an immediate attack. Canada wanted to suppress Article 10 altogether; and the Scandinavian delegations desired to provide for exceptions to the automatic application of economic sanctions under Article 16. Both these proposals gave rise to long deliberations. In the following year, the Assembly voted a resolution which prescribed *inter alia* that the Council would,

when need arose, " recommend the date on which the
enforcement of economic pressure under Article 16
is to be begun ", the effect being to give the Council
latitude to postpone and modify the application of
economic sanctions. In 1923 a resolution was proposed declaring that the decision what measures were
necessary to carry out the obligations of Article 10 must
rest with " the constitutional authorities of each member ". The effect of this resolution was to leave the
whole matter of military assistance to the discretion of
individual governments ; and its adoption was blocked
only by the adverse vote of one minor state. Although
neither Article 10 nor Article 16 had been formally
amended, it was clear from these discussions that their
practical application in time of crisis would lag considerably behind the strict letter of the Covenant. The
machinery of Geneva was evidently not likely to set in
motion that prompt military action which alone could
save France from invasion.

In these circumstances it is not surprising that
France continued to press Great Britain for some
additional guarantee of assistance against German
aggression. The conclusion of these efforts was, however, paradoxical. In January 1922, the British Government at length plucked up courage to offer France a
guarantee in approximately the same terms as those of
the abortive treaty of 1919. It so happened that the
French Prime Minister of the day was the obstinate and
short-sighted Poincaré, who believed in a policy of all
or nothing. Poincaré demanded that the guarantee
should be supplemented by a military convention de-
fining the precise nature of the assistance to be rendered

by the British army, and declared that, failing this, a mere guarantee treaty was worthless to France. The British Government was not prepared to commit itself so far. It had discharged its debt of honour; and it now abandoned for some time to come the apparently hopeless task of satisfying the French appetite for security.

THE SYSTEM OF ALLIANCES

Poincaré's high-handed attitude was explained in part by the success which France had meanwhile achieved in the other aspect of her quest for security : the building up of a system of alliances. A policy of military alliances was more congenial to French temperament and French tradition than the more abstract security of guarantees against aggression. It was this policy which had gained for France her supremacy in Europe in the eighteenth century, when she contained Austria by alliances with Austria's smaller neighbours. It was this policy by which she now sought to encircle Germany. In the west, the position was made secure in September 1920 by a military alliance with Belgium. Elsewhere fresh ground had to be broken. Russia had ceased to exist as a military power. But in her place the new republic of Poland had appeared on Germany's eastern frontier. In the south there had arisen, thanks to the victory of the Allies, the three new or much enlarged states of Czechoslovakia, Yugoslavia and Roumania, who were France's natural friends and clients. Out of this material France built up, in the three years after the war, an effective and closely knit system of alliances.

POLAND

The Polish republic which came into being at the
end of the war was not a new state, but the revival of an
old one. From the tenth to the eighteenth century,
Poland had been a large and powerful kingdom. In
the latter half of the eighteenth century, she incurred
the joint enmity of Russia, Prussia and Austria ; and
after three " partitions ", in which larger and larger
slices of territory were taken from her, she lost her
independence in 1791. The simultaneous eclipse in
1918 of the Russian, German and Austrian Empires
was a stroke of luck which made her re-birth certain.
But the first years were a period of great difficulty.
The Russian, German and Austrian Poles, who now
united to form a single state, had for a century and a
quarter lived under different laws and different systems
of administration, had served in different armies and
fought on opposite sides, and had acquired different
traditions and different loyalties. It required no small
stock of common patriotism to override these divergences of outlook. Moreover Poland, set in the midst
of the great European plain, had no clearly marked
geographical frontiers except on the south, where the
Carpathian Mountains divided her from Slovakia. Her
western and northern frontiers with Germany were
settled, in the manner already described, by the
Versailles Treaty. Everywhere else, the limits of the
new Poland were the subject of acrimonious debate
with her neighbours.

In the south-west the little district of Austrian

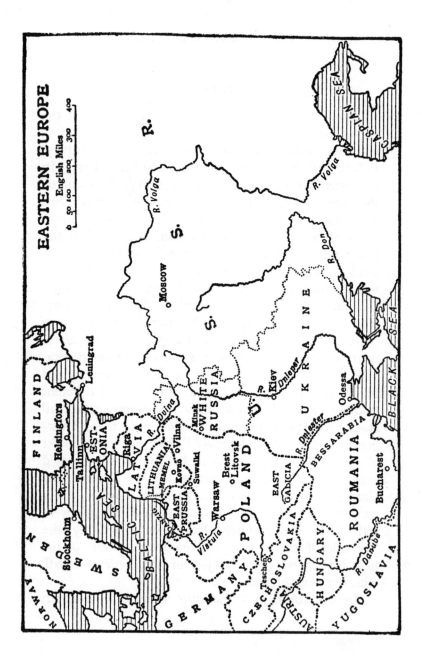

EASTERN EUROPE

English Miles

0   50 100   200   300   400

Silesia, an important coal-field inhabited by a mixed Czech-Polish population, provided an apple of discord between Poland and the new state of Czechoslovakia. Early in 1919 Polish and Czech forces came to blows in the disputed area; and a pitched battle was only averted by the mediation of French and British officers. It was decided to settle the dispute by a plebiscite. But as the time for the vote drew near, passions ran so high that the plan was dropped; and under strong French pressure, both sides agreed to a settlement. By this settlement, Czechoslovakia obtained the coal mines and Poland the principal town of Teschen (though not its railway station which remained in Czechoslovakia). It was a compromise which had no virtue except that of being a compromise; and both sides continued to regard themselves as deeply injured parties.

In Austrian Poland a different problem arose. Of the two provinces of West and East Galicia into which Austrian Poland was divided, the former was purely Polish in character. In East Galicia the landed gentry and most of the intellectuals (other than the Jews, who were here particularly numerous) were Poles. But the peasantry belonged to the same stock which peopled the whole of south-western Russia — being variously described as Little Russians, Ukrainians or Ruthenes. It is probable that the landless Ruthene peasant of East Galicia hated the Polish landowner rather because he was a landowner than because he was a Pole. But of the depth of the hatred there was no doubt. In the early months of 1919 East Galicia was the scene of a stubborn civil war between the ruling Polish minority and the subject Ruthene majority. Polish reinforcements were soon brought in; and in May the resistance of the Ruthenes, supported by nothing more effective than mild protests from the Allies in Paris against Polish high-handedness, came to an end. The Allies, helpless to alter the accomplished fact, offered Poland a mandate over East Galicia for twenty-five years, after which time the fate of the territory was to be decided by the League of Nations. The Poles rejected the proposal and remained in possession. In 1923 the Allies at last formally recognised Polish sovereignty over East Galicia in return for a promise (which was never carried out) to set up an autonomous régime there.

On the eastern frontier of Poland the same problem presented itself on a far larger scale. In the days of its greatness the kingdom of Poland had not been confined to lands where the indigenous population was Polish. It had embraced the whole of Lithuania, most of White Russia, and the whole of the Ukraine as far as the Black Sea. In these territories, vast tracts of country were in the possession of Polish landowners—a state of affairs which continued right down to the Russian revolution of 1917. After the revolution, these landowners took refuge in Poland. They not unnaturally put strong pressure on the Polish Government to reconquer their lands for them; and perfervid patriots dreamed of a restored Polish empire stretching from the Baltic to the Black Sea. A proposal from the Allies in Paris that the eastern frontier of Poland should be so drawn as to include only territories where the Polish population was in a majority was received as a bitter insult.

It was in such a mood that Marshal Pilsudski, the head of the Polish state and the commander-in-chief of the army, set out in the spring of 1920 to conquer the Ukraine for Poland. The Soviet army, disorganised by the civil war, made feeble resistance ; and Polish troops quickly reached Kiev. In June, however, the Soviet forces were able to launch a mass counter-offensive, which not only drove the Poles helter-skelter out of the Ukraine, but brought Soviet troops within a few miles of Warsaw. Here the fortunes of war underwent another sudden reversal. The Soviet offensive, like the Polish offensive before it, was exhausted. The Polish army advanced once more. This time, avoiding the Ukraine, they marched due east into White Russia ; and when the armistice was at last sounded, the line was some 150 miles east of the so-called "Curzon line" proposed by the Allies. But the Soviet Government was prodigal of territory and needed peace. In 1921 the Treaty of Riga confirmed the armistice line as the permanent frontier between Poland and Soviet Russia. Poland abandoned her claim to the Ukraine, but received a large, though sparsely populated, tract of White Russia.

Next came the turn of Lithuania. Here the chief bone of contention was the city and district of Vilna. Vilna had been the capital of the mediaeval empire of Lithuania (which in the sixteenth century had been united with Poland by a convenient royal marriage) ; and when in 1918 an independent Lithuania was revived, it promptly proclaimed Vilna as its capital. Unhappily, Vilna had an equally strong sentimental attraction for Poland. It was the seat of a famous Polish university and an ancient home of Polish learning. From the ethnographical standpoint, neither the Lithuanian nor the Polish claim was strong. The population of the city was Jewish (the Jews had an absolute majority), Polish and White Russian ; of the surrounding district, White Russian and Lithuanian. But where so many passions were excited, the wishes of the populations concerned (if indeed they had any) were unlikely to be decisive.

In July 1920, during the Soviet advance towards Warsaw, Lithuania had signed a treaty with the Soviet Government by which the latter recognised her claim to Vilna. But the subsequent Polish advance cut off Lithuania altogether from her Soviet friends, and she was left to face the Poles alone. Fighting soon began in the neighbourhood of Suwalki. It went less well for the Poles than might have been expected ; and in October an armistice was signed which left Vilna and district in Lithuanian hands. Three days later, an independent Polish general named Zeligowski collected some troops and, taking the Lithuanians completely by surprise, occupied Vilna. Officially, the Polish Government deplored this flagrant breach of faith. But it unblushingly stuck to the prize; and Pilsudski admitted, some years later, that the *coup* had been carried out with his knowledge and approval. Long negotiations conducted by the League of Nations failed to dislodge the Poles ; and in 1923, when the Lithuanians had put themselves out of court by their seizure of Memel (which had been occupied by the Allies since the Versailles Treaty), the Allies formally recognised Vilna as part of Poland.

The Polish state, thus constituted, had a population of over thirty millions—a figure which almost entitled it to the rank of a Great Power. It was rich in natural resources, possessing an abundance of coal and iron in the south-west, oil in East Galicia, extensive forests in the east, and good agricultural land almost everywhere. But it also had conspicuous weaknesses. Not less than 25 per cent of its population was non-Polish, including four million Jews ; and most of the minorities were actually or potentially hostile. Furthermore, Poland was, in these early days, on bad terms with all her neighbours without exception. There was constant friction with Germany over the treatment of the German minority and over Danzig ; and it seemed doubtful whether any German Government would stomach indefinitely the separation of East Prussia from the rest of Germany by the Polish corridor. Soviet Russia might some day regret her generosity. Czechoslovakia was sullenly resentful, Lithuania noisily indignant ; and there might be trouble again in East Galicia. Poland was the strongest Power in eastern Europe. But she could scarcely face the world alone.

In these circumstances, the French policy of alliance with the neighbours of Germany coincided perfectly with Poland's own needs. The Franco-Polish treaty of alliance of February 1921 was an instrument of close political co-operation. It was accompanied by a secret military convention, and was followed by the supply from France on easy terms of large supplies of war material for the equipment of the Polish army. Some cautious Frenchmen complained that so quarrelsome an ally was more of a liability than an asset, and that no French soldier would be willing to die for Poland. Some Poles grumbled at the patronising attitude of their French associates, and at the number and costliness of the French Military Mission in Warsaw. But the alliance was founded on a too solid basis of common interest to be shaken by any trivial discontents. In every important issue of international politics, France and Poland ranged themselves side by side. At Geneva, the French and Polish delegates were hand-in-glove in every private negotiation, and spoke and voted together in every public debate.

THE LITTLE ENTENTE

The Little Entente was the unofficial name for the alliance between the three states which profited most by the break up of the Austro-Hungarian monarchy: Czechoslovakia, Roumania and Yugoslavia.

Czechoslovakia, as the name (a recent coinage) indicates, was formed by the union of two neighbouring peoples. The Czechs and Slovaks are two branches of the same Slav stock, speaking closely related dialects of the same language. The history of the two peoples is, however, quite different. The Czechs, who formed in the Middle Ages the nucleus of an independent Kingdom of Bohemia, passed from 1620 onwards under the Germanic influence of the Austrian Empire. The old Czech aristocracy was completely Germanised; and the modern Czechs are thrifty, hard-working, well-educated middle-class and working-class people. Slovakia, on the other hand, had for a thousand years prior to 1918 been part of Hungary. The Slovaks were an illiterate peasant race; and Slovak culture was represented by a handful of intellectuals living abroad, mainly in the United States. These conditions made it inevitable that the army officers, the civil servants and the teachers of the new Czechoslovak state should be drawn principally from the Czechs. But this inequality was resented in Slovak circles; and the most representative Slovak party persistently demanded " national autonomy " for Slovakia.

The greater part of the soil of Czechoslovakia was agricultural; and the new state strengthened itself by an extensive agrarian reform, involving the expropriation of the larger landowners, mainly German or Hungarian, and the distribution of their land to Czech or Slovak small farmers and peasants. But Czechoslovakia was also a highly developed industrial state, and a large manufacturer of war material. Her former Austrian provinces contained some 80 per cent of the production of coal and iron and the heavy industry of the pre-war Austrian Empire. These advantages were in part set off by the weakness of her geographical position and the mixed character of her population. Of her population of more than fourteen millions the Czechs, who formed the ruling class, accounted for six and a half millions and the Slovaks for two millions more. The balance was made up of a compact and industrious German minority of more than three millions living on the fringes of Bohemia, and of Hungarian, Ruthene and Polish minorities. The Slovaks would be of uncertain value in a crisis; and the minorities would be hostile in almost any war in which Czechoslovakia might find herself engaged. Prague, the capital, was situated so near the frontier that it could be occupied by German troops within days, or perhaps hours, of an outbreak of hostilities with Germany; and the long, narrow territory of Slovakia would be difficult to defend against an attack from Hungary. Of all the states of Central Europe, Czechoslovakia was the most heterogeneous and, from the military standpoint, the most vulnerable.

Roumania had more reason to congratulate herself on the peace settlement than on her experiences during the war. She changed sides twice in the course of the fighting ; and at the end of it she acquired the greater part of Transylvania from Hungary and Bessarabia, in spite of the protests of the Soviet Government, from Russia, thereby doubling her territory and increasing her population from seven to seventeen millions. Like Czechoslovakia, she carried out an extensive measure of agrarian reform and redistribution of land to small-holders. Her minorities—Hungarian, Russian and Jewish—were not sufficiently important to be a menace to her national security. But Roumanian administration had a bad name for corruption ; and the quality of the Roumanian army, judged by Balkan standards, was not high. Roumania was the largest oil-producing state in Europe next to the Soviet Union ; and oil and wheat were her principal sources of wealth.

Internally, Yugoslavia was called on to solve the same problem as Czechoslovakia : the fusion of cognate races. Of the three elements which united to form the Yugoslav state, the Serbs had enjoyed independence since the final withdrawal of the Turkish garrisons in 1867. The Croats had been under Hungarian, and the Slovenes under Austrian, rule until 1918. The Serbs, who were from the first the dominant partners in the union, were excellent fighters, and had a rough-and-

ready gift for organisation. But politically and cultur-
ally they were inferior to the Croats and Slovenes, who
looked down on them as semi-barbarians. The friction
between the three partners became a serious handicap
to the new state and, combined with the political
immaturity of the Serbs themselves, made any parliamentary system unworkable. The Croat leaders persisted in the demand for autonomy ; and many of
them, in consequence, spent years in prison or in
exile—an unhappy condition of affairs the blame for
which must be shared by both parties. The prosperity
of the country depended mainly on its sturdy and
industrious peasantry, though its mineral resources
were also considerable.

Externally, Yugoslavia was the member of the Little
Entente with the most varied and extensive interests.
While Czechoslovakia belonged primarily to Central
Europe and Roumania to the Balkans, Yugoslavia
belonged equally to both. In the north her frontier
reached within a hundred miles of Vienna, in the south-
east within fifty miles of the Aegean. This multi-
plicity of interests gave her an exceptional position in
the partnership. The Little Entente was devised for
the purpose of common protection against Hungary ;
and Hungary was the only country mentioned by name
in the treaties which constituted the alliance. But, for
Yugoslavia, Hungary was never the first concern. The
portion of Hungarian territory which had fallen to her
share was smaller than the portions allotted to Czechoslovakia and Roumania ; and she had less to fear from
Hungarian irredentism. On the other hand, she was
intensely jealous of Italy's dominant position on the

Adriatic. Italy had appropriated far more Slav territory than was, in Yugoslav eyes, her due ; and it was
notorious that Italy hoped, and was perhaps intriguing,
for the disruption of the Yugoslav state. The Yugoslavs were good haters. The enmity of Yugoslavia for
Italy was one of the most persistent of all European feuds
in the period between the two wars.

The Little Entente came into being through treaties
of alliance concluded in 1920 and 1921 between each
pair of its members. It was not until much later that
France concluded political treaties with the Little
Entente states. But there were from the outset formal
or informal military understandings providing, as in
the case of Poland, for the appointment of French
military missions and for the supply of war material to
the Little Entente armies ; and Czechoslovakia, Roumania and Yugoslavia became France's faithful satellites
in foreign affairs at Geneva and elsewhere. France's
relations with the Little Entente rested on a different
foundation from her relations with Poland. The basis
of the alliance with Poland was a direct common interest
in keeping Germany in check. The understandings
with the Little Entente, on the other hand, implied a
tacit bargain. The three Little Entente Powers would
assist France to enforce the Versailles Treaty, in which
their own interest was negligible. France would support the Little Entente as a whole against Hungary, and
Yugoslavia in particular against Italy. The importance
of this move was that it enlarged France's conception
of her own security. She was now definitely committed
to the maintenance not only of the Versailles Treaty,
but of the whole European peace settlement. It was

no longer her concern merely to keep Germany at bay
on the Rhine and prevent her from strengthening her
position in the east. It became a recognised French
interest to support Poland against Lithuania, Czechoslovakia against Hungary, and Yugoslavia and Roumania
against Bulgaria, and even to save her friends from the
inconvenience of a too rigorous interpretation of their
obligations towards their minorities. In view of the
powerful influence which she could exercise in all these
questions, France was a patron well worth having.

During the period 1920–24 France, the possessor
of a large, well-equipped and victorious army and of
enormous stocks of munitions, reached the summit of
her prestige and power in Europe. She was the champion of the *status quo* and the sworn enemy of what came
to be known as " revisionism ". Her position was
comparable to that of Metternich after the peace settlement of 1815 ; and by her agreements with Poland and
the Little Entente she had built up a modern counterpart of the Holy Alliance.

43

THE years of French supremacy were also the years of Germany's deepest humiliation.   Home politics are not within the scope of this book.   But the internal affairs of Germany had, in the period between the wars, so direct an influence on the international situation that a few words must be said about them here.   Before 1914 Germany had lived under a combination of parliamentary democracy and military autocracy, which was perhaps well adapted to the stage of political development reached by the German people.   After the war, the universal enthusiasm for democracy swept over Germany ; and the form of government which emerged from the chaos of November 1918 was a republic with a Social-Democrat Government, the President being an ex-cobbler named Ebert.

The " Weimar Republic " (so called from the town of Weimar, where the National Assembly met in 1919 to approve its constitution) started life in the most discouraging conditions.   It was faced everywhere with disorder, disorganisation and destitution. Its first task was to ratify the Versailles Treaty ; and its name was thus associated in German minds with a national disgrace.   In 1815 the Powers who had overthrown Napoleon perceived that if they wished the restored monarchy to survive in France, they must treat it with consideration and respect. The victors of 1918 showed no such wisdom. It was in their interest that the pacific Weimar democracy should firmly establish itself in Germany. But instead of doing everything in their power to enhance its prestige, they exposed it to such constant humiliations that it could never hope to win the loyalty and affection of the German people. The territorial clauses of the Versailles Treaty have been described in the Introduction. The present chapter deals with those other provisions of the Treaty which played the largest part in Germany's international relations during the years 1920–24.

War Guilt and War Criminals

The articles of the treaty relating to " war guilt " and " war criminals " were not less eagerly approved in Great Britain than in France. The victors of previous wars, however ruthless in their treatment of the defeated foe, had thought it superfluous to pronounce any moral condemnation. But war propaganda both in Great Britain and in France had so persistently stressed the moral delinquencies of Germany (in particular, the violation of Belgian neutrality, the wanton devastation of the occupied territories, and the killing of civilians by bombing from the air and by unrestricted submarine warfare against merchant ships) that public opinion demanded some formal condemnation of her acts ; and insistence on Germany's guilt provided a justification, which was felt both in British and in American circles to be needed, for the severity of the peace terms. By an article placed at the head of the reparation chapter,

Germany was obliged to " accept the responsibility of Germany and her allies for causing all the loss and damage to which the Allied and Associated Governments and their nationals have been subjected as a consequence of the war imposed upon them by the aggression of Germany and her allies ". The position of the article was significant. The reparation provisions of the treaty were those which had excited most misgiving in American, and in some British, circles.

The origins of the first world war will probably be debated by historians for centuries to come. The verdict of history may well be that, of all the belligerent Powers, Germany and her allies bore the largest share of responsibility. But historical truth cannot be established by international treaty—least of all by a treaty imposed by victors on vanquished. The Allied Governments, in the passion of the moment, failed to realise that this extorted admission of guilt could prove nothing, and must excite bitter resentment in German minds. German men of learning set to work to demonstrate the guiltlessness of their country, fondly believing that, if this could be established, the whole fabric of the treaty would collapse. In Allied countries the futility of the war-guilt clause soon came to be recognised. But it was never formally annulled, and was left to perish with the treaty itself.

The articles of the treaty relating to war criminals (the chapter is entitled " Penalties ") were of more immediate practical import. In the first of them, the Allies " publicly arraign William II of Hohenzollern, formerly German Emperor, for a supreme offence against international morality and the sanctity of treaties ". The ex-Kaiser was to be tried by a court of five judges, American, British, French, Italian and Japanese, who were to " fix the punishment ". Immediately on the coming into force of the treaty, the Allies officially requested the Government of Holland (where the ex-Kaiser had taken refuge in November 1918) to hand him over to them. That Government replied, as was expected, that it would be contrary to international usage for them to surrender a " political refugee " ; and within a few months one of the most notorious articles of the treaty was consigned to oblivion. It was a fortunate ending. A public trial by the Allies might well have revived the ex-Kaiser's lost prestige in Germany, and turned him into a German national hero and martyr.

By the following articles Germany agreed to hand over to Allied military courts for trial any persons in Germany accused by the Allies of having " committed acts in violation of the laws and customs of war ". It is doubtful whether this provision, however reasonably interpreted, could have been put into effect without causing a revolution in Germany. But when it was discovered that the lists prepared by the Allies included the names of the Crown Prince, of Hindenburg, of Ludendorff, and of almost every prominent figure on the German side during the war, there was so fierce an outburst of indignation that compliance with the demand was out of the question. After a long wrangle between the German and Allied Governments, a compromise was reached by which the German Government agreed to bring twelve of the accused (against whom definite and flagrant breaches of the laws of war were alleged)

47

before the German Supreme Court at Leipzig, the Allied Governments acting as prosecutors. The trials took place in 1921. Six of the accused were convicted, and sentenced to terms of imprisonment. Thereafter nothing more was heard of these clauses of the treaty. Had the passions of the time permitted the Allied Governments to make the arrangement reciprocal, and had they themselves been willing to bring to trial any of their own nationals accused of similar offences by the German Government, the whole procedure might have been a valuable innovation and an earnest of the desire of mankind to make international law an effective reality.

DISARMAMENT AND DEMILITARISATION

It was a natural and necessary consequence of their victory that the Allies should desire to render their defeated enemies incapable for as long a time as possible of military action. Under the armistice Germany had surrendered the greater part of her fleet and her heavy artillery. The treaty imposed permanent restrictions on her military strength. Her army was limited to 100,000 men recruited by voluntary enlistment (conscription being prohibited), and her navy to six battleships with a corresponding number of cruisers and destroyers. She was to possess no submarines, no military aircraft, and no heavy guns, and to build no fortifications. The amounts of war material of every kind, and the number of factories capable of producing it, which she was allowed to retain, were strictly limited. Allied Naval, Military and Air Commissions, whose officer personnel numbered at one time nearly 2000, were stationed in Germany to see that these provisions were carried out, and were not finally withdrawn till 1927. The Germans made every effort to evade a strict application of these measures. A considerable amount of war material was probably saved from destruction by concealment; and secret preparations were everywhere made to rebuild Germany's military strength once the control was relaxed. But it may on the whole be said that, by 1924, Germany had been subjected to a measure of disarmament more rigorous and complete than any recorded in modern history.

It will be remembered that, under the Treaty of Versailles, the Rhineland was to be not only permanently demilitarised, but occupied by Allied troops for a period of fifteen years. The civil administration of the occupied area remained with the German authorities. But an Inter-Allied High Commission, consisting of French, Belgian, British and American representatives, had power to issue ordinances " so far as may be necessary for securing the maintenance, safety and requirements " of the Allied troops; and these ordinances had the force of law. In spite of the failure of the United States to ratify the treaty, American troops remained in the Rhineland till 1923, and the American Commissioner continued to attend the meetings of the High Commission, though without the right to vote.

The joint occupation of the Rhineland first brought to the surface that underlying divergence between the French and British attitudes towards Germany which has been so unsettling a factor in European politics since 1920. At the close of the war, anti-German feeling had been quite as bitter in London as in Paris;

49

and some of the most invidious clauses of the Versailles Treaty were whole-heartedly approved, if not inspired, by the British Government. But passions on the British side abated rapidly. While France feared even a defeated Germany, the destruction of the German fleet gave the British Empire a sense of perfect security. British reluctance to see any one Power dominate the continent of Europe is notorious; and it would have been contrary to this tradition to allow France to trample Germany utterly in the dust. Time-honoured British conceptions of fair play and chivalry to a beaten foe came into conflict with the legally precise French mind, anxious to extort the last ounce of flesh stipulated in the bond. While the French army occupying the southern sector of the Rhineland assumed the high and mighty airs of conquerors in a hostile land, the British troops, whose headquarters were at Cologne, soon established the friendliest relations with the German inhabitants. The British soldier, though in theory an unwelcome guest, made himself on the whole extremely popular; and it was frequently remarked that he in turn found the company of his ex-enemies more congenial than that of his ex-allies. Conditions were thus ripe for a series of episodes which would drive a wedge between French and British opinion about Germany.

The first of these episodes was the employment in the French army of occupation of a detachment of coloured troops. French tradition recognises no colour bar, and it is unlikely that the French authorities deliberately sent coloured soldiers to the Rhineland in order to inflict on the German people a fresh humiliation. But the Germans regarded it as such; and knowing that their own colour prejudice was shared in an even stronger degree by British and American opinion, they lost no opportunity of pressing this grievance. The " black shame ", and the alleged misdeeds of the coloured troops, provided German propagandists with a fruitful theme. For the first time since the war, British and American opinion sided emphatically with Germany against France.

The second episode was the encouragement given by France to the so-called " separatist " movement in the Rhineland. Having failed in the peace negotiations to secure the forcible separation of the Rhineland from Germany, certain French generals and officials, with the tacit approval of the French Government, now sought to achieve the same object by inducing the local population to throw off the authority of Berlin and proclaim an independent German state of the Rhineland. The movement was almost purely fictitious. It was more than a century since the greater part of the Rhineland had been incorporated in Prussia, and few Rhinelanders coveted a spurious autonomy under French patronage. But the French discovered or imported a handful of German renegades who, in return for liberal subsidies, were prepared to play the French game; and the semblance of a separatist movement was kept alive for three years. Then in the autumn of 1923 events took an ugly turn. In the Palatinate, which formed part not of Prussia, but of Bavaria, the local French representative of the High Commission recognised the separatists as an independent government; and the separatists, armed for the purpose by the French military authorities, expelled the German officials and took over the administration. In January 1924 the High Commission by a majority vote (the French and Belgian against the British) officially recognised the " autonomous government " of the Palatinate. This was too much for British opinion and the British Government. Strong pressure was brought to bear on the French Government, which sent orders to its representatives in the Rhineland to abandon their support of the separatists. The result was shattering. The whole movement collapsed in a few hours. There were riots in the principal towns of the Palatinate ; and a score or more of the separatists were lynched by the population before the troops could intervene. After February 1924 no more was heard of the separatist movement in the Rhineland.

The third and most important episode in the relations between Germany and the Allies, and between France and Great Britain, at this period, was the tangled question of Reparation, to which we now turn

REPARATION

During the war, democratic opinion in many countries had expressed itself against the practice embodied in most peace treaties of imposing a " war indemnity " by way of penalty on the defeated state. The Allied Governments bowed to this opinion and, in the Treaty of Versailles, limited their demands on Germany to " compensation for all damage done to the civilian population of the Allied and Associated Powers and to their property ". This was, however, a concession of no practical consequence ; for it soon became clear that Germany's resources would not be adequate for the payment even of this compensation. The important difference between the Versailles Treaty and previous peace treaties providing for a payment to be made to the victors by the defeated Power was that, on this occasion, no sum was fixed by the treaty itself. It was left to an Allied Commission, called the Reparation Commission, both to draw up the bill and to decide on the manner in which it should be paid. The assessment was to be made by May 1st, 1921 ; and prior to that date Germany was to pay on account the sum of £1,000,000,000. It was contemplated that the eventual payments would have to be spread over a period of at least thirty years.

In the exchange of notes between the Allied and the German Delegations prior to the signature of the Versailles Treaty, the Allies had undertaken to consider any offer which Germany might make of " a lump sum in settlement of her whole liability "—such an offer to take the place of the proposed assessment by the Reparation Commission. Discussions of the possible terms of this offer, and of the " deliveries in kind " (particularly coal) by which Germany hoped to discharge the preliminary payment of £1,000,000,000, were the principal features of 1920. At a Conference held at Spa in July of that year, the German Chancellor and Minister for Foreign Affairs for the first time met the leading Allied ministers round a table on equal terms. But the only agreement reached between them was one fixing deliveries of coal for the next six months ; and the chief decision taken by the Spa Conference in the reparation question was the allocation, as between the Allies themselves, of the hitherto non-existent receipts. France was to take 52 per cent, the British Empire 22 per cent, Italy 10 per cent and Belgium 8 per cent, the balance being left for distribution between the minor Allies. Belgium, in view of the special severity of her sufferings, was to have priority up to the amount of £100,000,000.

The divergence between the views of the German Government and of the Allied Governments about the " lump sum " which Germany might reasonably be expected to offer was too wide to permit of an agreement ; and in March 1921, on the ground of Germany's failure to complete the preliminary reparation payment and to carry out certain of the disarmament provisions, Allied troops occupied the three towns of Düsseldorf, Duisberg and Ruhrort on the east of the Rhine. On April 27th, 1921, in pursuance of the treaty, the Reparation Commission fixed Germany's total liability at £6,600,000,000. By this time saner opinion in the Allied countries had come to understand that Germany was in no position to foot more than a small proportion of this enormous bill. While the Allied Governments had not yet sufficient courage publicly to renounce any part of their claims, the German debt was divided into three sections, represented by three classes of bonds " A ", " B " and " C ". The " C " bonds, which accounted for £4,000,000,000, were to be held by the Reparation Commission until such time as Germany's capacity to pay was established ; and two-thirds of the whole debt was thus shelved indefinitely. For the rest, the Allied Governments drew up a " schedule of payments " under which Germany was to pay £100,000,000 a year plus 25 per cent of the value of her exports. The schedule was communicated to the German Government with an ultimatum that, if it were not accepted by May 12th, Allied troops would occupy the valley of the Ruhr, the centre of Germany's metallurgical industry, and the seat of more than 80 per cent of her production of coal, pig-iron and steel. There was a Cabinet crisis in Germany; and on May 11th the demand was accepted.

By August, Germany had paid the first instalment of £50,000,000 due under the schedule; and this was destined to be her last cash payment for more than three years. Before long, Germany was in the throes of a currency crisis. Already, by the middle of 1920, the mark had descended from its normal value of 20 marks to the pound sterling to a figure of about 250 to the pound. Here it remained for some time, being largely supported by foreign speculators who rashly assumed that it must some day return to its original value. But in the summer of 1921, when it was clear that Germany would require large amounts of foreign currency to meet her obligations under the schedule, the mark resumed its downward course. In November it had reached 1000 to the pound; and in the summer of 1922 its fall became rapid and catastrophic.

By this time financial experts everywhere recognised that Germany's capacity to pay reparation in cash was completely exhausted. Marks were valueless to the Allies; and the German Government, even if it had had the will to pay, had no means of purchasing other currencies. The British Government pressed for a two years' moratorium for all cash payments by Germany. In France, public opinion refused to admit that the debtor should thus evade his just obligations, while the victorious Allies were left to bear the crushing burden of the costs of war and reconstruction. The appetite of the French Government had been whetted by the 1921 ultimatum. If the Ruhr were occupied by the Allies, not only would French security be increased, but the profits of German industry could be forcibly transferred to the Allied exchequers. This plan, plausibly referred to as a policy of " productive guarantees ", proved irresistibly attractive to a number of French politicians, Poincaré among them. In December 1922 Germany failed by a small margin to fulfil the agreed programme of deliveries in kind ; and the Reparation Commission, against the vote of the British representative, declared her in " voluntary default ". The significance of this step lay in the article of the treaty which entitled the Allies, " in case of voluntary default by Germany ", to take " such measures as the respective governments may determine to be necessary ".

The way was now clear for the experiment on which the French had set their heart. On January 11th, 1923, after a vain effort to secure the co-operation, or at least the approval, of the British Government, French and Belgian troops entered the Ruhr. The German Government declared a policy of passive resistance. Germans were forbidden to co-operate in any way with the invaders ; and all voluntary reparation payments and deliveries were stopped. The French replied with a counter-boycott, drawing a line between occupied and unoccupied German territory across which nothing was allowed to pass. Recalcitrant officials and industrialists in the occupied area were expelled or imprisoned ; and an organisation was set up to extract reparation from the output of the Ruhr industries.

The British Government took the view that this isolated action of France and Belgium, taken on an inadequate pretext and without agreement between the Allies, was a contravention of the treaty ; and it had no belief in the efficacy of this method of obtaining reparation payments. Franco-British relations were distinctly strained. In the Rhineland the position became most difficult. Nearly all the decisions of the High Commission in 1923 were taken by a majority against the British vote ; and in so far as they arose out of the Ruhr occupation, the authorities in the British zone refused to apply them.

The occupation brought the whole economic life of Germany to a standstill. On the French side, the deliveries of coal and iron from the Ruhr were insufficient to cover the costs of the operation. On the German side, the most immediate result was the complete bankruptcy of the German exchequer. The mark, on the eve of the occupation, had already fallen to 35,000 to the pound. Throughout 1923 the decline was continuous, its value being sometimes halved from one day to the next. The foreigner who exchanged his " good " currencies at these fantastic rates could live sumptuously in Germany on a few pence a day, or travel all over the country for a few shillings. Before the end of 1923, 50,000 milliards of marks could be obtained for one pound.

There is no doubt that the original decline in the

mark was the result of causes beyond the control of the German Government—the economic chaos of the war, the disorganisation of the state machine and, finally, the claims of the Allies. But once the process was under way, the German authorities soon abandoned all efforts to arrest it. The vast and undefined reparation debt not only made it impossible for Germany to put her financial house in order, but paralysed her will to make any serious effort to do so ; for the sounder her finances, the more she would be able to pay. The downward race of the mark was watched with grim complacency by the German authorities, who reflected that it was carrying away with it the last Allied hopes of reparation. The last stages of the process provided a classic instance of inflation in the strict sense of the word, *i.e.* the unrestricted printing of paper money without regard to any consideration save the immediate needs of the exchequer.

The inflation was a greater disaster for Germany than the Treaty of Versailles. Every mortgage, every investment bearing fixed interest, every banking account in marks, was rendered valueless. All savings were wiped out at a stroke. The blow fell most crushingly on the large middle class. The aristocrat, though impoverished, still had his land, his stock and his houses. A handful of industrialists and speculators made their fortunes out of the inflation. The working class, used to living from hand to mouth, had at any rate nothing to lose ; and the wages of the worker were adjusted to the rise in prices more rapidly than the salaries of clerks and officials. The middle class, deprived of its savings, forfeited that small margin which raised it above the proletariat, and suffered all the humiliations of a loss of caste. It despised the working class, to whose level it had sunk, and the Jews, whom it regarded (in most cases, wrongly) as the profiteers of the inflation. From this dispossessed and degraded middle class, National Socialism would one day draw the great mass of its recruits.

The Ruhr occupation, which completed Germany's ruin, was however a turning-point in the post-war history of Europe. By September 1923, German resistance was broken. A new ministry had just taken office in Berlin, Gustav Stresemann, a politician hitherto unknown abroad, being Chancellor and Minister for Foreign Affairs ; and to Stresemann fell the task of bringing " passive resistance " to an end. But this retreat did not solve the problem of the Allied Governments. Before reparation payments on any serious scale could be resumed, Germany's finances would obviously have to be overhauled ; and at the end of the year the United States agreed to join with the British, French, Belgian and Italian Governments in appointing a committee of " experts " who were to examine, from a purely business and non-political standpoint, ways and means of putting Germany's financial house in order. In order to spare French susceptibilities, no mention was made, in the committee's terms of reference, of the necessity of considering Germany's capacity to pay reparation. But everyone knew what was meant. The American " expert ", General Dawes, was the chairman of the committee, which was known after him as the Dawes Committee. It began its work in Paris in January 1924.

The appointment of Stresemann as German Foreign Minister (he soon laid down the Chancellorship, and devoted himself entirely to foreign affairs) and the setting up of the Dawes Committee were two of the three events which heralded the coming change of spirit. The third event happened in France. There, too, people had come to realise that the occupation of the Ruhr had been a costly mistake, and that the bankruptcy of Germany meant also the bankruptcy of the policy of " productive guarantees ". France, threatened with a financial crisis of her own, had more need than ever of substantial reparation payments from Germany ; but some other method of obtaining them must clearly be tried. The French elections of May 1924 resulted in a victory for the Left. The ministry of Poincaré fell, and was succeeded by a radical ministry under Herriot ; and the date of this occurrence—May 11th, 1924—may be taken as marking the end of the first post-war period of trying to establish peace by force. Some Frenchmen regretted afterwards that Poincaré's policy of enforcing the treaty at all costs was ever abandoned. But in 1924 it was recognised by general consent to have failed ; and its continuance would have brought about an open breach between France and Great Britain.

WHILE the duel between France and Germany occupied the centre of the European stage, other conflicts, which had little or no connexion with this main issue, were being fought out in the wings. These may be grouped under three headings : the Danubian States, Italy and Soviet Russia.

THE DANUBIAN STATES

Before 1914, Central Europe, which may be more closely defined as the basin of the middle Danube, was occupied by the composite state of Austria-Hungary with 55,000,000 inhabitants, separated from the Black Sea by the small state of Roumania. After the war the Danube basin was occupied by five states, namely (in order of population) Yugoslavia, Roumania, Czechoslovakia, Hungary, Austria. This drastic rearrangement resulted in a multiplication of customs barriers and a dislocation of economic life from which the Danubian countries never fully recovered. During the period 1920–24 Yugoslavia, Roumania and Czechoslovakia were saved by French patronage from the worst consequences of this upheaval ; and thanks to French armaments and French loans, they remained throughout this time relatively strong and prosperous.

These states, which formed the Little Entente, have been described in Chapter 1. It remains to give some account of the two ex-enemy states of the Danubian basin : Austria and Hungary.

The republic of Austria had from the first an artificial character which rendered its permanent survival dubious. It had no national unity and no national will to exist. It was composed of the German-speaking populations of the old Austrian Empire. But these Germans, who had been loyal subjects of the Hapsburgs so long as Vienna was the capital of a polyglot Hapsburg Empire, had never desired to see German Austria a tiny independent state. The new republic was split into two sections : its overgrown capital, containing nearly one-third of its whole population, predominantly socialist and anti-religious, and its strongly Roman Catholic countryside, with a few provincial towns which tended to follow the lead of Vienna. The strength of Austria's position lay in the almost universal desire of her inhabitants, manifested from time to time in unofficial " plebiscites ", to join Germany. This acted on the Allies as a kind of silent blackmail. Since the Allies (particularly France and Italy) were determined to prevent union between Austria and Germany, it was necessary for them to give an independent Austria sufficient inducement to exist.

It was, therefore, policy rather than pity which made Austria the pensioner of the Allied Governments. First, an International Relief Committee, in which neutrals were invited to co-operate, was set up ; and the Austrian Reparation Commission abandoned the " first charge on all assets and revenues of Austria " conferred on it by the St. Germain Treaty, in order to permit of the issue of " relief bonds " secured on these assets and revenues. Between 1919 and 1921 the Austrian Government received about £25,000,000 in the form of " relief credits ".   Then the Allied Governments had the idea of referring the whole matter to the League of Nations ; and after further large advances from the British, French, Italian and Czechoslovak Governments to keep Austria afloat for a few months longer, a complete scheme for the financial reconstruction of the country, the stabilisation of its currency, and the issue of an international loan, was drawn up by the Financial Committee of the League, and accepted by the Austrian Government in October 1922. The loan protocol included a significant political condition.   Austria not only reiterated the obligation assumed under the St. Germain Treaty not to " alienate her independence " without the consent of the Council of the League, but undertook to enter into no economic agreements with other Powers which might compromise that independence.   On the basis of this protocol, an Austrian loan of a nominal amount of £30,000,000 was offered to the investing public of ten countries in the spring of 1923.   It was guaranteed in certain proportions by the British, French, Italian, Czechoslovak and some neutral governments, and was everywhere heavily over-subscribed.   This brilliant success not only solved the Austrian problem for several years, but provided a precedent for the loans to other European countries which were issued under League auspices at a later date.

Hungary was left materially in a better position than Austria. She had lost nearly half her pre-war population and more than half her territory. But this was in one sense a source of strength; for she had now no disaffected subjects of alien race. Economically, Hungary was a rich agricultural country, whose town population was not proportionately excessive. Politically, most of the forms of democracy were kept up. But the real power was in the hands of a ruling caste of large and small landowners, which controlled both the army and the administration. The peasant in Hungary lived in conditions more nearly approaching serfdom than in any other modern European state. The working class in the towns was small and unorganised; and after an abortive communist revolution in 1919, when Bela Kun held Budapest for nearly five months, any form of revolutionary propaganda was rigorously suppressed.

Hungary had, since the peace settlement, been second only to Germany in her resentment of the terms imposed on her and in her determination to reverse them at the first opportunity. This determination made her an object of apprehension to the three states which acquired Hungarian territory by the Treaty of Trianon—Czechoslovakia, Roumania and Yugoslavia—and was, as we have seen, the cause of the formation of the Little Entente. But the Little Entente states were also haunted by another fear. The abdication of the last Hapsburg, Karl IV, in November 1918 had not destroyed the traditional devotion of the Hungarian people to its monarch. The new constitution of Hungary was in form a monarchy; and the head of the state assumed the title of Regent, which implied the hope of a future restoration. On the other hand, the inhabitants of the ceded territories of Slovakia, Transylvania and Croatia, while they might have no love for their former Hungarian masters, were also believed to retain a lingering loyalty to the Hapsburg dynasty ; and a Hapsburg restoration in Hungary was therefore dreaded by the Little Entente governments as a potential source of unrest among their new subjects.

The nervousness of the Little Entente was not altogether unfounded. Twice during 1921 the impulsive and ill-advised Karl made an attempt to regain his Hungarian throne. Each time he arrived unannounced in Hungary from his home in Switzerland, apparently convinced that the whole country would rise in his favour. In fact, the Hungarian Government was in no state to face the war with the Little Entente which a Hapsburg restoration would have entailed ; and Karl's presence was a serious embarrassment to them. On the first occasion he was induced quietly to leave. On the second he was arrested, handed over to the Allies and conveyed to Madeira, where he was henceforth to live. The Hungarian Government was compelled, under Allied pressure, to pass a law excluding the Hapsburgs for ever from the throne of Hungary ; and the only result of Karl's escapades was a striking demonstration of the power and solidarity of the Little Entente. Six months later Karl died in Madeira, leaving as his heir a boy of nine, the Archduke Otto. It was clear that the Hapsburg question would cease to trouble Central Europe for several years to come.

The way was now open for financial reorganisation. The success of the League loan to Austria suggested a similar measure of assistance to Hungary, whose financial position, though less desperate than that of Austria, had also been dislocated by war and revolution. In 1923 a reconstruction scheme was drawn up by the Financial Committee of the League; and in the following spring a Hungarian loan of £12,000,000 was successfully issued to the public of eight countries. It differed from the Austrian loan in one important respect. There was no international guarantee; and the sole security for the loan was the credit of the Hungarian Government.

ITALY

Italy had been one of the five " Principal Allied and Associated Powers " who dictated the terms of peace. Yet her appetites, like those of Japan, were whetted, not satisfied, by the results of the war; and throughout the subsequent period she must be ranked, like Japan and like the ex-enemy countries, among the discontented and " troublesome " states. This discontent became so disturbing a factor in international affairs that some explanation must be given of its causes.

In the first place, Italy, like Germany, only attained her present political shape in 1870. In 1848, the Italian peninsula was still divided between eight different states, and Italian unity was the dream of a few enthusiasts. Italy in the nineteen-twenties was still in the period of turbulent and adventurous youth. She had not yet acquired the respectable, peace-loving traditions of the old-established nations. She remembered that she won her unity by fighting for it; and she still looked to war to extend her power and her territory. If it be asked why Italy proved less loyal to the League of Nations than the other Great Powers, one answer is that, if the

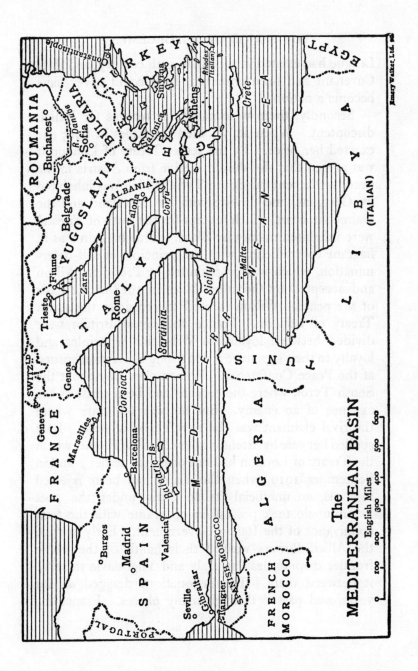

The MEDITERRANEAN BASIN

English Miles

0   100   200   300   400   500   600

League had existed in the nineteenth century, and if its Covenant had been observed, Italy could never have become a nation.

Secondly, there were particular reasons for Italian discontent. When Italy joined the Allies in 1915 she exacted her price. By the secret Treaty of London it was agreed that she should receive from Austria in the peace settlement the South Tyrol, which was inhabited by Germans, and Trieste with its hinterland and the Dalmatian coast, which (except for the town of Trieste) were inhabited mainly by Slavs. This bargain was in flagrant contradiction with the principle of self-determination, which was propounded by President Wilson and accepted by the other Allies in 1918 as the basis of the peace. Wilson refused to recognise the secret Treaty of London. France and Great Britain were divided between loyalty to Wilsonian principles and loyalty to their signature ; and a long altercation ensued at the Peace Conference. Wilson gave way about the South Tyrol, where the bargain had been made at the expense of an enemy. But he was obdurate where the rival claimant was the new Yugoslav state. Italy spoiled her case by extending her claims to Fiume, which the Treaty of London had not promised to her ; and in September 1919, when this claim had been rejected in Paris, an unofficial Italian army under the poet D'Annunzio took possession of Fiume with the tacit connivance of the Italian Government. Early in 1920 the Allied Powers washed their hands of the whole frontier dispute, leaving Italy and Yugoslavia to settle it between them. The negotiations dragged on for years, and passed through many phases. France in-

curred keen Italian animosity by her support of Yugoslavia. It was not till 1924 that a final settlement was
reached. Italy abandoned to Yugoslavia the whole
Dalmatian coast except the port of Zara, but elsewhere
obtained rather more favourable terms than those of
the London Treaty, including possession of the town of
Fiume.

In the meanwhile, Italy and Yugoslavia, whose relations were by this time chronically embittered, had
found a fresh bone of contention in the Albanian question. In 1913 Albania had been recognised as an
independent state. But during the war it fell into
complete chaos. By the London Treaty it was agreed
that Italy should receive the port of Valona and should
be charged with the conduct of Albania's foreign relations ; and at the end of the war Italian troops were in
occupation of almost the whole country. This position
they were unable to maintain in face of opposition both
within the country and from the Yugoslavs, who regarded the presence of an Italian army on the east coast
of the Adriatic as a menace to their own security. In
1920 the Italian troops were withdrawn, and Albania
was admitted as an independent state to the League of
Nations.

There remained, however, one delicate question.
Italy claimed that, in return for the abandonment of
her rights under the London Treaty, the Allies should
recognise her " special status " in Albanian affairs. In
November 1921 the Ambassadors' Conference in Paris,
which had succeeded the Supreme Council as the principal organ of the Allied Governments, passed a resolution in which it was declared that, in the event of any

threat to the independence of Albania, the British, French and Japanese Governments would instruct their representatives on the Council of the League of Nations to propose that the task of maintaining that independence should be entrusted to Italy. In form, this resolution had no immediate application whatever. It was, indeed, something of an absurdity, since the only Power likely to threaten Albania's independence was Italy herself. But Italy interpreted it as a recognition of her right to intervene in Albanian affairs to the exclusion of any other Power; and this claim was a source of constant irritation and apprehension in Yugoslavia.

A third article of the Treaty of London contributed to Italy's discontent and encouraged the feeling that she was not being fairly treated by her Allies. It provided that in the event of Great Britain and France increasing their colonial territories in Africa at the expense of Germany, Italy should obtain " equitable compensation " by a favourable adjustment of the frontiers between her existing African colonies and the contiguous colonies of Great Britain and France. This promise was sufficiently vague to account for a wide latitude of interpretation. It was not until 1924 that Italy and Great Britain were able to reach an agreement; the territory of Jubaland was transferred, in settlement of this obligation, from the British colony of Kenya to Italian Somaliland. Agreement between Italy and France proved still more difficult. A frontier rectification in North Africa in 1919 failed to satisfy Italy's extensive claims under this article; and the Italian grievance continued until 1935 to inject a further element of poison into Franco-Italian relations.

In October 1922, while the Italo-Yugoslav frontier was still unsettled, an important change took place in the form of government in Italy. The democratic régime, which had been discredited by its failure to maintain internal order, was overthrown by the Fascist party; and Italy passed for more than 20 years under the personal dictatorship of the Fascist leader, Benito Mussolini. This event had international repercussions of two kinds. The change from democracy to dictatorship was soon to be imitated by several other European states, the first to follow suit being Spain; and the advent of Mussolini to power heralded a more aggressive Italian foreign policy. Restless discontent had been characteristic of Italian policy under the postwar democracy. Under Mussolini, this discontent became more ambitious, more self-assertive, more calculating in its determination to turn the needs and embarrassments of other Powers to Italy's advantage.

Mussolini soon gave Europe a taste of his quality. In August 1923 the Italian representative on the commission which was marking out the frontier between Albania and Greece was shot, together with three of his assistants, by Greek bandits. The Italian fleet at once bombarded Corfu, killing several civilians, occupied the island, and demanded an indemnity—a demand which was endorsed by the Ambassadors' Conference in Paris. Greece, thoroughly frightened and, since the fall of Venizelos, without a friend in Europe, rashly appealed both to the League of Nations and to the Ambassadors' Conference. This division of authority enabled Mussolini to declare that he would not recognise the jurisdiction of the League. By private negotiations an agreement was reached under which Greece would deposit a sum of 50,000,000 lire with the Permanent Court of International Justice at the Hague, pending an award by the Court on the validity of the claim. At the last moment, however, the Italian Government rejected this solution; and Greece, under pressure from the Ambassadors' Conference, was compelled to pay the indemnity direct to Italy. The moral of these proceedings appeared to be that the Allied Governments were not prepared, through the League of Nations or otherwise, to take action against one of their number in defence of a small Power.

THE SOVIET UNION

The Union of Soviet Socialist Republics, which became in 1923 the official name of the country formerly known as Russia, must also be reckoned, in the years after 1918, among the disturbing forces in European politics, though for quite different reasons. It was not till 1920 that the civil war, in which the anti-Soviet forces had received the active support of the British, French Japanese, and (for a short time) American Governments, came to an end; and relations between the Soviet Government and the Allies continued for many years after to be marked by mutual hostility and mistrust. This hostility was natural and inevitable. European states since the Reformation had regarded themselves and one another as complete and independent national units. To undermine the security of another state by spreading disaffection among its subjects was an expedient which might be justified in time of war, but which was altogether contrary to the idea of normal relations. Soviet theory boldly rejected these fundamental assumptions. It denied that the Soviet Union was a national unit. It regarded the state as a transitory form of political organisation incompatible with the realisation of the communist ideal. The duty of every good communist was to spread throughout the world the same revolution which had been successful in Russia; and since the first Soviet leaders believed that the revolutionary government would be unable to maintain itself in Russia unless capitalism were overthrown elsewhere, there was a certain element of self-interest in their missionary zeal.

So long, however, as the capitalist states continued to exist, it was necessary for practical purposes to build up a system of relations between them and the Soviet Union. While the Communist International ("Comintern" for short), whose headquarters were at Moscow, worked through its local branches to overthrow the capitalist governments of other countries, the Soviet Government, whose directors were also the directors of Comintern, endeavoured to establish normal diplomatic relations with these same governments. This dual policy seriously embarrassed the Soviet authorities in their dealings with foreign Powers during the whole of this period.

At the outset, it was only with its smaller neighbours that the Soviet Union was able to establish official relations. The sincerity of the Soviet Government's disclaimer of national ambitions was shown by its readiness to recognise the newly formed states which had broken away from the Russian Empire. In 1920, it concluded treaties of peace with Finland (which had been a semi-autonomous Grand Duchy under the Empire) and with Estonia, Latvia and Lithuania (whose territories had been an integral part of Russia); and these were followed by the treaty with Poland (see p. 35) in the next year. The three Caucasian states— Georgia, Azerbaijan and Armenia—fared less well. None of them, except perhaps Georgia, possessed any of the elements of independence. The withdrawal of the Allied troops, under whose patronage they had come into being in the last year of the war, sealed their fate; and their territories reverted to the Soviet Union and Turkey. Early in 1921 the Soviet Union signed treaties of friendship with Turkey, Persia and Afghanistan. The treaties with Persia and Afghanistan had the result, if not the intention, of encouraging those countries to resist the pressure of British influence; and it seemed for a time as if the nineteenth-century rivalry between Russia and Great Britain in Asia was about to be resumed.

The Great Powers still shunned official relations with the Soviet Government. But the possibilities of trade with the Soviet Union (even though the latter refused to acknowledge the debts of Tsarist Russia) could not be neglected. In 1921 Great Britain made a commercial agreement with the Soviet Government and sent a " trade mission " to Moscow. This example was followed by Italy; and by the next year the Soviet Union was sufficiently recognised as a member of the family of nations to be invited to an economic conference of all the European Powers, including Germany, which was held at Genoa in April 1922. Lloyd George hoped to use the conference to bring about an agreement between the Soviet Union and the other Powers. But this hope was checkmated by the *intransigeance* of the French and Belgian Delegations, which insisted on recognition of Russia's pre-war debts as a condition of any parleying with the Soviet Government; and the only result of the conference was one which its conveners neither expected nor desired. A week after the conference assembled, the German and Soviet Delegations met quietly at Rapallo, a seaside resort a few miles from Genoa, and signed a treaty of friendship between the two countries. The terms of the treaty were unimportant. But its signature was a significant event. It secured for the Soviet Union its first official recognition by a Great Power ; and it was the first overt attempt by Germany to break the ring which the Versailles Powers had drawn round her. The indignation with which this treaty was greeted by the Allied Powers was understandable. But it was the direct consequence of their own policy of treating Germany and the Soviet Union as inferior countries. The two outcasts naturally joined hands ; and the Rapallo Treaty established friendly relations between them for more than ten years.

The policy of Great Britain in regard to the Soviet Union now unfortunately became a shuttlecock of party politics. The fall of Lloyd George, which occurred soon after the Genoa Conference, was attributed in part to his policy of " coquetting with the Bolsheviks ". The Conservative Government which followed thought it necessary to take a stiffer line ; and, by way of reaction, the Labour Government, which came into power in February 1924, at once granted official recognition to the Soviet Government. Throughout the summer negotiations proceeded in London ; and in August an agreement was signed between the British and Soviet representatives providing for the mutual cancellation of outstanding claims and for a guaranteed loan to the Soviet Government.

In the meanwhile, opposition to the Labour attitude towards the Soviet Union became the principal plank in the Conservative programme. The trade agreement of 1921 contained a clause by which the Soviet Government had undertaken to refrain from any form of revolutionary propaganda in the territories of the British Empire. Neither Conservative nor Labour Government had accepted the Soviet contention that the Soviet Government and Comintern were two entirely independent entities, and that the activities of the latter could not be held to constitute a breach of this pledge. During the summer of 1924 the Conservatives constantly embarrassed the Labour Government by drawing attention to Comintern propaganda in the British Empire ; and on the eve of the general election of October 1924, a Conservative newspaper published what purported to be a letter from Zinoviev, the president of Comintern, giving instructions to British communists for the conduct of communist propaganda in Great Britain. The Soviet Government stoutly denied the authenticity of the letter. But it was generally believed in, and helped to give the Conservatives a large majority. This incident, and the return to power of a Conservative Government, destroyed all chance of the ratification of the agreement negotiated during the summer. Relations between Great Britain and the Soviet Union once more became strained, though there was no actual breach.

This tension was, however, not typical of the international situation of the Soviet Union at the end of 1924. The official recognition of Great Britain had been followed by that of Italy, France, and Japan and of most European states. The United States was the only Great Power which still refused to have any relations with the Soviet Government. Moreover on the Soviet side there had been, since the death of Lenin in January 1924, a distinct tendency to relegate world-revolution to a secondary place in the party programme. The most significant aspect of the " Zinoviev letter " affair had been the eagerness of everyone in the Soviet Union to deny its authenticity ; for there was nothing in the letter, whether genuine or not, which conflicted with the hitherto declared policy of the Soviet leaders. The struggle for leadership between Trotsky and Stalin which began in 1924 turned on this very point. Trotsky maintained the traditional thesis that the Soviet Government could not maintain itself indefinitely in the midst of a capitalist world, and that the spread of revolution was therefore the primary aim of Soviet activity. Stalin stood for the new policy which came to be known as "building up socialism in a single state ". The expulsion of Trotsky from the Communist Party in 1927 proclaimed to the world that this policy had won, and that hopes of world-revolution, while not formally abandoned, would not in future be allowed to interfere with the establishment of normal relations between the

Soviet Government and capitalist states. The Soviet Union had thus at length accepted the fundamental basis of international relations, and its full return to the international community of states was only a matter time.

PART II

THE PERIOD OF PACIFICATION:
THE LEAGUE OF NATIONS

(1924–1930)

THE second period of European history between the wars—the period of pacification—began with a solution of the two questions which had caused most trouble during the first period : the problem of reparation, and the problem of French security. The solutions of these problems which were found in 1924 and 1925— the " Dawes Plan " and the Locarno Treaty—were incomplete and, as we now know, short-lived. But for half a decade they were accepted as definitive; and these years, with all their uncertainties and imperfections, were the golden years of post-war Europe.

THE DAWES PLAN

On May 11th, 1924, the date of the general election which made Herriot Prime Minister of France, the Dawes Committee had just presented its report to the Reparation Commission. In Germany Stresemann, the Foreign Minister, was already the most influential figure in political life. In Great Britain the Labour Government of Ramsay MacDonald was in power. These three statesmen now set to work to settle the reparation problem on the lines of the Dawes report.

The first preoccupation of the Dawes Committee had been the re-establishment of the German currency, without which foreign payments by Germany were clearly out of the question. By the end of 1923 the German mark had in effect lost all value. The German Government had provisionally brought into existence a new currency at the old parity of 20 to the pound, which it called the Rentenmark. But the position of the Rentenmark was precarious unless some solid reserve of gold or foreign assets could be formed to back it. The Dawes Committee recommended the creation of a new currency at the same parity, the Reichsmark, which would be controlled by a Bank of Issue independent of the German Government.

Assuming the establishment of a stable currency, the Committee considered that Germany could pay to the Allies, on reparation account, annuities beginning at £50,000,000 and rising, from the fifth year onwards, to a standard maximum of £125,000,000. The security for these payments was to take three forms : bonds of the state railways, bonds of German industrial enterprises, and revenue receipts from the customs and the taxes on alcohol, sugar and tobacco. Lest, however, these payments should once more disturb the exchange, it was proposed that they should be made by Germany in marks, and that the responsibility for the transfer of these sums into foreign currencies should rest with the Allied Governments. In order to ensure the fair working of these arrangements in the interest of the creditors, the Reparation Commission was to have the right of appointing Allied commissioners to the board of the Bank of Issue, to the railways and to the management of the " controlled revenues " (*i.e.* of the earmarked tax receipts) ; and there was to be an " Agent for Reparation Payments " in charge of the whole plan. Finally, there were two indispensable conditions for the success of the scheme : that the Ruhr occupation should be abandoned, and Germany restored to full economic control of her whole territory ; and that Germany should receive a foreign loan of £40,000,000 for the double purpose of providing a currency reserve and of helping her to pay the first annuity which would fall due before the benefits of the plan would have had time to mature.

After preliminary discussions between MacDonald and Herriot, the " Dawes Plan " was submitted to a conference held in London in July and August, which was also attended by Stresemann. In the new atmosphere of conciliation, the plan was accepted without much difficulty, though many complicated details required settlement, and the Germans, mindful of the Ruhr, sought and obtained an undertaking that penalties would not again be imposed except in the event of deliberate large-scale default. In October the German loan was issued and (except in France, where it was taken up privately by the banks) everywhere over-subscribed. Rather more than half the total amount was subscribed in the United States, and more than a quarter in Great Britain. France, Belgium, Italy, Switzerland and Sweden took the balance. Though the Dawes loan was not issued under the auspices of the League of Nations, there is little doubt that the precedent of the League loans to Austria and Hungary contributed materially to its success. In the middle of November the last French and Belgian troops were withdrawn from the Ruhr.

The Dawes Plan had. many merits. It limited its demands to sums which Germany, in favourable conditions, might be able to pay, though the necessity of satisfying French expectations had perhaps encouraged the experts to err on the side of optimism. It separated the question of payment from the question of transfer, and left the latter for the creditors to deal with. It gave the creditors the security of certain specified revenues—instead of a vague general charge on Germany's resources. Above all, it removed reparation from the sphere of political controversy, and treated it like an ordinary commercial debt. It took the whole problem out of the hands of the unsatisfactory Reparation Commission, and ensured that it would be handled from an impartial, non-political standpoint, more especially as the " Agent for Reparation Payments " was to be an American citizen.

In these points the Dawes Plan represented so immense an advance on anything that had gone before that its enthusiastic reception is not difficult to understand. But it had serious flaws. It provided for annual payments, but it failed to prescribe their duration or to make any pronouncement on Germany's total indebtedness; for no French Government at this period would have dared to confess that it had formally abandoned any part of the full reparation claim of £6,600,000,000. Germany was still, therefore, in the hopeless position that any increase in her financial well-being would entail an increased obligation, and she was deprived of any incentive to accumulate savings, which would merely pass into the Allied exchequers. Worse still, the Dawes Plan set up the fatal precedent of lending Germany the wherewithal to pay reparation. The success of the Dawes loan was followed by an orgy of German borrowing. During the next five years every important German municipality, and nearly every important German business concern, raised large loans or credits in the United States, and sometimes also in Great Britain. This influx of capital seemed providential. It created a wave of prosperity which enabled Germany to pay the Dawes annuities without undue strain on her resources, and solved the transfer problem by placing an abundance of foreign currency at her disposal. The Dawes Plan appeared throughout these years to have been an unqualified success. Few people had the insight to realise that Germany was paying her debts out of American money, and that her solvency depended on the continued popularity of German loans in Wall Street.

INTER-ALLIED DEBTS

This is the most convenient place to mention another set of claims which, though different in origin, became inextricably intertwined with the reparation problem and eventually shared its fate. During the war Great Britain had lent vast sums to her European Allies including Russia, and had in turn borrowed more than half the total amount from the United States, from whom some of the Allies had also obtained loans direct. This complex of indebtedness soon threatened to become a burden as unwieldy and intractable as that of reparation. In the matter of inter-Allied war debts, America was only a creditor, the Continental Allies were only debtors (France was also creditor for a small sum), and Great Britain occupied an intermediate position, being part debtor, part creditor.

When in 1922 the United States Government began seriously to press for repayment, France declared that she could only pay her war debts if and when Germany paid reparation ; for it was intolerable that victorious France should pay her Allies if defeated Germany failed to pay her.   Great Britain, balanced between debit and credit, would have liked to see a complete cancellation of all war debts.   In August 1922, she addressed to her European Allies a communication (commonly referred to as the " Balfour note ") declaring that she would expect to receive from them in settlement of their debts only such amounts as she herself was obliged to pay to the United States in settlement of hers.   This over-clever attempt to place the whole odium of debt collection on the United States was widely resented in that country, and further hardened American opinion against cancellation.

In view of the American attitude, the British Government considered that they had no option but to honour their obligation.   In December 1922 an agreement was concluded under which the British debt to the United States, together with interest, would be discharged by sixty-two annual payments of about £33,000,000.   Until 1926 Great Britain received nothing from the European Allies.   Then, following the Dawes settlement, agreements were reached, on the same lines as the British-American agreement, for the payment by annual instalments of the debts due from France, Italy, Roumania, Yugoslavia, Greece and

Portugal to Great Britain and to the United States. A detailed account of these transactions cannot be given here. But it is worth noting that, while the American settlement with Great Britain represented (reckoning interest at a standard rate of 5 per cent) a reduction of less than 30 per cent of the original debt, the British settlements represented reductions, in the case of Italy, of more than 80 per cent and, in the case of the other Allies, of more than 60 per cent. Moreover, the combined receipts of Great Britain from inter-Allied debts and from reparation never reached the level of her debt payments to the United States; so that in effect all debt payments, wherever made, found their way into the American exchequer.

The vast transfers of funds provided for in these debt settlements, like the transfers under the Dawes Plan, were rendered possible by loans and credits from the United States to the debtor countries. The League of Nations continued the policy which it had so happily inaugurated in Austria and Hungary. Between 1924 and 1928, loans were raised under League auspices by Greece, Bulgaria, Estonia and the Free City of Danzig, and were mainly subscribed in the United States and in Great Britain. The abundant flow of credit across the Atlantic, both to Germany and to other European countries, not only supported the whole cumbrous structure of reparation and war debt payments, but created a general atmosphere of prosperity and well-being in Europe; and this prosperity was an essential condition of the improvement in political relations between the principal European states, which was the most striking feature of the period.

THE GENEVA PROTOCOL

Having concluded in London, in August 1924, the agreement to adopt the Dawes Plan for the settlement of German reparation, MacDonald and Herriot attended in the following month the Assembly of the League of Nations at Geneva; and here they made an important attempt to settle the other outstanding problem of French security.

Since the French rejection in 1922 of the British proposal for a guarantee pact (see p. 29), the search for French security had been diverted into different channels. In 1921 the League had begun its efforts (which will be described in a later chapter) to tackle the vexed question of disarmament; and in 1922 the French Government first put forward the thesis, which it maintained with the utmost tenacity, that France could only reduce her armaments if her security were increased. The French point of view had widened since the demand for security had first been heard in 1919. France now had clients in Eastern and Central Europe whose safety had become part of her own. What was required was a general guarantee of additional security both for France herself and for her allies. The Geneva discussions about disarmament gave an excellent opportunity for demanding such a guarantee. If it were obtained, French policy would have secured a notable success. If it were not obtained, France and her allies would admit no obligation to disarm.

The British Delegation at Geneva, without perhaps

88

realising the full implications of its action, tacitly accepted this assumption ; and the Temporary Mixed Commission (the body appointed to investigate the disarmament question) submitted to the 1923 Assembly a draft " Treaty of Mutual Assistance ", which contained somewhat vague provisions for future disarmament and extremely precise guarantees for present security. Any outbreak of hostilities was to be followed within four days by a decision of the Council of the League which party was the aggressor, and members of the League were then to be under an automatic obligation to render military assistance against the aggressor. The effect was therefore not merely to counteract the whittling-away process which Article 16 of the Covenant had undergone in the Assembly resolutions of 1921 (see p. 28), but to strengthen that Article by making military sanctions automatic and obligatory.

The 1923 Assembly, which was not attended by responsible ministers of any of the Great Powers, could do nothing but refer this draft to the governments for consideration. It was enthusiastically approved by France, by most of her allies and by the smaller states of Eastern Europe, but decisively rejected by Great Britain, by the British Dominions, and by the Scandinavian states and Holland—countries which were more concerned to avoid an increase in their commitments than to obtain an increase in their security. But when in the following year MacDonald and Herriot appeared together at the Assembly, the atmosphere had so much improved all round that a compromise between the two opposing views seemed in sight; and the 1924 Assembly drafted, and unanimously recommended to the governments for their acceptance, the agreement which came to be known as the " Geneva Protocol ". Its full title was the " Protocol for the Pacific Settlement of International Disputes ".

The principal novelty of the Protocol was its attempt to improve on the Covenant and to provide additional security through compulsory resort to arbitration. The Covenant left the door open for war, not only in cases when the Council, voting without the parties, failed to pronounce a unanimous judgment on a dispute, but also in cases where the subject of the dispute was ruled to be a matter within the domestic jurisdiction of one of the parties. The Protocol sought to close these two "gaps". It provided that all disputes of a legal character should be submitted to the Permanent Court of International Justice, whose decision would be binding. In other disputes, the procedure of the Covenant was maintained. But should the Council fail to reach a unanimous conclusion, this would not entail, as under the Covenant, liberty for the disputants to go to war. The Council was to refer the dispute to a committee of arbitrators whose decision was binding. As regards the second gap, the Protocol provided (the proposal had come from the Japanese delegates) that disputes about matters of domestic jurisdiction, though excluded by the Covenant from a formal judgment of the Council under Article 15, should be submitted to the procedure of conciliation under Article 11, and that no Power should be judged an aggressor in such a dispute if it had brought the matter before the League under that Article. Finally, in order to keep the balance between security and disarmament, the Protocol proposed that the Disarmament Conference should meet on June 15th, 1925, provided sufficient states had ratified it by that time.

The Geneva Protocol did nothing to strengthen the powers of the Council under Article 16 of the Covenant or to make military sanctions obligatory ; and it therefore went less far to satisfy the French demand than the draft Treaty of Mutual Assistance. The fact that it was accepted as adequate by the French Government of 1924 was strong evidence of the conciliatory note which had found its way into French policy since the fall of Poincaré. The Protocol did, however, satisfy the one vital interest of France and her allies—the maintenance of the peace settlement of 1919 and, in particular, of its territorial arrangements. A demand for the revision of a treaty provision was not a " dispute " to which the procedure laid down in the Protocol (or, indeed, in the Covenant itself) would apply ; and lest there should be any doubt on this point, it was specifically emphasised in the report of the committee which had drafted the Protocol. In other words, the Protocol accentuated what was afterwards attacked as one of the weaknesses of the Covenant : its tendency to identify security with the maintenance of the 1919 settlement, and its failure to provide adequate machinery for the revision of that settlement. But in 1924 this criticism was scarcely heard. Germany was not yet a member of the League. The lesser ex-enemy states still had more fear of suffering aggression than hope of being strong enough to commit it ; and they gladly signed the Protocol.

General enthusiasm over the Protocol prevailed until

the end of the Assembly. Then reaction set in. The first trouble came over the clauses providing that disputes on matters of domestic jurisdiction might be brought before the League under Article 11 of the Covenant. The motive of Japan in bringing forward this proposal was well known. Canada, Australia and New Zealand had recently followed the example of the United States in excluding Japanese immigrants from their territories (see p. 153); and Japan wished to establish her right to protest against these restrictions at Geneva. The text of Article 11 seemed sufficiently wide in itself to confer that right. But the British Dominions were most reluctant to admit in terms that their domestic legislation on immigration questions could in any event be discussed or challenged by the League; and it soon became clear that on this ground, if on no other, they would refuse to ratify the Protocol.

Study of the other provisions of the Protocol also provoked reflexion, both in the Dominions and in Great Britain. Compulsory arbitration was a novelty to which British public opinion did not easily reconcile itself; and though successive British Governments proclaimed their unalterable loyalty to the Covenant, sanctions had never been popular in any part of the British Empire. The Protocol had, it was true, not modified Article 16. But there was no escaping from the argument that an increase in the number of disputes in which the Council could determine the aggressor meant an increase in the number of disputes in which sanctions might have to be imposed.

In these circumstances, the opposition of the

Dominions, combined with the well-known reluctance of the House of Commons to agree to any increase of Great Britain's obligations under the Covenant, might well have prevented the acceptance of the Protocol even if the government which signed it had remained in power. But in November, after the " Zinoviev letter " election, the Labour Government of MacDonald was succeeded by the Conservative Government of Baldwin. This sealed the fate of the Protocol. In March 1925 Austen Chamberlain, the new Foreign Secretary, formally announced to the Council of the League that Great Britain had decided not to accept it.

THE TREATY OF LOCARNO

The Geneva Protocol was dead. The French quest for security had once more run into a dead end ; and once more it was, in French eyes, the fault of Great Britain. The way out could only be found in a return to the original plan of a specific guarantee by Great Britain of France's Rhineland frontier. But this guarantee was to take a new form. The solution was found, surprisingly enough, in a proposal which had first emanated from the German Government two years before.

At the end of 1922 the German Government had proposed to the French Government to enter into a mutual pledge, in which Great Britain and Belgium would be included, not to resort to war against one another for a generation. The proposal was made through the United States Government, which was invited to act as " trustee " of the arrangement. The scheme seemed, on the eve of the Ruhr occupation, more advantageous to Germany than to France (for there was more danger of France attacking Germany than *vice versa*); and it was unceremoniously rejected by Poincaré. The German Government persisted, without success, during the next two years. Then the rejection of the Geneva Protocol, combined with the feeling that it was time to have a political, as well as a financial, settlement with Germany, gave the scheme a new attraction. The co-operation of the United States in a political question affecting Europe was indeed no longer to be thought of. But Great Britain, whose role as a mediator between France and Germany had been clearly established by her independent attitude at the time of the Ruhr occupation, was ready to step into the breach. She was prepared, acting alone (for the Dominions would not, in this matter, associate themselves with her), to guarantee the Franco-German frontier against aggression by Germany (which was what France had always asked). She was also prepared, in order to keep the balance even, to guarantee the same frontier against aggression by France.

Such was the basis of the famous Locarno Treaty. Throughout the summer of 1925 negotiations proceeded through diplomatic channels, and the details of the scheme slowly took shape. The frontier between Germany and Belgium was placed on the same footing, and was to enjoy the same guarantee, as the frontier between Germany and France. The guarantee was to apply not only to the frontiers, but to the de-militarised zone in which Germany was forbidden to maintain troops or construct fortifications. Italy came in as an additional guarantor. It was stipulated that after the signature of the treaty Germany should join the League of Nations and obtain a permanent seat on the Council.

There were two main difficulties. The first arose over Germany's frontiers with Czechoslovakia and Poland. Germany, while willing to reaffirm her acceptance of the Versailles frontiers in the west, was not prepared to do the same for the other Versailles frontiers. She frankly admitted that she did not regard her eastern frontier as final, though she disclaimed any intention of attempting to alter it by force. The attitude of Germany in this respect corresponded with that of Great Britain, who was ready to guarantee Germany's western, but not her other, frontiers. The difficulty was met, in so far as it was possible to meet it, by the conclusion of arbitration treaties between Germany and Poland, and between Germany and Czechoslovakia, and of guarantee treaties between France and these two countries.

The second difficulty arose out of Germany's friendship with the Soviet Union dating from the time of the Rapallo Treaty (see p. 75). Germany feared that the Western Powers might one day desire to take military action against the Soviet Union under Article 16 of the Covenant, and call on Germany to participate in such action. This fear was met by a letter in which the other Locarno Powers informed Germany that, according to their interpretation, a member of the League was bound to co-operate in support of the Covenant only " to an extent which is compatible with its military situation and takes its geographical position into account ". This was understood to mean that Germany, as a disarmed state, would not be expected to take any part in military sanctions against the Soviet Union.

In October the ministers of all these states assembled at the Swiss lakeside town of Locarno, where, on October 16th, the following agreements were drafted and initialled :

(1) the treaty guaranteeing the Franco-German and Belgo-German frontiers (the " Locarno Treaty " properly so called) ;

(2) arbitration treaties between Germany on the one hand and France, Belgium, Czechoslovakia and Poland on the other ;

(3) treaties of mutual guarantee between France on the one hand and Czechoslovakia and Poland on the other.

The whole series of treaties was formally signed in London on December 1st, 1925.

The treaties thus concluded contained certain important implications which none of the signatories would have cared to admit, but which became more apparent as time went on. In the first place, there was a tacit assumption that the voluntary endorsement by Germany of her western frontier gave that frontier a more sacrosanct character than had hitherto attached to it, or than now attached to her other frontiers ; and this implied that obligations imposed by the Versailles Treaty were morally, if not legally, less binding than obligations voluntarily accepted. Secondly, the readiness of Great Britain to guarantee certain frontiers and her refusal to guarantee others had the practical effect of grading frontiers, from the point of view of security, into first and second class ; and while the British Government firmly protested that all its obligations under the Covenant would be honoured, the impression resulting from the Locarno Treaty was that Great Britain was not prepared to take military action to defend frontiers in Eastern Europe. In the long run, the Locarno Treaty was destructive both of the Versailles Treaty and of the Covenant. It encouraged both the view that the Versailles Treaty, unless confirmed by other engagements of a voluntary character, lacked binding force, and the view that governments could not be expected to take military action in defence of frontiers in which they themselves were not directly interested. Ten years later, nearly all governments appeared to be acting on these assumptions.

Amid the spirit of universal good-will and optimism prevailing in 1925, these implications could safely be ignored ; and it would be difficult to exaggerate the contribution of the Locarno Treaty to the pacification of Europe. It struck, for the first time since the war, a fair and impartial balance between French and German needs. It completed the work which the Dawes Plan had begun by bringing Germany back into the family of Great Powers, not indeed on terms of complete equality (for the servitudes of disarmament and demilitarisation remained), but as a full and respected member. Austen Chamberlain described it, with pardonable pride in his achievement, as " the real dividing-line between the years of war and the years of peace ".

THE years 1924 to 1930 were the period of the League's greatest prestige and authority. Prior to 1924, members of the League had been normally represented at Geneva by delegates who, however distinguished, had not been the ministers responsible for the foreign policy of their countries. When MacDonald and Herriot came in person to Geneva for the Assembly of 1924, they set a precedent of far-reaching importance. Thereafter the foreign ministers of Great Britain, France and (during her period of membership) Germany normally attended some part of every session of the Assembly, and of nearly every session of the Council. This example was soon followed by the foreign ministers of most other European Powers, so that Geneva in September came to be a recognised meeting-place for the statesmen of Europe. In one year (1929), the Assembly was attended by every European Foreign Minister. The non-European countries were perforce represented on most occasions by their diplomats resident in European capitals or by professional delegates stationed at Geneva.

THE LEAGUE AT FULL STRENGTH

When the Locarno Treaties were signed, a special session of the Assembly was summoned for March

1926, at the same time as the regular session of the
Council, in order that Germany might be formally
admitted to membership of the League and to a permanent seat on the Council.   The occasion was felt to
be a turning-point in the history of the League. Hitherto, the influence of the neutral members, and of the
lesser ex-enemy states which had been admitted in the
first years of the peace, had not been strong enough to
refute the common charge that the League was an
association of the victorious Powers designed primarily
to uphold the terms of the settlement of 1919.   The
election of Germany as a member of the League and a
permanent member of the Council would redress the
balance, and give the League a fresh start on a more
impartial basis.

At this crucial moment, by a grave error of judgment,
a hitch was allowed to mar the arrangements.   Under
the original text of the Covenant, the Council was to
consist of the five victorious Great Powers—Great
Britain, France, Italy, the United States and Japan—as
permanent members, and four non-permanent members
elected by the Assembly.   Additions to the permanent
membership of the Council could be made by a unanimous vote of the Council approved by a majority of
the Assembly.   The defection of the United States
reduced the number of permanent members to four;
and in 1922, as the result of pressure from the lesser
Powers, the number of non-permanent seats was increased to six.   There matters stood when, in March
1926, the Council assembled to pronounce on Germany's application for a permanent seat.

The provision in the Covenant for an eventual

increase in the number of permanent members of the Council was admittedly designed for the benefit of the absent Great Powers—Germany and Russia. During the Locarno discussions the possibility of the admission of another Power to a permanent seat had never been mooted. When, however, the German application was known to be pending, Poland, Spain and Brazil all put forward claims to permanent seats on the Council. The demand of Poland, in particular, was not devoid of plausible foundation. Poland, though not within the magic circle of Great Powers, occupied a key-position in European politics, and was not far inferior to Italy in population or wealth. The Locarno Treaties had shown that France was ready, if necessary, to subordinate Polish interests to her own ; and Poland felt that she needed a seat on the Council in order to counteract any tendency on the part of France and Great Britain to come to terms with Germany at her expense. On the other hand, Germany could plead that the promise of a permanent seat had been made to her alone as part of the Locarno bargain. If the value of that seat was now debased by the admission to the same privilege of a Power whose vote on all important issues would neutralise her own, the bargain was not being carried out in the spirit in which it had been struck.

There is no doubt that public opinion in Great Britain, as well as the majority of delegates at Geneva, regarded the German plea as well-founded, and was opposed to any other addition to the permanent membership of the Council. Unfortunately, Austen Chamberlain committed himself to support the Spanish claim ; and thus encouraged, Briand, the new French

Foreign Minister, espoused the cause of Poland. Both Spain and Brazil (unlike Poland) were non-permanent members of the Council, whose vote was therefore necessary for Germany's admission ; and they refused to give that vote unless their own claim were admitted. The imbroglio was complete. The Council could reach no decision, and the Assembly dispersed without having done anything at all. Germany, in spite of Locarno, remained outside the League.

During the summer of 1926, feverish efforts were made by a committee of the Council to clear up the situation. The solution eventually found was to increase the number of non-permanent members from six to nine, and to make three of the non-permanent members re-eligible at the end of their triennial term by a two-thirds vote of the Assembly. Thus a new category of semi-permanent members of the Council was created to meet the needs of states occupying an intermediate position between major and minor states. Both Poland and Germany accepted this compromise, the former on the understanding that she would receive one of the new semi-permanent seats. Spain and Brazil rejected it, but, unwilling to face the odium of using their votes to block Germany's admission, withdrew from the League. At the Assembly of September 1926 Germany entered the League amid scenes of enthusiasm and took her place as a permanent member of the Council. Nevertheless, an unpleasant impression remained in German minds that Germany could not count on a square deal at Geneva. For the moment, Stresemann's influence sufficed to heal the wound. But encouragement had been given to the already strong anti-League party in Germany. It was significant that in April 1926, at the height of the controversy about the permanent seat, Germany concluded a fresh treaty with the Soviet Union, in which parties reaffirmed their loyalty to the Treaty of Rapallo, and each undertook to remain neutral in the event of an attack on the other.

The admission of Germany brought the League up to its maximum strength ; and the occasion may be taken for a brief review of its membership in the later 'twenties. In North and South America, the three largest countries—the United States, the Argentine and Brazil—were all absent ; and the bevy of smaller Central and South American states contributed little materially (for their subscriptions were almost always in arrears), and nothing morally, to its support. In the Far East, Japan, China and Siam, as well as India, were members, and in the Middle East, Persia ; but Turkey held aloof. In Africa, the Union of South Africa usually sent active delegates to the Assembly ; but Liberia and Abyssinia were members with somewhat dubious qualifications. Australia and New Zealand represented the fifth continent. But Europe was the kernel of the League ; and here, when Spain returned to the fold in 1928, its membership was complete except for the Soviet Union—the only Great Power which was still openly hostile.

The attitude of the Soviet Government to the League of Nations was a reflexion of its attitude to the capitalist states which composed the League. Relations between the Soviet Union and Great Britain continued from 1924 onwards to deteriorate. In 1926 indignation was caused by the support received from the Soviet Union for the general strike. In the next year the British Government high-handedly raided the premises of Arcos, the official Soviet trading organisation ; and having discovered there documents proving Soviet intrigues against the British Empire, they cancelled the trade agreement of 1921 and broke off diplomatic relations with the Soviet Government. This quarrel was, however, an exception to the general course of Soviet relations during this period. Relations with France and Italy underwent a gradual improvement. Relations with Germany had not been seriously impaired by Germany's entry into the League. In 1927, though Soviet spokesmen continued to pour ridicule on the League itself, the Soviet Government began to follow the example of the United States by regularly co-operating in the economic, humanitarian and disarmament activities of the League. During that year, Soviet representatives came to Geneva for the first time to attend the meetings of a general economic conference (see p. 110) and of the Preparatory Commission for the Disarmament Conference (see p. 177).

THE LEAGUE AS PEACEMAKER

The principal business of the League was, and was bound to remain, the prevention of war by the peaceful settlement of disputes. Its jurisdiction was, indeed, even in the days of its greatest power, not universal. When in 1926 the Nicaraguan Government appealed to the League against Mexico, whose government was alleged to be assisting its political enemies, the United States Government hurriedly sent a squadron of ships to Nicaragua " for the protection of American and foreign lives and property " ; and the League accepted this intimation that the maintenance of peace and order in Central America was not a matter in which it need interest itself. The peculiar relations between Great Britain and Egypt (which had been recognised as an independent state in 1922) excluded Egypt from membership of the League, and prevented differences of opinion between Great Britain and Egypt from being treated as international disputes. Disputes between China and the Great Powers over the treaties which gave foreigners special rights in China were not considered proper matters for submission to the League. But notwithstanding these exceptions, the sphere of action of the League was far-reaching ; and during these years disputes were referred to it from many quarters of the world. By way of illustration, three of these disputes, all of them involving possible danger of war, will be described here.

The first arose under the treaty of peace with Turkey, which provided that the frontier between Turkey and the mandated territory of Iraq should, in default of agreement between the British and Turkish Governments, be determined by the Council of the League. In the autumn of 1924 the Council, on which Turkey (though not yet a member of the League) was represented for this purpose, appointed a neutral boundary commission to recommend a frontier line. The disputed area was the vilayet or district of Mosul, which was inhabited by a mixed Kurdish, Turkish and Arab population, and which had been in British occupation since the armistice. While the boundary commission was at work, the Kurds in Turkey, a hardy race of mountaineers, revolted against the Turkish Government. The revolt was put down with traditional Turkish ferocity. Many Kurds fled into the Mosul area, and there were serious clashes on the existing provisional frontier. The situation seemed so menacing that the Council of the League, early in 1925, sent out a second commission to report on these disturbances. The report was extremely unfavourable to Turkish methods of administration, and may have assisted the Council to fix a frontier which included practically the whole vilayet of Mosul in the mandated territory. During the last stage of the proceedings Turkey withdrew her representative from the Council, and went back on her previous undertaking to accept the Council's decision as final. The Permanent Court of International Justice, to which the matter was referred, gave its opinion that, under the Lausanne Treaty, the votes of the parties were not required to make the decision of the Council binding. After some hesitation, Turkey made the best of a bad job, and accepted the new frontier, which was confirmed by a treaty between Great Britain, Turkey and Iraq in June 1926.

The next dispute came from the Balkans. For many years after the war, the frontier between Greece and Bulgaria had been the scene of minor raids and disturbances, principally the work of Macedonian brigands (see p. 12). In October 1925 one of these incidents culminated in the murder of the commander of a Greek frontier post and one of his men. By way of reprisal, a Greek army marched into Bulgarian territory. The Bulgarian Government appealed to the League under Article 11 of the Covenant. The Council promptly met in Paris, exhorted the Greek Government to withdraw its troops, and requested the British, French and Italian Governments to send military officers to the spot to see what was happening. These measures exercised a deterrent effect on the Greek Government. The Greek forces retired from Bulgarian soil, and Greece was condemned to pay compensation to Bulgaria for the violation of her territory on a scale fixed by a League commission. Greece accepted the verdict. But there was some bitter comment on the different conception of justice which had prevailed two years before, when Greece suffered aggression, in precisely similar circumstances, at the hands of Italy (see p. 72).

The third dispute was one which had its roots in events already described. The Lithuanian Government, refusing to recognise the decision of the Allied Governments by which Poland had been left in possession of Vilna (see p. 36), severed relations with the Polish Government and proclaimed a " state of war " between the two countries. The frontier had ever since remained closed to traffic by road, rail or river ; and this unnatural situation was aggravated by frequent frontier incidents and provocative pronouncements on both sides. In the autumn of 1927 Voldemaras, the stubborn little dictator of Lithuania, seized the occasion of an expulsion of some Lithuanians from Vilna to refer the whole matter to the League under Article 11 of the Covenant. On December 10th there was a memorable meeting of the Council at which the dictators of Lithuania and Poland (it was Pilsudski's only appearance at Geneva) confronted each other. This confrontation produced an agreed resolution of which the most notable feature was the declaration that " a state of war between two members of the League was incompatible with the spirit and the letter of the Covenant ", and that Lithuania in consequence no longer considered herself in a state of war with Poland. The rest of the resolution was less promising. The " difference of opinion " about Vilna was not affected by it. The recommendation to the two governments to " enter into direct negotiations " on the other questions was not carried out, and there was no resumption of diplomatic or commercial relations. Nevertheless, the ventilation of this long-standing Polish-Lithuanian quarrel at Geneva did in fact lead to a lasting relaxation of tension, if not to a reconciliation, between the two countries ; and it constituted a substantial success for the League.

The treatment of these three disputes by the League provokes some general reflexions. Both the Mosul and the Polish-Lithuanian disputes were disputes between states of very unequal strength. In both cases, the stronger state was not only in possession of the disputed territory, but had at any rate formal right on its side. In both these cases, the League performed the useful function of enabling the weaker state to climb down from an untenable position without loss of *amour-propre*. The Greco-Bulgarian dispute was between weak and equally matched states, neither of which had powerful friends on the Council. These factors made it particularly suitable for League action.

It was easy for the Council to take an impartial decision and to secure its acceptance by the parties. No such fortunate conjunction of circumstances thereafter occurred in a dispute threatening an outbreak of hostilities; and this incident therefore remained the high-water mark of League achievement in preventing war.

The most noteworthy fact about all these successes of the League was, however, that they were achieved by methods of conciliation. In the two last cases, the procedure was governed by Articles 4 and 11 of the Covenant. Both parties to the dispute sat at the Council table, as provided by Article 4, with the full rights of members, including the right to vote; and this meant, under the unanimity rule, that no decision could be taken without the assent of the parties themselves. In the earlier stages of the Mosul dispute, exactly the same procedure was applied, though Turkey was not a member of the League; and though, in the final stage, this procedure was altered by the somewhat unexpected verdict of the Permanent Court based on the terms of the Lausanne Treaty, there was never any question of enforcing a decision. In all these cases it was recognised that the Council could proceed only by methods of persuasion. During this period of its greatest power and prestige, the League relied solely on its moral authority; for Article 11 of the Covenant conferred on it no other powers. Before 1932, no attempt was ever made to resort to the procedure of judgment and penalty provided in Articles 15 and 16.

OTHER ACTIVITIES OF THE LEAGUE

But though the preservation of peace was the League's most important and conspicuous function, no history of international relations after 1919 would be complete without some mention of what may be called the routine activities of the League, many of which became a recognised part of international life.

Some of these activities were political. The Mandates Commission, a body composed of eleven experts in colonial government, met twice a year at Geneva to receive annual reports from the Mandatory Powers on the territories administered by them, and to submit these to the Council with its comments and recommendations. The Council considered them and, if necessary, made recommendations on them, the Mandatory Power (whether a regular member of the Council or not) being represented on the Council for this purpose. A procedure of a different character had been devised for the execution of the minorities treaties (see p. 12). Petitions on behalf of minorities were submitted, together with the reply of the government against whom the complaint was made, to a committee of three members of the Council. The committee discussed the matter with the government (but not with the minority, which had no right to be heard), and generally concluded either by exonerating the government or by obtaining from it an undertaking to remedy the grievance complained of. If the committee failed to obtain satisfaction, it could refer the petition to the Council, on which the defendant government was, of course, represented.   Thus both mandates and minorities procedures were based on the same principle as Article 11 of the Covenant, *i.e.* that decisions were reached by methods of persuasion and with the consent of the government concerned.

The League had other occasional political functions. It successfully administered the Saar territory, through a governing commission, from 1920 to 1935, and in January 1935 conducted the plebiscite there.   No other territory was ever placed under direct League administration.   But the League guaranteed the constitution of the Free City of Danzig, and was represented there by a High Commissioner, whose function was to arbitrate on disputes between the Free City and Poland.   Both parties had the right of appeal to the Council against the High Commissioner's decisions.   Before 1934, when the German-Polish agreement altered the position (see p. 200), no question appeared more frequently on the agenda of the Council than disputes between Poland and Danzig ; and the League machine achieved a high degree of efficiency in dealing with these disputes.

The League provided a new and elaborate machinery for international co-operation in the economic sphere.   Financial and economic committees composed of experts from various countries met annually at Geneva, and directed the work of the financial and economic sections of the League secretariat.   The financial committee was responsible for the issue and supervision of the various League loans.   A general financial conference was held at Brussels in 1920, and an economic conference at Geneva in 1927, the former being concerned with post-war financial reconstruction and the latter with the reduction of tariffs and other trade barriers.

The social and humanitarian work of the League was in part a co-ordination of sporadic international activities which had begun before the war, and in part broke fresh ground. The campaign against slavery was the most ancient of all these activities. A Slavery Convention was concluded at Geneva in 1925 ; and in 1932 the League decided to set up a Permanent Slavery Commission. Other League organisations dealt with the traffic in dangerous drugs, the traffic in women, the protection of children, the relief and settlement of refugees, and health and disease in their international aspects.

Finally, there were two international organisations which, though borne on the League budget, were administratively independent of the League : the International Labour Organisation and the Permanent Court of International Justice.

The International Labour Organisation, which had its seat at Geneva, was created by the peace treaties to provide for the improvement of labour conditions by international agreement. Its constitution was modelled on that of the League, its Annual Conference, Governing Body and Office corresponding respectively to the Assembly, Council and Secretariat. The International Labour Organisation was now composed of all the members of the League, together with the United States and Brazil. Each national delegation to the Annual Conference consisted of four delegates, two appointed by the government, one by employers' organisations and one by workers' organisations

A large number of international conventions dealing with various aspects of labour were concluded, but not all of them were generally ratified.

The Permanent Court of International Justice was established by the League under Article 14 of the Covenant for the purpose of deciding " any dispute of an international character which the parties thereto submit to it ", and of giving " advisory opinions " on questions referred to it by the Council or the Assembly. It had a panel of fifteen judges appointed every nine years by the Council and the Assembly, and sat at the Hague. The statute of the Court contained a so-called " Optional Clause ", signatories of which bound themselves to submit to it for decision any international dispute of a legal character between themselves and other League members ; and about fifty states, including most of the Great Powers, signed this clause, some some of them with certain reservations. The American Government twice made a move to adhere to the Permanent Court (on which there was always an American judge). But the proposal on each occasion fell through. Between 1922 and 1939, the Court pronounced more than fifty decisions and opinions.

CHAPTER 6 : THE CAMPAIGN AGAINST WAR

THE Locarno Treaties had not brought to an end the quest for security. France was not prepared to rely on Locarno to the extent either of abandoning her continental alliances or of disarming herself. Security remained in the forefront of her programme. It was necessary to her allies, for whom Locarno had done nothing; and the need of it was used by France herself as a bulwark against growing pressure to disarm. The tactics which the French Delegation at Geneva had first pursued in 1922 now became a regular part of French policy. Every time the British (or, after 1926, the German) Delegation reminded the League or its organs of the importance of disarmament, the French, Polish and Little Entente Delegations harped no less emphatically on the need for security as a prior condition of disarmament. Members of the League tended to split into two camps : those who thought that disarmament would bring about an increase of security, and those who thought that increased security must precede disarmament. But nobody contested the doctrine of the close interdependence of disarmament and security ; and this doctrine, which had been the implied basis of the draft Treaty of Mutual Assistance and of the Geneva Protocol, continued to dominate the proceedings of the League in the post-Locarno period.

The disarmament negotiations, which were set on foot by the creation in 1926 of a Preparatory Commission for the Disarmament Conference, will be discussed in a later chapter. But the simultaneous efforts of the League to tackle the security problem must be dealt with here; for these theoretical attempts to provide fresh procedure for the settlement of disputes and to prevent war were characteristic of the period of optimism which followed Locarno, and were the pendant of the practical activities of the League described in the last chapter.

LEAGUE CONVENTIONS

The years 1926 to 1929 were particularly fertile in schemes for strengthening security against war, each Assembly hailing the birth of some fresh proposal.

In 1926, the Finnish Delegation produced a plan, obviously suggested by the success of the League loans, for enabling states which might be attacked to obtain financial support on favourable terms from their fellow members of the League. Such support would be the positive counterpart of the refusal of financial facilities to the attacking state prescribed by Article 16 of the Covenant. The proposal eventually took shape as the Convention on Financial Assistance which was adopted by the Assembly of 1930. Since, however, its coming into force was made conditional (in accordance with the principle of the interdependence of disarmament and security) on the conclusion of a disarmament convention, it remained no more than a project.

When the Assembly of 1927 met, the Preparatory Commission for the Disarmament Conference was already in sight of rocks ahead, and a limited naval conference at Geneva during the summer had suffered shipwreck. These untoward events drove the Assembly heavily back on the security problem. For the first time since 1924, whispers were heard of an attempt to resuscitate the Geneva Protocol; and the Netherlands Delegation invited the Assembly " to resume the study of the principles of disarmament, security and arbitration which are expressed in the Covenant ". The Assembly accordingly invited the Preparatory Commission to set up a Committee on Arbitration and Security, " whose duty would be to consider the measures calculated to give to all states such guarantees of security as will enable them to fix the level of their armaments at the lowest possible figure in an international disarmament treaty ".

In the interval between the 1927 and 1928 Assemblies, the Committee on Arbitration and Security pursued its work with untiring enthusiasm. It found inspiration in a suggestion which had been put forward during the Assembly by the Norwegian Delegation. The experience of 1924 had shown that all members of the League were not prepared to travel equally far along the path of arbitration. More progress might, it was now suggested, be made by drafting, not a general convention like the Geneva Protocol for acceptance by the League as a whole, but a series of " model treaties " to be accepted by pairs or groups of states as applicable between themselves. Thus the most advanced states could conclude agreements for the arbitration of all disputes between them. The less advanced might agree on the submission to arbitration of all disputes of a legal character. Those who were not yet ready to accept compulsory arbitration at all, might agree to procedures of conciliation or to other methods of minimising the danger of war. The Committee prepared for the use of the 1928 Assembly no less than ten such " model treaties " of varying degrees of stringency.

Faced with this plethora of material, the Assembly chose a course which seemed calculated to combine the advantages of the " model treaty " with those of a general convention. It took three of the most promising drafts and converted them into the three first chapters of a General Act for the Pacific Settlement of International Disputes. The first chapter provided that each pair of signatories of the Act should set up a permanent conciliation commission, whose duty it would be to recommend an amicable, though not binding, settlement of disputes between them. The second chapter prescribed the submission of all legal disputes to the Permanent Court of International Justice, whose decision would be binding. The third chapter prescribed the submission of non-legal disputes to a committee of arbitrators whose president, failing agreement, would be chosen by the Permanent Court of International Justice. A fourth chapter provided that members of the League could subscribe to one or more chapters of the Act, and could if they liked make reservations excluding particular categories of disputes from those to be dealt with under the Act.

This seemed elastic enough to suit all tastes. But the Act had no great success. Chapter I was felt to have little value in itself. Provision for conciliation commissions had been made in treaties between the

United States and other countries before the war and in the Locarno Treaties between Germany and her neighbours. But no use had ever been made of them. Chapter II was already covered by acceptance of the Optional Clause of the Statute of the Permanent Court. Chapter III revived one of the chief stumbling-blocks of the Geneva Protocol with the surprising difference that it completely short-circuited the Council of the League, which was not even called on (as under the Protocol) to appoint the committee of arbitrators. Within two years of the approval of the General Act by the 1928 Assembly, only Belgium, Norway, Denmark and Finland had accepted the whole of it, while Holland and Sweden had subscribed to the first two chapters.

THE PACT OF PARIS

In the meanwhile, a fresh initiative had come from another quarter. A few days before the 1928 Assembly met, Paris was the scene of a striking and important ceremony : the signature of a pact for the renunciation of war, commonly known as the Pact of Paris or the Briand-Kellogg Pact. It is a little unfair that none of the immense public applause which greeted this event should have been bestowed on the League. For during the Assembly of 1927, which had already devoted so much thought to the problem of preventing war, the Polish Delegation had proposed a solemn declaration " that all wars of aggression are, and shall always be, prohibited " ; and this declaration was unanimously adopted. Historically, however, the Pact of Paris had a different ancestry. In April 1927, inspired by a body of influential American citizens, Briand proposed to the American Government the conclusion of a pact between France and the United States renouncing war as an instrument of national policy between the two countries. Since it was difficult to imagine any national interest which could possibly lead to war between France and the United States, such a pact would have had little practical importance. But it would have conferred a certain prestige on France as the particular friend and associate of the United States in Europe ; and it was perhaps for this reason that the American Secretary of State Kellogg, after a long delay, replied with a counter-proposal that the suggested pact should be of universal application. This proposal was in due course accepted. On August 27th, 1928, the representatives of the six recognised Great Powers (the United States, Great Britain, France, Germany, Italy and Japan), the three other " Locarno Powers " (Belgium, Poland and Czechoslovakia) and the British Dominions and India, assembled in Paris to sign the pact. Every other independent state in the world was invited to accede to it.

The sense in which the signatories interpreted their undertaking to renounce war " as an instrument of national policy in their relations with one another " is explained in the correspondence between them which preceded its signature. The original authors of the pact had already declared that it did not ban war in self-defence. It was not an acceptance of the pacifist doctrine of non-resistance. Great Britain further made it clear that the right of self-defence included, in her case, the right to defend " certain regions of the world the welfare and integrity of which constitute a special and vital interest for our peace and safety ". In the case of the United States, self-defence included any action required to prevent an infringement of the Monroe Doctrine. These explanations (for they were not treated as formal reservations) threw into relief the general character of the pact. It was regarded by many as a declaration of principle rather than a contractual obligation. Each state remained the sole judge of its own actions. No machinery for the interpretation or enforcement of the pact was set up or contemplated.

Imperfect though it was, the Pact of Paris was a considerable land-mark. It was the first political agreement in history of almost universal scope. The Argentine, Brazil, Bolivia and Salvador, aggrieved by the reassertion of the Monroe Doctrine, held aloof. But every other state, with insignificant exceptions, hastened to accede. The Soviet Union, after an initial moment of hesitation, was so enthusiastic that it proposed and concluded a special agreement with its neighbours to bring the Pact of Paris into force as between themselves in advance of the general ratification. No less than sixty-five states accepted the pact—a number exceeding by seven the current membership of the League of Nations. It is indeed probable that some states acceded rather from a desire to conform than from any belief in the utility of the pact. Flagrant violations of it were soon committed by Japan and Italy, the one thinly disguised as a police operation, the other, still more thinly, as a defensive war. But this did not destroy the significance of the fact that the nations, acting together, had been prepared to pronounce a ban on war as a normal and legitimate method of settling international disputes. The term " outlawry of war " used by the American sponsors of the Pact implied the existence of a universal, unwritten law against which war was declared to be an offence. No authority existed to punish violations of the law, or even to pronounce that the law had been violated. But the conception itself struck root in the political thought of the world.

The enthusiastic reception of the Pact of Paris naturally looked like a challenge to the League. The Covenant contained no absolute ban on the use of war as an instrument of national policy. It only circum-scribed within the narrowest limits which appeared practicable to its authors the conditions in which a member of the League might legitimately go to war. Now that practically every member of the League had accepted an obligation not to go to war at all (except in self-defence), common sense seemed to demand that the Covenant should be strengthened by the incorpora-tion in it of this new obligation. Nobody was surprised when the British Delegation submitted to the Assembly of 1929 a series of amendments to the Covenant designed to effect this result. The Labour Govern-ment, which had just come into power in Great Britain, was eager to reverse the negative policy of its predecessor.

The process proved, however, far less simple than it looked. The Pact of Paris was a moral declaration, based on a general sense of the sinfulness of war. The Covenant was a political treaty based, in its essen-tial provisions, on what the statesmen of 1919 deemed practicable and expedient. The Pact condemned all wars, but punished none. The Covenant allowed some wars, and prohibited others; but prohibited wars it punished. To fuse together instruments so different in spirit, and to make a neat job of the fusion, was a superhuman task. If you merely pitchforked the articles of the Pact into the Covenant, you produced a document of which one part prohibited war altogether, and another part allowed it in certain conditions—a flagrant contradiction. If you attempted a more organic fusion, you were left with an amended Covenant which prohibited all wars, but made only some wars punishable—an unwelcome admission that some parts of the Covenant could be violated with impunity.

Both these courses seemed pusillanimous and unworthy of the League. The remaining alternative was to make the sanctions of Article 16 apply not only to wars prohibited by the existing Covenant, but to all wars prohibited by the Pact of Paris. This would not only strengthen the Covenant by making the prohibition of war absolute, but would give new force to the Pact of Paris by making violations of it, as between members of the League, punishable. Such was the proposal put forward in 1929 by the British Delegation and heartily supported by the French Delegation, which saw in it a welcome contribution to security. The strongest objection was one of those which had proved fatal to the Geneva Protocol, *i.e.* that any extension of the incidence of Article 16 automatically increased the obligations of those Powers who would be most concerned in the application of sanctions. But this time the British Government, the principal objector in 1925, had not allowed itself to be deterred by this fear; and the proposed amendments seemed likely to have an easy passage.

It is indeed possible that, had the amendments been put to the vote in 1929, they would have met with unanimous approval, though this might not have prevented them from sharing afterwards the fate of the Geneva Protocol. But the discussion of them in committee was postponed till the Assembly of 1930; and by this time a breath of scepticism was already in the air. The British and French Delegations stood to their guns. But strong opposition came from the Scandinavian countries and Japan. The amendments could still have been carried by a handsome majority. But there was serious doubt about the ratification of amendments adopted by a majority vote; and the prudent decision was taken to postpone the question to the next Assembly. By September 1931 Great Britain was in the throes of a financial crisis and a change of government. The period of optimism was over; and the proposed amendments were talked out.

The valiant attempt led by the British Delegation to incorporate the Pact of Paris in the Covenant was the last important episode in the quest for increased security through the League, which had begun in 1922 and had been resumed, after the fiasco of the Geneva Protocol, in 1927. After the Assembly of 1930 the clouds gathered rapidly. The ratification by the British and French Governments in the summer of 1931 of the General Act, and the signature at the 1931 Assembly of a not very important Convention to Improve the Means of Preventing War (which had started life as one of the

" model treaties " of the Committee on Arbitration and Security) were flashes which no longer kindled the old enthusiasm. The Assembly of 1930 was the last at which it was possible to feel (as many people had felt since Locarno) that the world was becoming year by year a safer place, and that the League was slowly building up machinery which would prove effective in preventing war.

THE YOUNG PLAN

The tranquillity and optimism of the period of inter-war history which we have called " the period of pacification " were, as we have already seen, due principally to the sudden improvement in Franco-German relations brought about by the Dawes Plan and the Locarno Treaty. The trio of Locarno statesmen— Stresemann, Briand and Austen Chamberlain—continued to direct the foreign affairs of their respective countries till the summer of 1929. The mutual confidence and friendship which grew up between these three men was an important element in the stability of Europe during these years ; and this asset must be credited to the League, since it was the regular meetings of the Council and Assembly which alone made these personal relations possible. The inveterate hostility between France and Germany was suspended, and was scarcely visible at Geneva except in the discussions about disarmament.

Nevertheless, the Franco-German problem, though momentarily out of sight, was never forgotten. During the Assembly of 1926, which saw the admission of

Germany to the League, Briand and Stresemann had a long private meeting at the village of Thoiry, near Geneva. A *communiqué* was issued to the effect that the two ministers had discussed all matters of common interest to the two countries, had " brought their points of view into agreement in regard to the general solution ", and were referring to their respective governments for approval. The nature of this provisional agreement was not officially disclosed. But it was understood that Stresemann begged for the immediate evacuation of the Rhineland and the return of the Saar to Germany, offering in return concessions in the form of reparation payments, and that Briand was personally disposed to close with this offer. The French Government was, however, not prepared for this drastic anticipation of the time-limits fixed by the Versailles Treaty for the Allied occupation of the Rhineland and League control of the Saar ; and Stresemann's offer of a large capital payment on reparation account was financially impracticable. The Thoiry conversation had no sequel. But this disappointment caused no immediate set-back in Franco-German friendship. In December agreement was reached to bring Allied military control in Germany to an end ; and the Inter-Allied Commission was withdrawn on January 31st, 1927.

The two principal topics of the Thoiry conversation —the Rhineland and reparation—dominated Franco-German relations for the next two years. The Treaty of Versailles had divided the occupied Rhineland into three zones, to be evacuated respectively in five, ten and fifteen years after the coming into force of the Treaty. The first zone had been evacuated, several months late, at the end of 1925. The second and third zones were not due for evacuation till 1930 and 1935. Now that relations had improved, it became a cardinal object of Germany to secure the immediate liberation of the whole of the Rhineland from Allied occupation ; and a subsidiary point in the programme was to induce the French Government to restore the Saar at once to Germany without waiting for the plebiscite in 1935. Stresemann still hoped to purchase these concessions by a new reparation agreement. The Dawes Plan was admittedly provisional. It was in the interest of both sides that there should be a final settlement of Germany's obligations, the total of which was still undefined ; and now that payments were being made regularly and easily, Germany also hoped to secure the removal of the galling control over her finances involved in the Dawes Plan.

Time worked on the German side. Public opinion in Great Britain was impatient to see the occupation of the Rhineland wound up ; and even in France it came to be recognised that the occupation was a wasting asset which should be disposed of as soon as possible for what it would fetch. During the Assembly of 1928, the delegates of Germany and of the five principal reparation Powers came to an agreement that negotiations should be opened for " the early evacuation of the Rhineland " and that a committee of financial experts should be appointed to prepare " a complete and definite settlement of the reparation problem ". The terms of the agreement might have suggested that two questions were to be discussed simultaneously. But the French Government made it clear from the outset that the evacuation could only follow the reparation settlement ; and it was on this, therefore, that attention was first concentrated.

The " committee of financial experts " met in Paris in February 1929. It was composed of two experts drawn from each of the countries which had concluded the Geneva agreement and two from the United States (for whose appointment, however, the United States Government disclaimed official responsibility). The senior American expert, Owen Young, was elected chairman ; and the committee was known after him as the " Young Committee ". Its deliberations, which were arduous, lasted for four months. On June 7th, 1929, it adopted and submitted to the governments the " Young Plan ".

The " complete and definite solution of the reparation problem " devised by the Young Committee was to take the form of thirty-seven annual payments averaging £100,000,000 (as against the maximum Dawes annuity of £125,000,000) followed by twenty-two smaller annual payments sufficient to cover the war-debt payments of the Allies to the United States, which were due to continue till 1988. The foreign control imposed on Germany by the Dawes Plan was removed. The responsibility for transferring the sums paid would rest no longer on the creditors but on the German Government. One safeguard against exchange difficulties was, however, introduced. About one-third of each annuity (£33,000,000) was to be treated as an " unconditional " obligation. The balance was subject to a proviso which allowed Germany, in the event of exchange difficulties, to postpone transfer for a maximum of two years. Finally, the Plan recommended the establishment of a Bank of International Settlements, whose role was to receive and distribute reparation payments, to issue an international loan secured on the unconditional annuities, and in general to perform the functions of an international central bank.

It now remained to secure the adoption of the experts' report by the governments and to settle the details of the evacuation of the Rhineland. A conference for these purposes was convened at the Hague in August 1929. The principal British delegates were the new Labour Chancellor of the Exchequer, Philip Snowden, and the new Labour Foreign Secretary, Arthur Henderson.

The adoption of the Young Plan was not achieved without serious and unexpected difficulties. They came not from Germany, but from Great Britain. In recent years British policy had shown a marked inclination (for which Austen Chamberlain had been criticised in some quarters) to fall in with the French view of international questions. The British experts on the Young Committee seemed to have been unduly affected by this tradition. In order to make the scheme palatable to France, they had agreed to a substantial increase, at the expense of Great Britain, in the percentage of reparation payments allocated to France by the Spa agreement of 1920 (see p. 54). Of the unconditional annuities, more than three-fourths were to go to France ; and though arrangements were made to compensate Great Britain for this sacrifice in the event of the conditional annuities not being transferred, these arrangements were complicated and unsatisfactory.

Snowden showed no tenderness for these French privileges. He demanded a return to the Spa percentages ; and he fought his case with a pugnacity and stubbornness which made him for a few weeks the *bête noire* of French politicians and the most popular man in Great Britain. He obtained the greater part of his demands ; and the conference ended by endorsing a revised version of the Young Plan.

Meanwhile the negotiations for the evacuation of the Rhineland were conducted by Stresemann, Briand and Henderson in the political commission of the Conference. The advent of the Labour Government to power in Great Britain had intensified the general desire to bring the occupation to an end ; and a public statement by Henderson that the British troops would be withdrawn in any event virtually settled the issue. An attempt by the French Government to make the evacuation dependent on the setting up of a committee to " verify " the observance of the permanent restrictions on the militarisation of the Rhineland, was rejected. The Conference reached an agreement that all Allied troops should be withdrawn from the Rhineland by June 30th, 1930 (nearly five years in advance of the due date), assuming that the Young Plan had been put into force by that time.

There was no further hitch. Hjalmar Schacht, the Governor of the Reichsbank, who had been the senior German expert on the Young Committee, warned the world that its requirements would prove to be beyond Germany's capacity. But this prognostication was not taken very seriously. A second conference was held at the Hague in January 1930 to clear up a few outstanding points and reach a similar settlement of what little was left of Hungarian and Bulgarian reparations. On May 17th the Young Plan came into effect. Six weeks later, the last Allied troops left German soil.

The evacuation of the Rhineland, and the "final" settlement of the reparation question which was destined to be so soon undone, were the last important events of the period of pacification. Before passing on to the next period, it remains to note a few of the landmarks which announced the transition from one to the other. Of the trio of statesmen whose co-operation had been responsible for so many of the successes of the years 1925–29, Austen Chamberlain was the first to go, resigning with the Conservative Government in May 1929. In October, five weeks after the end of the first Hague conference, and before any of its fruits had been garnered, Stresemann died. Almost at the same moment a panic occurred on the New York Stock Exchange. Its effect in Europe would have been more immediate if it had been realised how utterly the whole structure of reparation and Allied debt payments depended on the willingness of the American investor and speculator to send dollars across the Atlantic. For some months longer, the world continued to live in a fool's paradise. A successful Naval Conference was held in London from January to April 1930 (see p. 181). In the summer of the same year, as the last French troops were preparing to leave the Rhine, Briand declared that the time had come to create the United States of Europe, and circulated a memorandum on the subject, which was politely referred by the League Assembly to a committee.

But the illusion did not last much longer. During the Assembly of 1930 the results of the German Reichstag elections were announced; and the gain of a hundred seats by a hitherto insignificant party, the National Socialists or Nazis, led by a magnetic orator named Adolf Hitler, caused general astonishment. In December the Preparatory Commission for the Disarmament Conference produced a draft convention of which almost every clause was the subject of profound and bitter disagreement. By 1931 the storm had broken with full force over Europe; and " crisis " became the most familiar word in the vocabulary of international affairs.

PART III

THE PERIOD OF CRISIS : THE RETURN OF POWER POLITICS

(1930–1933)

THE causes of the economic crisis which reached its culminating point in 1931 are still a matter of debate among economists. This chapter will deal only with its symptoms and effects in the international sphere. The first international manifestation of the crisis was the complete cessation of American loans to Europe in the autumn of 1929 ; and this was rapidly followed by a drying-up of purchasing power all over the world, resulting in a general and catastrophic fall in prices. The European debtor countries were doubly hit. They could no longer borrow from America the dollars with which to pay their debts ; and the commodities with which they might have paid them now possessed only a fraction of their value before the slump. Only one possibility remained. Most of the 1930 reparation and debt payments were made by transfers of gold ; and these transfers once more doubly aggravated the situation. In the first place, this abnormal flow to the United States created an artificial scarcity of gold, which (since gold is the measure of value) still further depressed commodity prices. Secondly, it compelled countries subject to this drain on their gold reserves to prohibit the export of gold ; and this step was taken by the majority of European states in the course of 1931. Moreover, these countries, in a desperate effort to keep their own agriculture and industry alive and to maintain a favourable balance of trade, were driven to every kind of expedient in the form of tariffs, import restrictions and quotas, export subsidies and exchange restrictions, amounting in some cases to a complete state control of foreign trade. The normal flow of commerce was almost completely interrupted. Unemployment figures rose everywhere by leaps and bounds. Half Europe was bankrupt, and the other half threatened with bankruptcy.

THE CRISIS IN GERMANY

In Germany, for several reasons, the crisis was particularly acute. Germany was the largest debtor state, and had been during the past five years the largest recipient of foreign loans. The Dawes Plan, which did not remove the threat of undefined liabilities when the debtor could afford to pay, had given Germany little inducement to pursue a thrifty and cautious financial policy; and the opportunity to borrow lavishly, coming on top of a period of privation, was an irresistible temptation. It was calculated that, during the five years of the Dawes Plan, Germany had paid barely £500,000,000 on reparation account and received about £900,000,000 in foreign loans and credits. The surplus was spent on vast programmes of building and reconstruction by the state, by the municipalities and by private enterprise. No serious attempt was made to balance the budget, since deficits could easily be covered by short-term borrowing. Germany's finances, public and private, floated on a constant stream of borrowed money.

The crash therefore found Germany in a particularly vulnerable condition. She was left for the first time to face, without the aid of foreign loans, a reparation debt of £100,000,000 a year, other public and private obligations abroad whose annual charge did not fall far below that sum, and a budget deficit of £60,000,000. The country had no internal capital resources on which to fall back. Savings and reserves had been wiped out by the inflation of 1923, and had never been built up again. German industry was in no position to come to the rescue of the government. It, too, lost the stimulus of plentiful credit from abroad; and simultaneously, it was deprived of its best foreign markets by the general slump and the raising of tariff and quota barriers. German exports, the value of which had reached £630,000,000 in 1929, fell by 1932 to £280,000,000; and German imports fell still more steeply during the same period from £670,000,000 to £230,000,000. The number of registered unemployed rose from under 2,000,000 in 1929 to a peak figure of over 6,000,000 in March 1932.

In a country where the political balance was always precarious, so great an economic upheaval was bound to have drastic consequences. In March 1930 a government was formed which, for the first time in the history of the Weimar Republic, contained no Social-Democrats. Brüning, a member of the Centre, became Prime Minister, whilst Curtius, who had succeeded Stresemann, retained the portfolio of Foreign Affairs. In the following month, all-round tariff increases and agrarian subsidies were introduced—Germany being one of the first countries to experiment in these dubious specifics against economic depression. At the general election of September 1930, the National Socialists or Nazis, whose policy consisted of bitter denunciation of the Jews, the Social-Democrats and the Versailles Treaty, increased the number of their seats in the Reichstag from 12 to 107. The ministry remained unchanged. But democracy had now virtually broken down ; and Germany was governed for many months by a system of presidential decrees which could be reconciled with the letter, but hardly with the spirit, of the Weimar constitution.

Early in 1931 there was a fresh shock to German political stability. The committee appointed by the League Assembly of 1930 to consider Briand's scheme of European Union (see p. 129) held its first business meeting in January 1931. The original scheme had been predominantly political. But the crying need of the moment was clearly economic co-operation ; and the committee began to discuss plans for the lowering of trade barriers between European countries. It achieved no concrete result. But the discussions started a new train of thought in an unexpected quarter. It occurred to Curtius and the Austrian Chancellor (who had come to Geneva for the committee) that a close economic union between Germany and Austria would not only contribute to the lowering of trade barriers, but would do something to satisfy those ambitions for political union between the two countries which had been vetoed by the peace treaties. The conversations were conducted in profound secrecy ; and on March 21st a surprised world learned that Germany and Austria had signed a treaty providing for the establishment of a customs union between them. Other neighbouring countries were to be invited to join the union.

The principle of regional economic agreements had already been commended at the 1930 Assembly by supporters of European union. But this application of the principle was in the highest degree distasteful to the French Government and to the Little Entente. It was notorious that a customs union between a large and a small Power inevitably led to the political domination by the former of the latter. If the scheme went through, the independence of Austria would become a myth. Moreover, Czechoslovakia, whose principal markets were Germany and Austria, could scarcely afford to remain outside the union. Other Danubian states might follow; and Germany would secure economic, and in the end political, control of the Danube basin. France and her partners prepared to resist this conclusion at all costs. Legal ground for their objection could be found, not only in the treaty veto on the alienation of Austria's independence, but in the undertaking which Austria had given in the loan protocol of 1922 (see p. 63) to enter into no economic agreements likely to compromise that independence.

The attitude of the British Government was hesitant. Generally speaking, Great Britain had everything to gain from the removal of customs barriers in the Danube basin. Neither the scheme itself nor the extension of it to other Powers would have been inimical to British interests. But it seemed likely that the project would cause grave political disturbances, if not war, in Central Europe; and the appeal to treaty obligations could not be ignored. In May, the Council of the League unanimously decided to refer to the Permanent Court of International Justice the question whether the proposed customs union between Germany and Austria was contrary to the terms of the peace treaties and of the 1922 protocol.

The matter was, however, not eventually settled by a legal decision. The point of law was doubtful; and France was not prepared to risk the possibility of a decision in favour of the union. She redoubled her efforts to induce Austria to abandon the scheme; and these efforts were assisted by a serious financial crisis in Austria which will be described later in this chapter. Exactly what passed between the French and Austrian Governments during the summer can only be guessed. But on September 3rd the Austrian Chancellor announced to the Committee on European Union, the German delegate assenting, that the project had been abandoned. Two days later the Permanent Court issued its judgment. By a majority of eight votes to seven, it had decided that the customs union would be contrary to the treaties and to the protocol. The fact that the majority included the French, Italian, Polish and Roumanian judges, and the minority the British, German and American judges, gave the judgment a certain political colour, which did not enhance the prestige of the Court as an independent legal tribunal.

In its immediate consequences the veto on the German-Austrian customs union was a misfortune for Europe. In Central Europe the rejection of the project ushered in a long period of political uncertainty and economic chaos from which no escape could be found. In Germany it precipitated the final collapse of the Weimar Republic. Between 1920 and 1933 the prestige of every German Government depended in the last resort on the success or failure of its foreign policy. When the customs union project fell through, Curtius, the last representative of the policy and principles of Stresemann, retired in disgrace. Brüning, the Chancellor, took over the portfolio of foreign affairs; and the Nazis redoubled their propaganda against the humiliations of the Versailles Treaty.

THE YEAR OF DISASTER

Throughout 1930, it was still possible to believe that the crisis was a disagreeable, but passing, phase in the economic life of the world which would be surmounted without any fundamental disturbance of the organism. But the winter of 1930–31 shattered the last defences of optimism ; and serious people began to talk of the impending collapse of civilisation. In 1931 critical events rained so thickly on a distracted world that the history of the year is an almost uninterrupted catalogue of disaster.

By the spring of 1931 the overloaded machinery of international payments was lumbering to a standstill, the only uncertainty being the precise point at which the mechanism would break down. The point proved to be Vienna ; and the crash came at the height of the customs union dispute, though there is no evidence to connect the two events. In May the most important private Austrian bank, the Kredit-Anstalt, was found to be insolvent. In order to prevent a general panic, the

Austrian Government passed a decree guaranteeing the foreign obligations of the Kredit-Anstalt ; and the Bank of England advanced £6,000,000 to the Austrian State Bank in a vain endeavour to stem the tide. The Bank of France, in view of the customs union project, refused to help.

But by this time the collapse of the Kredit-Anstalt was seen to be only one symptom of world-wide bankruptcy and failure of confidence. The panic spread across the frontier to Germany. Foreign creditors hastened to call in their short-term loans, and in three weeks the Reichsbank lost gold to the value of £50,000,000. The smaller states of Central and South-East Europe, with the exception of Czechoslovakia, were all faced with default on their foreign debts, including the loans which Hungary, Greece and Bulgaria had obtained with the help of the League of Nations.

In the southern hemisphere, Australia and the Argentine had been forced by the calamitous fall in agricultural prices to suspend gold payments at the end of 1929 ; and Brazil, bankrupted by the collapse of the market in coffee, followed suit in the following year. These misfortunes were a serious blow to Great Britain, who had large financial interests in all three countries. For months past there had been a constant outflow of gold from the Bank of England, mainly to France, now the strongest financial Power in Europe ; and in the summer of 1931 this process was accelerated. In June it was calculated that 60 per cent of the world's supply of gold (excluding that held in Soviet Russia) was either in the United States or in France. Further payments in gold would soon become impossible.

A general default seemed imminent when, on June 20th, President Hoover of the United States, issued to the world an offer to postpone for one year all payments due from foreign governments to the United States Government on condition that a similar postponement was applied to all other inter-governmental debts including reparations. This tacit recognition of the part played by Allied war debts in the economic crisis was an act of great courage and statesmanship. The recognition was belated ; and one of the motives of the proposal was admittedly to restore the credit and purchasing power of Germany, and of Europe in general, for the benefit of the American bondholder and exporter. But these considerations do not diminish the credit due to Hoover. The Allied Governments had been equally slow in facing the realities of the international financial position, and far less intelligent in appreciating where their true interest lay.

Hoover's offer evoked widespread enthusiasm. Its moral effect was so great that for a few days it looked as if confidence might be completely restored. But France was once more the obstacle. France had a larger excess of reparation receipts over war-debt obligations than any other Power. She was far more interested in the continuance of reparation payments, and far less in Germany's financial and commercial recovery, than Great Britain or *a fortiori* than the United States. Alone in Europe, France demurred to the Hoover moratorium. When she at last agreed, it was on condition that the unconditional annuities of the Young Plan should be formally paid by Germany to the

Bank of International Settlements, but immediately re-
lent to the German State Railway Company, and that
interest should be charged on the whole of the postponed annuities.   It took a fortnight of hard bargaining
to achieve even this result; and the delay was fatal
to the momentary confidence which Hoover's offer
had generated.   The atmosphere of crisis grew thicker
than ever.   On July 13th, just a week after the Hoover
moratorium had been accepted by all concerned, one of
the largest German banks suspended payment.

The Hoover moratorium had disposed for the time
being of the debts of governments to one another.   But
even when this stumbling-block was removed, private
debts remained and presented an insoluble problem.
Germany was in a state where any further transfer of
marks abroad would bring about a repetition of the
catastrophe of 1923.   Her foreign creditors had no
option but to agree to a moratorium on all German
debts;   and this caused serious embarrassment to
financial concerns in London which had large sums
locked up in Germany in short-term obligations.

Great Britain herself was now in the throes of an
acute financial crisis.   In April 1925, at the beginning
of the boom period, the British Government took
what experience has shown to have been the foolhardy
step of re-establishing sterling on a gold basis at its pre-
war rate.   Some time later, France, Italy and several
other European countries also reverted to the gold
standard, but on terms which represented a substantial
reduction of the original gold value of their currencies.
Thus French francs, which before the war were worth
25 to the pound sterling, were now worth only 125 to

the pound. There is little doubt that France and some other countries, though probably not by design, stabilised their currencies at an unduly low rate. The result of this proceeding was to keep wages and other costs of production in most European countries substantially lower than in Great Britain, and to stimulate the export trade of these countries at the experse of British exports. Moreover, every important country except Great Britain followed the policy of penalising imports by high tariffs. The recommendations of the economic conference of 1927 (see p. 110) for a reduction of tariffs and removal of other trade barriers were ignored ; and a proposal made by the British Government in 1929 for a " tariff truce ", *i.e.* an agreement not to increase existing tariffs, received scant support.

So long as prosperity lasted and world trade continued to expand, Great Britain still managed to pay her way. But she shared less than any other important country in the trade boom of 1925–29. Her adverse trade balance increased year by year. In 1930 Germany for the first time outstripped her (by some £30,000,000) as the biggest exporting Power ; and the United States, the third Power on the list, was ahead of Great Britain in all markets except those of the British Empire, the British Dominions (other than Canada) and Scandinavia. When the crisis broke, this decline in competitive power proved fatal to Great Britain s stability; and the collapse of world trade hit particularly hard a country which had always derived a large revenue from the transporting and financing of other people's commerce. The balance of payments became increasingly unfavourable. Confidence was further sapped by the rapid falling off of tax receipts, which produced, by July 1931, a budget deficit of £100,000,000. Foreign creditors took fright. In one week at the end of July £21,000,000 of gold were withdrawn from Great Britain. A large credit from the Bank of France barely arrested the flight from sterling, which continued throughout August. On August 24th the Labour Government resigned and was succeeded by a National Government, which introduced a supplementary budget designed to cover £70,000,000 of the budget deficit by economies in expenditure and by increased taxation. But a minor outbreak of discontent in the fleet over the pay cuts shattered confidence once more ; and on September 21st the government prohibited the export of gold. In the familiar phrase, sterling " went off gold " ; and within a few days its value had fallen, in terms of gold and gold currencies, by about 25 per cent.

The position of sterling as one of the great international currencies was so strong as to produce a paradoxical and unexpected result. The fall of sterling, instead of raising the price level in Great Britain (the normal and natural consequence of a decline in the national currency), carried the world price level down with it. While therefore its effect in Great Britain was entirely beneficial, giving an impetus to a flagging export trade and laying the foundation of a slow but sure recovery, its first effect abroad was still further to aggravate the evil of low and unremunerative prices. Moreover, the general election of October 1931, which gave the National Government an overwhelming majority, paved the way for the abandonment by Great Britain of her traditional free-trade policy and the introduction of an all-round tariff on manufactured goods and quotas for many agricultural products ; and in 1932, at the Ottawa Conference, Great Britain and the British Dominions concluded a number of preferential tariff and import quota agreements, from whose benefits foreign states were excluded.   These measures were in all probability a necessary condition of the revival of British trade.   But the fact that Great Britain had adhered, though belatedly, to the now almost universal policy of economic nationalism placed a new and formidable obstacle in the way of a return to normal conditions as hitherto understood.

The abandonment of the gold standard by Great Britain, whose example was quickly followed by the Scandinavian countries, by New Zealand and (somewhat later) by South Africa, was the culminating point of the crisis ; and the winter of 1931–32 was perhaps the darkest period since 1918.   It had its political as well as its economic preoccupations.   On September 19th, Japan embarked on the military adventure which made her in less than a year mistress of the fertile Chinese province of Manchuria.   On February 2nd, 1932, the Disarmament Conference opened at Geneva ; and few well-informed people could regard its prospects with anything but profound pessimism.   The Japanese action in Manchuria and the Disarmament Conference will form the subject of the next two chapters.   The remainder of this chapter will trace the further course of the economic crisis down to the middle of 1933.

THE END OF REPARATION

The countries of Europe were now divided into three categories : those which maintained free export of gold and were effectively on the gold standard—France, Italy, Poland, Belgium, Holland and Switzerland (sometimes called " the gold *bloc* ") ; those which had formally abandoned the gold standard—Great Britain, Sweden, Norway, Denmark, Finland and Estonia (sometimes referred to as " the sterling *bloc* "), together with Spain, Portugal and Greece ; and the remainder, which had effectively abandoned the gold standard by prohibiting the export of gold, but maintained their currencies at an artificial gold parity by controlling all transactions in foreign exchange.

Of the last and most numerous category, Germany was the outstanding example; and the final step in the long reparation controversy presented the creditor governments with a new bone of contention. The German Government, through the Reichsbank, now had a virtual monopoly of Germany's foreign exchange. France argued that the German Government was under an obligation to transfer the unconditional annuities of the Young Plan in advance of all other foreign payments. Great Britain answered, firstly, that this argument, if logically applied, was absurd, since essential German imports must clearly be paid for first ; and secondly, that it was more essential for the restoration of Germany's credit that she should discharge her commercial debts (in which Great Britain was far more interested than France) than that she should pay reparation. Agreement might never have been reached on this delicate point of priority. But in January 1932, before the Hoover moratorium expired, Brüning solved the problem by declaring that Germany neither could nor would in any circumstances resume payment of reparation. This attitude was dictated partly by considerations of internal politics. The National Socialist campaign against the Versailles Treaty was gaining ground ; and no government could now afford to take a less "patriotic" line on the reparation question.

This being the case, the essential point was to reach some agreement before the Hoover moratorium came to an end on July 1st, 1932. The French Government, though privately reconciled to the inevitable, could not yet face a public admission that reparation was dead. It was not till June that a conference assembled at Lausanne and agreed to cancel all reparation claims in return for a single payment by Germany of £150,000,000 in the form of 5 per cent redeemable bonds. The creditor governments signed a separate agreement cancelling war debts as between themselves, and made their ratification of the main agreement conditional on a satisfactory settlement of their debts to the United States. But the position was now such that the ratification or non-ratification of the Lausanne agreement (it was, in fact, never ratified) was of little practical account. It was unthinkable that anyone would renew the attempt to make Germany pay reparation. A long chapter of history had been closed once and for all.

The expiry of the Hoover moratorium did, however, reopen in a practical form the question of Allied debts to the United States.   Fortunately the next instalments were not payable till December 15th ; but unfortunately a presidential election was due in the intervening November.   Although the rumblings of the economic crisis had first been heard in the United States, the full force of the storm was felt there somewhat later than in Europe ; and it scarcely reached its height before the autumn of 1932.   The election took place in an atmosphere of profound pessimism.   The majority of the electors found it difficult to believe that anything which President Hoover had done was right.   It was at any rate clear that the Hoover moratorium had not helped America ; and it was no time, when the United States Treasury was faced with a deficit of £800,000,000, to talk of cancelling the debts of Europe.   Whatever the result of the election (in fact, Franklin Roosevelt won a sweeping victory), the request of the Allied Governments for a revision of their obligations could only have met with a blank refusal.   In these circumstances, Great Britain, with some hesitation, paid the December instalment.   The French Government proposed to do likewise.   But the Chamber of Deputies rejected the proposal ; and France, together with the other principal debtor states, defaulted.

The payment by Great Britain in December 1932 was the last to be made in full by any debtor state.   In June and December 1933 Great Britain made nominal payments of £2,000,000 each, which were treated by the United States Government as sufficient to avoid an admission of default.   Before the next instalment was due, fresh legislation in the United States prevented a repetition of this fiction ; and nothing more was ever paid. In effect, the year 1932 saw the last act in that confused drama of reparation and inter-Allied debts which had tormented the world for more than ten years. The Lausanne Conference buried them both in the same unhonoured grave.

THE WORLD ECONOMIC CONFERENCE

It was decided at Lausanne to hold in the following year a general economic conference—the first since the Geneva conference of 1927; and the United States Government accepted an invitation to participate on condition that inter-Allied debts were not discussed. Before the conference met, much happened in America. During the winter of 1932–33 the crisis reached its peak in the United States with a conjectural figure (for no official records were kept) of 15,000,000 unemployed. When Franklin Roosevelt was installed as President in March 1933, the whole financial system was on the verge of a breakdown. In the following month, the United States abandoned the gold standard, and the value of the dollar quickly depreciated by about 30 per cent.

It was under the shadow of this event that the World Economic Conference met in London in June 1933. It was the largest assembly of states on record, sixty-four countries being represented; and it was a striking tribute to the still persistent faith in the collective wisdom of mankind. But a strange parallel was soon revealed between the economic problem and the disarmament problem. Just as France and her allies had for years pleaded that security was a necessary prelude to disarmament, so France appeared at the World

Economic Conference as the leader of a group of nations which insisted on currency stabilisation as a condition of any agreement to reduce tariffs or abandon quotas. The prospects did not at first seem quite hopeless. The British Government, while pressing strongly for tariff reductions, paid tributes to the desirability of stabilisation and professed willingness to negotiate. So did Cordell Hull, the American Secretary of State and head of the American Delegation. But the United States Treasury, new to the experience of a flexible currency, was more keenly alive to its advantages than to its drawbacks. President Roosevelt issued a statement which amounted to a disclaimer of the conciliatory attitude of the American Delegation; and an expert hurried over from Washington to defend the Treasury view against the assaults of the stabilisers. This rather undignified incident was the death-blow of the conference. It dragged on till the end of July, concluding subsidiary agreements about the marketing of wheat and the price of silver, and adjourned *sine die*. It had performed the important function of demonstrating beyond any manner of doubt that the world economic crisis could not be cured by any universal formula.

THE LAST PHASE

The World Economic Conference failed because the delegates, whatever their opinions as to the next step, were all seeking ultimately to bring back a now irrevocable past—the régime of low tariffs and fixed currencies. Its failure turned the thoughts of statesmen into new channels. It was clear that economic nationalism and state regulation of trade had come to stay, and must be faced as basic facts of the future world organisation. In spite of these obstacles an improvement, scarcely noticeable at first, then gathering force, set in. In Great Britain, the starting-point seems to have been the successful conversion in July 1932, on a 3½ per cent basis, of the large mass of public debt represented by the 5 per cent War Loan. In the United States a rise in commodity prices and a revival in foreign trade dated from March 1933, and received a powerful stimulus from the depreciation of the dollar and President Roosevelt's " New Deal ". The revival began slowly to spread elsewhere. It was confined at first to those countries which had abandoned gold. But these, comprising as they did the sterling *bloc*, the United States and Japan, accounted for considerably more than half the world's trade (Great Britain alone representing about one quarter), and determined the prevailing mood. Bilateral commercial agreements between pairs of states based on direct bargaining took the place of large-scale schemes of international co-operation. International investment of capital was still virtually suspended. Each state fended for itself. Economic panaceas went out of fashion ; and the financial and economic organisations of the League devoted themselves to routine and research.

Great Britain took the lead in the new policy of bilateral agreements. In the year following the World Economic Conference, agreements involving mutual tariff reductions and undertakings to purchase were concluded with the Argentine, with the Scandinavian and Baltic countries, and with Soviet Russia and Poland.

Agreements with France, Germany and Holland were defensive measures designed to meet threatened discrimination by these countries against British goods, and did not lead to any substantial increase of trade. In June 1934, President Roosevelt obtained from Congress powers to conclude with other states trade agreements involving reductions in the United States tariff ; and such agreements were signed with many American countries, including Canada, and with some European states. Prosperity returned more slowly to countries remaining on the gold standard. In 1934 and 1935, Italy, Poland and Belgium all seceded from the gold *bloc*, the two first by establishing exchange control, the last by an official devaluation of her currency ; and the gold standard finally ceased to exist in September 1936, when France, Switzerland and Holland devalued their currencies.

While, however, it cannot be claimed that economic and financial stability was ever fully restored, the year 1933 may be said to mark the end of that specific period of contemporary history known as the world economic crisis. For three years the world had been brooding over its economic troubles and finding no solution. In 1933, the first rift in the economic clouds coincided with a fresh darkening of the political horizon. Political preoccupations—the withdrawal of Japan and Germany from the League and the imminent breakdown of the Disarmament Conference—once more dominated world affairs and, though themselves in large measure due to economic causes, caused the purely economic aspects of the crisis to take a subordinate place in men's thoughts.

THE position of Japan in the Far East could be compared to that of Germany and Italy in Europe. Her native resources were insufficient to maintain a rapidly growing population. She felt that she was treated as an upstart, and that the other Great Powers jealously resisted the fulfilment of her aspirations. At the Washington Conference, the Anglo-Saxon Powers obliged her by joint pressure to relinquish her war-time gains in China and to subscribe to the doctrine of China's integrity. In 1923 a disastrous earthquake further compelled her to renounce any immediate thought of military enterprise. But the American Immigration Act of 1924, which virtually excluded Japanese settlers from the United States, was felt as a grave insult ; and American policy in this matter was imitated by several of the British Dominions. In 1925 the decision of the British Government to carry out a long-standing project for a first-class naval base at Singapore seemed like a further bar to Japanese ambitions. The Asiatic mainland remained the only field for Japanese expansion, and the only place where Japanese could appear not merely as equals, but as conquerors. But it was not until September 1931 that Japan resumed the offensive which the Washington Conference had induced her to abandon ; and before arriving at this event, it is necessary to note the main outlines of China's relations with foreign Powers during the intervening years.

China after the Washington Conference

The revolution of 1911 left China a prey to internal dissension ; and by 1919 the province of Canton was completely independent of the Peking Government, which exercised a somewhat shadowy control over the rest of the country. In 1922, within a few months of the Washington Conference, civil war broke out over the whole of northern and central China, which was divided between the authority of rival Tu-chuns or provincial governors. In the extreme north, Manchuria became virtually independent under the energetic Chang Tso-lin. In the centre, Wu Pei-fu was the most powerful of several Tu-chuns, but never succeeded in unifying the country. In the south, Canton was the headquarters of the Kuomintang, or nationalist party, led by young Chinese intellectuals who had been educated in Western Europe or the United States, or in American colleges in China, and had imbibed ideals of democracy and self-determination. The president of Kuomintang, Sun Yat-sen, was the most striking personality in China, combining the qualities of a visionary and a prophet with those of an astute politician. In 1923 Sun Yat-sen became head of the Canton Government, and took as his chief adviser a Russian named Borodin, who soon concluded a working alliance between Soviet internationalism and Chinese nationalism.

These internal dissensions were closely bound up

with the other main issue in Chinese politics—resistance to foreign domination.   During the nineteenth century the Great Powers had imposed on China the so-called " unequal treaties ", by which China conceded a

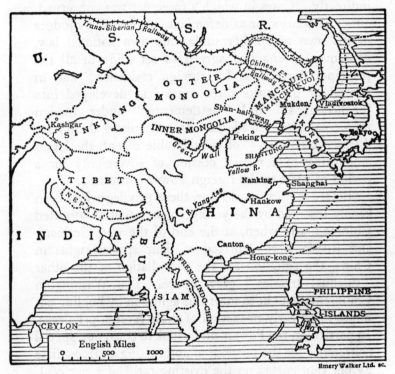

THE FAR EAST

number of special privileges to subjects of these Powers living and trading in Chinese territory. Of these special privileges, two were of outstanding importance. Firstly, the Chinese customs tariff on imports and exports was limited by agreement to a maximum of 5 per cent. Secondly, the Great Powers enjoyed extra-territorial jurisdiction in China. Their nationals were not subject to Chinese law or to Chinese courts, and paid no Chinese taxes except such as were levied indirectly. Cases in which a foreigner was concerned, either as accused or as defendant, were tried by judges of his own nationality under his own national law. Moreover, China had agreed to set aside in all the principal ports areas for foreign residence; and in several of the ports these areas had developed into " concessions " and " settlements " under foreign municipal administrations. At other places there were " leased territories " of considerable extent, the leases amounting to a virtual cession of sovereignty for a period of years to the foreign Power concerned.

Before the first world war, these privileges had been keenly resented by the younger generation of educated Chinese; and when, at the end of the war, Germany and Russia were deprived of their special rights in China, the agitation for the cancellation of the other " unequal treaties " grew apace. The Washington Conference sought to meet this agitation by holding out hopes of an early relaxation of these foreign privileges. In particular, the Powers undertook to convene a special conference for the purpose of authorising an immediate $2\frac{1}{2}$ per cent surtax on the existing tariff of 5 per cent, and eventually increasing the tariff to $12\frac{1}{2}$ per cent; and somewhat more vaguely, they promised to set up a commission to investigate and report on the extra-territorial rights of foreigners and the administration of justice in China. Once, however, the Washington Conference had dispersed, there was no great haste to implement

these promises. The civil war provided ample reason
for delay ; and there seemed little chance in such dis-
turbed conditions of the suppression of li-kin (or duties
levied on goods in transit in the interior), which had been
one of the conditions for raising the customs tariff.

The delay, however excellent the reasons that could
be found for it, played into the hands of Kuomintang,
which appeared as the champion of Chinese national
independence. In March 1925 Sun Yat-sen died.
But his death gave him a recognised status in China as
the patron saint of Chinese nationalism ; and his name
became a symbol of the national revolt against foreign
control. Under Soviet influence, anti-foreign feeling
developed into a bitter and implacable feud. Borodin
did his best to direct it primarily against Great Britain,
the original sponsor of the " unequal treaties " and the
principal enemy of his own country. The enormous
extent of British interests in China made her an easy
target. But Borodin's influence might not have
availed but for an unhappy incident in the International
Settlement at Shanghai in May 1925, when Chinese
students, engaged in a peaceful demonstration against
conditions of labour in the Japanese-owned cotton
mills, were fired on by the municipal police under
British officers. The drastic action of the police seems
to have lacked justification ; and the subsequent hand-
ling of the affair by the British authorities added fuel to
the flame. A further and still more serious shooting
incident occurred a few weeks later in the British
concession at Canton. A wave of indignation swept
through China ; and a boycott of British goods was
instituted.

Meanwhile, the spread of Kuomintang influence, ably seconded by Borodin, was having a disintegrating effect on the power of the northern Tu-chuns. The special conference for tariff revision had at last set to work at Peking in the autumn of 1925. But early in 1926 it was compelled to abandon its task owing to the absence of any authoritative government with which to negotiate. Peking, though still the seat of the foreign legations, had already ceased to be the capital of China. The centre of gravity had shifted southwards. In October 1926 the Nationalist Government in Canton once more took the initiative by beginning to levy the $2\frac{1}{2}$ per cent surtax, in the ports under its control, without awaiting the authorisation of the Powers.

The British Government now had the wisdom to perceive that it was time to come to terms with the rising tide of nationalism—the only real force in China. In December 1926 it took two steps which created a considerable impression. The British Minister went to Hankow to meet the Foreign Minister of the Nationalist Government—a first move towards its recognition as the Government of China ; and the British Legation in Peking issued a memorandum emphasising the sympathy of the British Government with the Chinese nationalist movement. The memorandum declared that the idea of imposing foreign tutelage on China was obsolete, expressed readiness to discuss treaty revision, and proposed as a first step that the Powers should forthwith authorise the levying of the $2\frac{1}{2}$ per cent surtax throughout China.

Before there had been time for this declaration

of policy to produce its effect, the storm broke. On January 1st, 1927, the Nationalist Government trans-ferred its headquarters from Canton to Hankow, a more central situation for a national capital. A few days later, the British concession at Hankow was overrun by a Chinese mob ; and a division of British troops was hurried to Shanghai to protect the Inter-national Settlement there from a similar assault. In February the British Government concluded with the Nationalist Government an agreement legalising, under certain conditions, the transfer of the concession at Hankow from British to Chinese control. The policy of conciliation, tempered by a determination to safe-guard British lives and property, was soon justified by its results. The year 1927 proved to be a turning-point in two important respects.

In the first place, it saw the sudden and dramatic end of Borodin's influence. The alliance between the revolutionary internationalism of Moscow and the patriotic nationalism of Kuomintang had always been to some extent artificial. They had worked well enough together so long as the object was the liberation of China from foreign control. But when, at the begin-ning of 1927, the Nationalist Government established itself in Hankow and developed pretensions to become the central authority for the whole of China, Kuomin-tang split into two factions. The left wing aimed at continuing the revolutionary traditions of the party in co-operation with Borodin. The right wing, strongly influenced by the new attitude of Great Britain, coveted respectability and recognition by the Great Powers It so happened that at this time the right wing found a vigorous leader in General Chiang Kai-shek, who had no sympathy with communism and no desire for the assistance of Russian advisers. Chiang Kai-shek set up a rival Kuomintang Government at Nanking, and sent a demand to the Hankow Government for the expulsion of Borodin and the communists. In July the demand was complied with. Borodin and his Russian assistants were sent back to Moscow, and many Chinese communists were thrown into prison. The seat of government was transferred from Hankow to Nanking, which remained thereafter the capital of China.

Secondly, the year 1927 witnessed an important change in China's international relations. For two years Great Britain had borne the brunt of China's resentment of the foreigner. Japan, true to the policy of self-restraint accepted by her at the Washington Conference, had remained in the background, and her trade had profited by the boycott on British goods. But the prospect of the re-establishment of a unified national government in China reversed the position, and brought out the fundamental difference between British and Japanese policy in China. Great Britain, whose interests in China were purely commercial, sincerely desired an orderly and united country where trade could prosper. Japan, whose concern in her neighbour's affairs was above all political, preferred to see China weak, divided and incapable of contesting Japanese supremacy or thwarting Japanese ambitions. In particular, Japan regarded with distaste any prospect of North China coming under the effective control of a central government.

When, therefore, in May 1927 Nationalist forces

marched northwards and reached a point on the Yellow River some 500 miles south of Peking, the Japanese Government took alarm. Japanese troops were landed in the province of Shantung, and occupied certain strategic points with the evident intention of barring the Nationalist advance. This act, which showed that Japanese designs on Shantung, abandoned at Washington under the pressure of the Powers, were still alive, produced a strong reaction throughout China. The hostility displayed two years earlier against Great Britain was now directed against Japan, and it was the turn of Japanese goods to be boycotted by Chinese patriots. In face of Japanese opposition, the whole of North China as far as Peking recognised the authority of the Nationalist Government. But about Manchuria, Japan was adamant; and when in April 1928 Chang Tso-lin showed signs of coming to terms with Nanking he was killed in a mysterious bomb explosion which many regarded as a Japanese plot.

Thus by the middle of 1928 the situation in China had clarified itself, and the stage was set for the dramatic events of 1931. Civil war continued intermittently. In some provinces of central China, communism was still in the ascendant. The control of the government was weak or non-existent in the outlying provinces. In Manchuria Japanese influence prevented any co-operation with Nanking. But in name China was once more united under a central government. Internationally, Japan resumed her role as China's principal bogey; the ever-present fear of Japan had a sobering effect on China's attitude to other foreign interests. At no time since 1919 had there been less friction in the conduct of China's international relations than between 1927 and 1931.

JAPAN CONQUERS MANCHURIA

Precisely what circumstances decided the date of Japan's first overt act of aggression is a matter for conjecture. There had long been rivalry in Japan between the civil and the military authorities. Both were equally anxious to establish Japan's position as a Great Power. But while the civilian political leaders believed that this could best be achieved by conciliating British and American opinion, the military party (whose position was strengthened by the fact that the army was responsible not to the civil government, but direct to the Emperor) sought to found Japan's greatness on a policy of military conquest. The civilian party had won at the Washington Conference, and for nearly ten years were strong enough to restrain the army from action. But since 1927 the provocative attitude of China towards Japanese interests had tried Japanese patience. The economic crisis, which between 1929 and 1931 cut the value of Japan's foreign trade almost in half, threatened serious internal unrest. In the summer of 1931, the murder of a Japanese officer in Manchuria by Chinese bandits was used to inflame opinion ; and in September the army took the matter into its own hands. The moment chosen was, by accident or design, one at which Great Britain was in the throes of a financial and political crisis.

By the treaty which ended the Russo-Japanese War, Japan had acquired the right to maintain some 15,000 soldiers in Manchuria for the protection of the South Manchurian Railway, the line which runs southward from the Trans-Siberian Railway to Port Arthur. These guards were confined to the railway zone, their headquarters being at Mukden. On the night of September 18th–19th, 1931, a Japanese patrol near Mukden discovered, or was alleged to have discovered, a detachment of Chinese soldiers attempting to blow up the main line. The Japanese guards were promptly called out, and a minor battle ensued, as the result of which the 10,000 Chinese troops in Mukden were disarmed or dispersed. Within four days, all Chinese towns within a radius 200 miles north of Mukden, some of them far outside the railway zone, were in Japanese occupation. The Chinese Provincial Government, of which a son of Chang Tso-lin was the head, was driven out of Mukden, and maintained a shadowy existence at Chinchow. By the middle of November the vast and thinly populated territory of northern Manchuria was in Japanese hands. The Japanese forces then turned southwards, bombing aeroplanes being used in this phase of the operations. Chinchow fell on December 28th, and on January 4th, 1932, the Japanese reached Shanhaikwan on the Great Wall, the frontier station between Manchuria and China proper. The Japanese conquest of Manchuria was complete.

The Japanese plan of campaign had been carried through without regard to the embarrassments of the Council of the League of Nations, which had been in almost continuous session during this time. The Chinese Government had at once appealed to the League under Article 11 of the Covenant—the Article under which decisions could be taken only by a unanimous vote, and under which the League had scored all its past successes.   The Japanese delegate disclaimed on behalf of his government any intention of annexing Chinese territory, and explained the operations of the Japanese army by the necessity of protecting Japanese lives and property from Chinese bandits.   The Council, recalling the methods by which it had triumphed in the Greco-Bulgarian quarrel (see p. 105), drew up a resolution designed to pave the way for a Japanese retreat.   The resolution recited an assurance given by the Japanese delegate that his Government would " continue as rapidly as possible the withdrawal of its troops . . . into the railway zone in proportion as the safety of the lives and property of Japanese nationals is effectively secured ", and expressed the hope that this and other measures for the " restoration of normal relations " would be speedily completed.   On September 30th, 1931, this resolution was unanimously accepted ; and the Council adjourned for a fortnight, anxious but not despondent.

The Pact of Paris prohibited recourse to war ; and the Nine-Power Treaty concluded at Washington (see p. 21) bound its signatories to respect the independence and integrity of China.   It was for this reason that Japan so firmly insisted that her Manchurian venture was to be regarded not as an act of war, but as " police operations ", and that she had no intention of annexing Chinese territory.   As the days went on, however, this pretence became more and more difficult to keep up.   When the Council reassembled on October 13th, it was clear that Japan was in process of

164

breaking not only the Covenant of the League, but the Pact of Paris and the Nine-Power Treaty; and this at once brought the United States on the scene. The leaders of American opinion were quick to realise that the Japanese action had opened a new chapter in the struggle for power in the Pacific. The American Government not only applauded the efforts of the Council with rare warmth, but supported them by diplomatic representations at Peking and Tokyo; and it was intimated to Briand, the President of the Council, that an invitation to participate in the proceedings of the Council would be not unwelcome at Washington.

The Council, carried off its feet by this flattering and surprising offer, now made its first mistake. When Briand laid before it the proposal to invite the American Government to send a delegate to the Council, the Japanese delegate at once objected to the proposal as unconstitutional. Article 17 of the Covenant prescribed the only condition in which non-members of the League could be invited to be represented at the Council; and that condition was not present. After a long debate, this objection was overruled. By a somewhat sophistical argument, the other members of the Council decided that the invitation to the United States was a matter of procedure which could be carried by a majority vote; and on October 16th an American delegate took his seat at the Council table, declaring that he would participate in the discussions only in so far as they related to the upholding of the Pact of Paris. The enthusiasm was enormous. Optimists whispered that the League, if it had lost Japan, had won America. But events soon showed that optimism was premature.

The American Government was too frightened of anti-League opinion in the United States to permit its delegate to play any active part ; and when the Council resumed its meetings in the following month, American co-operation was once more confined to private and unofficial conversations with individual members of the Council.

Meanwhile the dispute about American participation had widened the rift between Japan and the other members of the Council. The attitude of both sides stiffened. Japan demanded direct negotiations with China as a preliminary to withdrawal, and refused to inform the Council what her terms would be. The other members of the Council continued to insist on the withdrawal of the Japanese troops into the railway zone as a preliminary to negotiations. On October 24th a resolution was put to the vote calling on Japan to complete this withdrawal " before the date fixed for the next meeting of the Council ", *i.e.* November 16th, and was rejected by the single adverse vote of the Japanese delegate. Conciliation had definitely broken down. The procedure of Article 11 was exhausted.

So great, however, was the prestige which Article 11 had acquired in the prosperous days of the League, and so strong the reluctance to resort to the procedure of Article 15, under which a verdict could be pronounced against the vote of the parties, that this conclusion was not immediately drawn. During a long session in Paris, lasting from November 16th to December 10th, the Council continued to wrestle with the problem under the terms of Article 11. The deadlock was complete. But an open admission of failure was postponed

by the unanimous decision to send to the Far East a
League Commission to investigate on the spot " any
circumstances which, affecting international relations,
threatens to disturb peace between China and Japan ".
The sole limitation on the competence of the Commission was that it was not to " interfere with the military
arrangements of either party". It was composed of
representatives of the five Great Powers (Great Britain,
the United States, France, Germany and Italy); and its
president was the British representative, Lord Lytton.

Before the Lytton Commission could start its work,
other striking developments occurred. The Chinese
had replied to Japanese aggression with their traditional
weapon—a boycott of Japanese goods ; and feeling ran
so high that incidents were of frequent occurrence.
At the end of January 1932 one such incident, in which
a party of Japanese monks in Shanghai were attacked,
and one of them killed, gave the Japanese military command an excuse to teach the Chinese a lesson. A large
Japanese force was landed at Shanghai and, using the
International Settlement as its base, attacked the
Chinese troops in the suburb of Chapei, which was
bombed from the air and practically burnt out. But
the permanent occupation of Shanghai was no part of
Japan's present programme ; and the arrival of the
Lytton Commission in China early in March stimulated
Japanese anxiety to wind up this discreditable side-
show. After prolonged negotiations, in which the
British Minister acted as intermediary, the Japanese
troops were withdrawn from Shanghai in May. In
Manchuria Japan had meanwhile consolidated her
conquest by setting up a puppet Republic of Manchukuo

and appointing as its president the last survivor of the old Manchu dynasty, Pu Yi. Later in the year Japan officially recognised the republic, which was in fact administered by Japanese advisers, as an independent state.

The situation at Geneva had also developed. On January 29th, in the midst of the Shanghai fighting, the Chinese Government had at last demanded the application of Article 10 and Article 15 of the Covenant, and had followed this up by requesting the convocation of a special Assembly. The motive for transferring the matter to the Assembly was clear. The smaller Powers, who had most to fear from aggression, had from the first shown greater eagerness for the coercion of Japan than the Great Powers on whom would fall the brunt of enforcing sanctions ; and in the Assembly, the small Powers were in a large majority. The special Assembly met in March and listened to a number of excellent speeches. But it could not well pronounce its verdict until it received the report of the Lytton Commission, which could not be ready till the autumn. During the summer Geneva was in the throes of the Disarmament Conference, and reparation was being disposed of at Lausanne ; and the Far Eastern problem was half forgotten.

At the end of September the report of the Lytton Commission reached Geneva, and in November it was submitted to the Council. It was a long and exhaustive document which dealt not only with the Manchurian episode, but with almost every aspect of Chinese-Japanese relations. It rejected unhesitatingly the various pretexts on which Japan had endeavoured to justify her invasion of Manchuria, and declared the independent Manchukuo state to be a complete fiction. On the other hand, it did not deny that the Chinese attitude towards Japan in the past had been incorrect and provocative. It declared that neither the restoration of the *status quo* nor the maintenance of the fictitious Manchukuo state would be a satisfactory solution of the dispute, and recommended that an autonomous régime should be set up in Manchuria as the result of negotiations between China and Japan under the auspices of the League.

The Lytton report was successively considered by the Council, by the Assembly and by an Assembly Committee, which was charged with the task of drafting the report required by Article 15 of the Covenant. This report followed closely the lines of the Lytton report. It recommended that China and Japan should negotiate, under the auspices of a committee to be set up by the Assembly, for the withdrawal of the Japanese troops and the establishment of an autonomous régime in Manchuria under Chinese sovereignty. It proposed that members of the League should refuse to recognise the existing régime in Manchuria ; but it equally rejected any return to the *status quo*.

The most significant feature of the report was, however, the skill with which it avoided any pronouncement which might have entailed the application of sanctions under Article 16 of the Covenant. It pointedly recited the obligations of the Covenant, the Pact of Paris and the Nine-Power Treaty. But it abstained from drawing the conclusion that these obligations had been violated by Japan. It did not formally accept the

Japanese thesis that the Manchurian campaign had been a mere matter of police operations. But it quoted and endorsed the opinion of the Lytton report that " the present case is not that of a country which has declared war on another country without previously exhausting the opportunities for conciliation provided in the Covenant of the League of Nations, neither is it a simple case of the violation of the frontier of one country by the armed forces of a neighbouring country ". The importance of this passage was obvious. If Japan had not resorted to war, she had not broken the Covenant, and the application of Article 16 did not arise. Sanctions were, in fact, never discussed. The only penalty recommended in the report was one which had been originally suggested by the American Secretary of State, and in which the American Government was prepared to co-operate : non-recognition of Manchukuo.

On February 24th, 1933, the report was voted on by the Assembly. Of the forty-four delegations present, forty-two accepted it. Siam abstained, and Japan voted " no " ; but the adverse vote of one of the parties to the dispute did not affect the unanimous adoption of the report. As soon as the result was announced, the Japanese Delegation left the hall in a body. A month later, Japan gave formal notice to terminate her membership of the League.

After adopting its report, the Assembly appointed a committee " to follow the situation . . . and to aid the members of the League in concerting their action and their attitude among themselves and with the non-member states ". The Soviet Government still refused to have anything to do with the political organs of the League. The American Government cordially agreed to co-operate, and appointed a representative to the committee. But the League effort was now virtually exhausted. The deliberations of the committee were limited to two specific points : the export of arms to the Far East, and the practical consequences of the non-recognition decision. As regards the first question, nothing was achieved. The British Government rather illogically placed an embargo on shipments of arms from Great Britain to both China and Japan. But when nobody followed this example, the embargo was withdrawn ; and no further attempt was made to limit the supply of arms to either party. As regards the second question, the committee unravelled some of the complications of postal and commercial relations with an unrecognised state, and of the status of foreign consuls resident there. Manchukuo enjoyed most of the practical advantages of intercourse with the outside world. But its existence was not officially recognised by any country of importance except Japan.

THE CONSEQUENCES TO THE LEAGUE

The Japanese conquest of Manchuria was one of the most important historical landmarks since the first world war. In the Pacific, it denoted the resumption of the struggle for power which had been suspended by the Washington Conference. In the world at large, it heralded a return to " power politics ", which had been in abeyance, at any rate in this naked form, since the end of the war. For the first time since the peace

171

settlement, war had been waged (though under the guise of police operations) on an extensive scale, and a vast territory had been annexed (though under the guise of an independent state) by the conqueror. For the League of Nations, whose Covenant and whose ideals had been flouted, the consequences were incalculable. It was difficult to resist the conclusion that members of the League (and in particular the Great Powers on whom the main burden of upholding the Covenant must necessarily fall) were not prepared to resist an act of aggression committed by a powerful and well-armed state.

Many excuses were urged in mitigation of this failure. The test had come at a moment when the whole world was suffering from a wholesale and disastrous contraction of international trade. It was plausibly argued that to break off financial and economic relations with Japan, as the Covenant demanded, would mean a gratuitous aggravation of the prevailing economic distress. The British navy was the only first-class fleet possessed by a League member other than Japan; and should Japan reply to economic sanctions by attacking the possessions of sanctionist Powers in China, the British navy, so far from its normal bases, could scarcely provide an adequate defence. The feeling grew up that this was an exceptional case which could not be treated as a precedent. The distances were too great. The framers of Article 21 of the Covenant and the makers of the Locarno Treaty had wisely recognised the regional character of security. States could not be expected to apply sanctions on the other side of the world; and the abnormal status of

China, carefully emphasised in the Assembly report, justified the failure to apply strict League rules. Because the Covenant had broken down in the Far East, it did not follow that it would not prove an effective instrument nearer home. During the later stages of the Manchurian dispute, this consoling reflexion seems to have satisfied everyone except the Chinese delegate, who pathetically remarked that China "cannot be expected to admit that the operation of treaties, covenants and the accepted principles of international law stops at the border of Manchuria".

The League had, moreover, drawn one uncontestable advantage from the Manchurian affair: the goodwill of the United States. The participation of an American delegate in the proceedings of the Council had, indeed, been short-lived. It remained uncertain whether the United States would have co-operated with the League in economic sanctions, if these had been applied. It was clear that American military co-operation could not in any case have been counted on. American membership of the League was as far off as ever. But in spite of all these qualifications, a decided change came over the attitude of American opinion towards the League. The United States Government publicly applauded every decision of the League on this question—a novel departure in American politics. The movement might have gone further but for the discouraging effects of American participation in the Disarmament Conference.

In the midst of the Manchurian dispute, the League found itself with two other wars on its hands—both in South America; and here too the United States

Government encouraged and supported League action. The first of these conflicts concerned the Chaco, a remote uninhabited region which had for many years been contested between Bolivia and Paraguay. In 1932 regular fighting broke out, and in the next year Paraguay formally declared war. The dispute was dealt with by the League, first under Article 11, then under Article 15, of the Covenant. Nearly all members of the League, as well as the United States, imposed an embargo on supplies of war material to both belligerents. But every effort proved fruitless. The war ran its course, and ended in 1935 in a victory for Paraguay. The other dispute arose from the seizure by Peru of the small Colombian settlement of Leticia with its adjacent territory. Colombia appealed under Article 15 to the Council, which, in March 1933, issued a report calling on Peru to withdraw. At first Peru defied the summons. Presently, however, internal events in Peru produced a more reasonable frame of mind ; and later in the year a League commission visited Leticia to superintend the return of the district to Colombia. But neither the League's failure in the Chaco, nor its success at Leticia, diverted public anxiety from the graver problems of Manchuria and the Disarmament Conference.

It is a matter for speculation whether the Disarmament Conference would have succeeded if it had been convened in the period between 1925 and 1930. What is certain is that, when it finallly met in February 1932 at the height of the economic crisis and of the Japanese attack on Shanghai, its chances of success had almost disappeared. Its failure, following hard on the Manchurian fiasco, marked the culmination of the period of crisis which had begun in 1930. The account of the Conference itself must, however, be prefaced by a brief review of the ten years of preparation which had led up to it.

THE DISARMAMENT PROBLEM

In the Versailles Treaty, the Allied Powers had declared that the purpose of the drastic disarmament of Germany was " to render possible the initiation of a general limitation of the armaments of all nations " ; and by Article 8 of the Covenant members of the League recognised " that the maintenance of peace required the reduction of national armaments to the lowest point consistent with national safety ". On the one hand, therefore, the Allied Governments had given Germany a promise (which was morally, if not legally, binding) to proceed to a general measure of disarmament when Germany was disarmed. On the other hand, they had accepted " national safety " as an overriding factor in any reduction of armaments. The conflict between these two principles constituted the problem of disarmament.

Article 8 of the Covenant placed on the Council of the League the duty of formulating plans for the reduction of armaments " for the consideration and action of the several governments ". In November 1920 the Council appointed a " Temporary Mixed Commission ", composed of civilians and representatives of the fighting services, to assist it in this task. But the first success in the field of disarmament was won at the Washington Conference. There the navies of the chief naval Powers were limited by a straightforward numerical scheme of tonnage and ratios (see p. 20). It remained for the League to apply the same principle to the all-important matter of military establishments (for air power was still in its infancy) ; and in 1922 the British delegate on the Temporary Mixed Commission proposed a numerical scheme for the limitation of armies. Armies were to be divided into imaginary units of 30,000 men ; and a certain number of these units (like battleships) was to be allocated to each Power. Thus France was to have six units, or an army of 180,000 men, Italy four units, Great Britain three and so on. Unfortunately this simple plan was condemned by the military experts of nearly every European country. It was plausibly urged that, whereas a battleship of a certain tonnage was a more or less standard article and its maximum complement of guns was known, a unit of 30,000 men was not in itself a measurable force, and its strength could vary almost indefinitely in proportion to its armaments. The first concrete scheme of land disarmament was ignominiously shelved.

But Article 8 remained, and something must be done about it. It was at this point that the French Delegation, relying on the " national safety " stipulation, introduced the thesis of increased security as a necessary condition of disarmament, and won the assent of the British Delegation to their view (see p. 88). The next three years were the years of the draft Treaty of Mutual Assistance, the Geneva Protocol and the Locarno Treaties. During the whole of this period nothing was done in the field of disarmament, except for an unsuccessful attempt to limit the naval armaments of the smaller Powers on the basis of the Washington agreement, and a convention, which never came into force, for controlling international trade in arms.

It was the signature of the Locarno Treaties and the impending entry of Germany into the League which once more galvanised the disarmament machine into action. In the final protocol of the Locarno Conference, the signatories committed themselves to the view that the conclusion of these agreements would " hasten on effectively the disarmament provided for in Article 8 of the Covenant "; and from this time onward Germany's insistence on the disarmament of the other Powers became a determining factor in the proceedings. In December 1925 the Council appointed a Preparatory Commission for the Disarmament Conference, which met for the first time in May 1926.

Germany, the United States and the Soviet Union were all invited to become members of this Commission. The first two accepted immediately, and the Soviet Union in the following year.

Progress was nevertheless slow. The greater part of 1926 was occupied by the work of two " technical " sub-commissions labouring to define the nature of the armaments which were to be limited and reduced. It was not until March 1927, when the British and French Delegations submitted draft disarmament conventions, that the Preparatory Commission really came to grips with its subject. These drafts were in fact only dummy conventions. They contained no figures, but presented framework designed to show what should be limited and how. But even so they revealed wide differences of opinion, and many of these were fundamental. In the question of military personnel, the French Delegation wished to limit only men on service ; the British, American and German Delegations wished to limit all trained personnel. In the question of military material, the German Delegation demanded a specific numerical limitation of all important categories of armament such as had been imposed on Germany under the Versailles Treaty ; the French Delegation wished to limit military material by the indirect means of limiting budgetary expenditure on it (the only form of limitation which had not hitherto been imposed on Germany) ; the British and American Delegations deemed any limitation of military material impracticable. In the question of naval material, the French and Italian Delegations wanted only a limitation of the total tonnage of navies ; the British and American Delegations wanted separate limitation of each category of ship. In the question of budgets, the French Delegation wanted a limitation of expenditure; the British and Italian Delegations wanted detailed publicity of expenditure in an agreed form ; the American and German Delegations wanted no budgetary stipulations of any kind. The Commission recorded these divergent views and adjourned for further reflexion.

In the meanwhile, the American Government had made an unexpected proposal. Impatient of these delays, it invited the other signatories of the Washington Naval Treaty to attend a conference for the purpose of dealing with those classes of ships which had not been limited by that treaty. France declined the invitation. She was prepared in the last resort to make naval concessions in return for counter-concessions on matters more vital to her ; but it would be manifestly disadvantageous for her to discuss naval disarmament as a separate topic. Italy followed suit. But Great Britain and Japan accepted ; and a Three-Power conference accordingly assembled at Geneva in June 1927.

Both American and British Governments seem to have seriously underestimated the difficulty of extending the Washington limitations to non-capital ships. The American Delegation proposed a simple extension of the Washington ratio of $5:5:3$ (see p. 21) to cruisers, destroyers and submarines, and put forward limitation figures on this basis. The British case was more complicated. The British Government maintained that, owing to the extent of Empire communications, the minimum British need in cruisers was seventy —a number considerably in excess of those already built or building. They therefore proposed that cruisers should be divided into two classes, divided according to tonnage and calibre of guns—a larger class which should be subject to the Washington ratios, and a smaller which should be free from all limitation. They also suggested a reduction in the size of capital ships. In brief, the British Government wished to economise by an all-round reduction in the size of ships, but claimed a free hand, or at any rate a high limitation, in respect of small cruisers. The American Government saw no reason to reduce the size of ships of any category. They refused to consider a limitation figure for cruisers in excess of existing numbers, and suspected a desire on the part of the British Government to escape from the principle of equality accepted at Washington. The Japanese Delegation occupied an intermediate position and gave an impression of willingness to accept whatever the two protagonists might agree on. But the divergence on the cruiser issue proved irreconcilable; and the conference ended with a confession of failure. It was the first open defeat for the cause of disarmament.

The failure of the Geneva Naval Conference cast a gloom over the 1927 Assembly, which, adopting the course now customary at Geneva whenever disarmament prospects looked black, recommended a further study of the problem of security. The autumn session of the Preparatory Commission was enlivened by the first appearance of a Soviet Delegation under M. Litvinov, who made an eloquent plea for total and universal disarmament. This proposal met with no support; and progress on more orthodox lines was barred by the unresolved deadlock of the spring session. In these conditions the Commission took its cue from the Assembly resolution and appointed the Committee on Arbitration and Security whose labours have already been chronicled (see p. 115). For two years disarmament once more receded into the background.

It was not till 1929 that the sky showed signs of clearing. In March of that year Herbert Hoover took office as President of the United States, and three months later MacDonald's second Labour Government came into power in Great Britain. These changes perhaps hastened a reconciliation which both sides had long desired. In the autumn MacDonald visited the United States ; and as the result of this visit it was decided to convene another naval conference to meet in London in January 1930. This time France and Italy, as well as Japan, accepted the invitation, though France reiterated her view of the interdependence of naval, military and air armaments.

The course of the London Naval Conference was very different from that of its predecessor. Great Britain had reduced her requirements in cruisers from seventy to fifty ; and this figure made agreement possible, though it represented, both for Great Britain and the United States, a measure of rearmament rather than of disarmament. It was France who now succeeded to the role previously played by Great Britain. Her delegates insisted that the extent of her colonial possessions made it essential for her to maintain a large fleet of cruisers, and rejected both the Anglo-American proposal for the extension to non-capital ships of the Washington ratios, and the Italian claim to parity with

France. More important, Japan for the first time expressed open dissatisfaction with the inequality imposed on her by the Washington treaties, and put forward a tentative claim to parity with Great Britain and the United States in all categories. She was finally persuaded, with considerable difficulty, to accept the Washington ratio (which gave her 60 per cent of British or American tonnage) for large cruisers, on condition that she was granted 70 per cent in small cruisers and destroyers, and parity in submarines ; and in April a limitation treaty was signed on this basis. French objections, however, proved intractable, and the agreement was confined to Great Britain, the United States and Japan. All five Powers agreed at the same time to extend the Washington treaty for a further five years.

This partial success spurred the League to renew its efforts. Germany, having secured the evacuation of the Rhineland, was free to concentrate on disarmament; and German pressure at Geneva for more rapid progress grew stronger month by month. It was decided that the Preparatory Commission should hold a final session in the autumn of 1930, and that, whatever the issue, the long postponed Disarmament Conference should then be convened. The final session did little to remove those differences on the principles of limitation which had dogged the earlier proceedings of the Commission. But a dummy draft convention (from which figures were still absent) was passed by majorities of varying size, the dissentients recording their objections and reservations in footnotes. Such a document was of little practical value ; and it was in fact not used by the Conference when it met. But it served to register and explain those fundamental divergences of opinion about disarmament which the Conference would have had to face. So much had been achieved by the five years' labour of the Preparatory Commission. The way was now clear. The Conference was summoned for February 2nd, 1932.

THE DISARMAMENT CONFERENCE

The Conference was attended by representatives of sixty-one states, including five non-members of the League of Nations, and presided over by Arthur Henderson. At the time of his appointment in the summer of 1931, Henderson was Foreign Secretary in the British Labour Government. But in August the Government resigned, and in the ensuing general election Henderson lost his seat in Parliament. It was therefore as a private individual that he presided over the Conference. This was an unforeseen misfortune. A president holding high office in the British Government would have been in a strong position to oblige the Conference to face the issues and take its decisions. The ultimate result would probably have been the same. But the prolonged falterings and evasions which discredited the Conference might have been avoided. Both the French and British Governments aggravated the difficulties by failing to appoint ministerial delegates to reside at Geneva and assume continuous direction of policy. The internal situation in Germany exercised a still more untoward influence ; for in May 1932 the weak and conciliatory government of Brüning was succeeded by the sly and truculent Papen, who was keenly conscious of the importance of stealing the thunder of the National Socialists. These minor handicaps, added to the graver disasters of the economic crisis and Japan's invasion of Manchuria, sealed the fate of the Conference.

The Preparatory Commission had provided more signposts to the pitfalls of disarmament than to promising lines of advance ; and it is not surprising that the Conference, though it passed a resolution adopting the Commission's draft convention as a " framework " for its labours, should in fact have steered an altogether different course. The French Delegation secured the initiative by proposing, in a memorandum circulated to the Conference, the creation of a League of Nations police force. Powers possessing capital ships, large submarines or heavy artillery were to hold them at the disposal of the League force, which was also to have a monopoly of bombing aeroplanes. This proposal was supported by several minor European Powers. But it was highly distasteful to Great Britain and the United States, who had always opposed the idea of a supernational military force, and to Germany, who regarded the plan as yet another manœuvre to shelve the real issue of disarmament. France did not attempt to press the proposal for a League force. But whenever the Conference embarked on the discussion of some concrete measure of disarmament, the French Delegation could be relied upon to remind it that some addition to French security was an unalterable condition of French approval.

The course of the Conference was more directly affected by a proposal made by the British Foreign

Secretary in his opening speech. Sir John Simon suggested that the Conference should consider what came to be known as " qualitative limitation ", *i.e.* limitation of armaments not by numbers (the main form of limitation contemplated by the Preparatory Commission), but by the complete abolition of certain forms of armament particularly lending themselves to offensive rather than defensive warfare. This clear-cut proposal received widespread support ; and heavy guns, tanks, submarines, bombing aircraft and gas were among the weapons instanced by several delegations as specifically offensive. When, however, the question was referred to three commissions composed respectively of naval, military and aeronautical experts, it became apparent that no distinction between offensive and defensive weapons would command general acceptance. Thus, while the British and American Delegations thought submarines offensive and battleships defensive, others thought precisely the opposite. Many delegations regarded all tanks as offensive. But the French Delegation attributed an offensive character only to a tank of over seventy tons (a hitherto non-existent phenomenon), and the British Delegation suggested a limit of twenty-five tons. The German Delegation alone had a consistent criterion : all armaments prohibited by the Versailles Treaty were offensive, all others defensive. But even this criterion did not save them from a glaring inconsistency ; for while they maintained that all military aircraft were offensive, they stoutly opposed any suggestion for the control of civil aircraft, which had been overlooked in the Versailles Treaty. Only the Commission on Chemical Warfare unanimously recommended that the use of noxious gases in war should be prohibited (a result already achieved by an international convention of 1925). But no scheme could be devised to restrict the manufacture or possession of such gases.

It was not until June that the various commissions reported these meagre results. A further delay was caused by the diversion of interest to the Lausanne Conference (see p. 147). An American proposal based on the principle of an all-round reduction of one-third in existing armed forces and armaments was politely, but coldly, received by Great Britain, who saw in it a sinister design to reduce the number of British cruisers; and when in the middle of July the delegations began to consider a resolution to report progress prior to the summer recess, they were embarrassed by the absence of any achievement to record. On July 20th a resolution was submitted to the Conference recording agreement (1) to prohibit air bombardment, to limit the number of aircraft and to regulate civil aviation, (2) to limit heavy artillery and tanks above a maximum size not yet determined, and (3) to prohibit chemical warfare. Forty-one delegations voted for this resolution, eight (including Italy) abstained, and two (Germany and the Soviet Union) voted against it. The German delegate, who had throughout insisted on the principle that the other Powers must either disarm down to the Versailles level or recognise Germany's right to rearm, announced that Germany would participate in the further work of the Conference only if there were ' a clear and definite recognition of equality of rights between nations ".

Negotiations during the recess led to no result ; and when the Conference reassembled in October Germany's place was vacant. For two months the work of the Conference was virtually suspended, the only noteworthy features being a new French security plan, and a French proposal to make the manufacture of arms in all countries a state monopoly. The German issue dominated everything else ; and at length, on December 11th, a formula was found. Great Britain, France and Italy recognised Germany's claim to " equality of rights in a system which would provide security for all nations ", and on these terms Germany agreed to return to the Conference. The principle of equality had been conceded, though the necessity for a " system of security " still left France with a trump card in her hand. The first year of the Disarmament Conference ended on this note of restrained hope.

The Conference resumed at the end of January 1933. But the only practical result of the December compromise had been to bring the French demand for security and the German demand for disarmament into sharper opposition. In the middle of March, when a complete deadlock had been reached, the British Prime Minister came to Geneva and laid before the Conference what came to be known as the " MacDonald Plan ". This plan put the Conference in possession for the first time of a complete draft convention containing figures of limitation of men and material for practically every country in Europe. It was cordially received. But faith in the possibility of a disarmament convention was almost dead. The debates on the plan during the next four weeks showed once more how little agreement

existed on fundamental points ; and in June the Conference adjourned with the now customary expression
of hope that private negotiations during the recess
would clear up the outstanding points of difference.

Hitler had been German Chancellor since the end
of January, and the Nazi régime was now firmly
established. This fact naturally increased the reluctance of the French Government to concede German
claims.   Yet it made it all the more imperative to come
to terms with Germany without further delay.   Unfortunately the only scheme evolved during the summer
recess of 1933 was a French plan for dividing the disarmament convention into two periods.   In the first,
or trial, period of four years, a system of international
supervision over armaments would be established, and
the reorganisation of national armies begun ; limitation
proper would take effect only in the second period.
The British and Italian Governments fell in with this
proposal.   On October 14th Sir John Simon formally
endorsed it in the Bureau of the Conference ; and
within a few hours Germany announced her withdrawal from the Disarmament Conference and the
League of Nations.

The withdrawal of Germany was a grave blow ; for
Germany had become more and more the focal point of
the disarmament problem.   The Conference came to
a standstill for six months, while the principal Powers,
including Germany, exchanged their views in diplomatic notes.   In February 1934 Eden visited Paris,
Berlin and Rome.   During his stay in Berlin, Hitler
made an offer to accept any limit for the German
army which was equally accepted for the French,

Italian and Polish armies, and to fix the German air force at 30 per cent of the combined strength of the air forces of Germany's neighbours or 50 per cent of the strength of the French air force, whichever figure was the lower. The French Government returned a reply protesting against the proposed " legalisation of German rearmament ", and insisting on guarantees and penalties for non-fulfilment as essential conditions of a disarmament convention. The British Government enquired whether, in the event of satisfactory guarantees being given, the French Government was disposed to agree to Hitler's offer. Finally, on April 17th, the French Government answered that the recently published German military budget showed the clear intention of Germany to rearm and that France was therefore not prepared to discuss the German proposals.

This answer was the real end of the Conference. It dragged on for a few months longer, while its committees considered such subsidiary matters as the manufacture of and trade in arms and the publicity of military budgets. But its sessions became intermittent, and its whole existence fitful and unreal. After the end of 1934 it ceased to meet, though it was never formally wound up, or even, like the World Economic Conference, adjourned. Its president died in the autumn of 1935.

The lingering death of the Disarmament Conference was the final episode in the period of post-war history which began with the onset of the economic crisis in 1930 ; and it overlapped by some months the new period which began when Hitler seized the reins of power in Germany. The two events stood, indeed,

189

in the closest relation to each other, and jointly marked the transition from one period to the next. The failure of the Allied Powers to carry out their promise to disarm justified, or at any rate explained, the rearmament of Germany. This rearmament necessarily led to increased apprehension and increased armaments in other countries ; and the vicious circle which the statesmen of 1919 had hoped to break was once more complete. The return to power politics, which had first declared itself in 1931 in the Far East, spread in 1933 all over the world.

The Four-Power Pact

A brief postscript may be added here about an event which, though it had only an accidental connexion with the Disarmament Conference, also stands on the border-line between the two periods and is significant of Italian policy on the eve of the re-emergence of Germany as a military Power. When in March 1933 the British Prime Minister brought the " MacDonald Plan " to Geneva, he continued his journey to Rome, accompanied by Simon, to discuss the disarmament problem with Mussolini. Mussolini himself had never believed in disarmament, and preferred to talk of other things. Immediately on their arrival in Italy, the guests were presented with the draft of a proposed Four-Power Pact to be concluded between Italy, Great Britain, France and Germany.

The principal aim of Italian policy during the past decade had been to assert Italy's equality with France, the other Latin Great Power. In particular, Italy resented France's colonial superiority and the strength in Europe which France drew from her alliances with Poland and the Little Entente. Her colonial ambitions must await a more convenient season. But in the meanwhile she sought to counteract French influence in Central Europe by supporting Hungary against the Little Entente, and in the Balkans by supporting Bulgaria against Yugoslavia. Her patronage of two states whose whole foreign policy was directed to the revision of the peace treaties made Italy a champion of " revisionism ". This gave her a common platform with the greatest of the revisionist Powers, Germany; and since 1929 Italian relations with Germany had been increasingly close. The aims of Italy in the spring of 1933 were therefore to restore Germany as rapidly as possible to a position of equality with the other Great Powers ; to weaken France's satellites, Poland and the Little Entente ; and to promote a revision of the peace treaties.

These aims were apparent in the draft agreement communicated to the British ministers. Under the terms of this draft, the four Powers declared their intention of co-ordinating their European policy in such a manner as to secure its adoption " in case of necessity by other Powers as well ". They thus clearly arrogated to themselves the hegemony of Europe ; and France's allies were relegated to a secondary role. Secondly, the four Powers declared that one of the points of their common policy would be to consider a revision of the peace treaties. This was a further blow to the Little Entente and Poland. Thirdly, the four Powers agreed that, if the Disarmament Conference failed to find a solution of the problem, they would recognise Germany's right to rearm by stages. Lastly, they undertook to co-ordinate their policy in all "extra-European questions", as well as "in the colonial sphere". Since two of the four Powers had colonial ambitions, this suggested an intention to study the means by which these ambitions might be satisfied.

Except for the colonial clause, there was nothing in this draft directly affecting any British interest. But the British ministers perceived that much of it would be highly distasteful to the French Government to which (as well as to the German Government) it had been simultaneously communicated; and they wisely refrained from committing themselves. The opposition in France was, in fact, considerable, and was intensified by the indignant protests of Poland and the Little Entente. The French Government decided, however, instead of rejecting the proposal outright, to work for the elimination of its obnoxious features; and this was achieved by a series of diplomatic negotiations lasting for more than two months. In the revised text, the four Powers undertook to co-operate with all Powers "within the framework of the League of Nations". They reaffirmed Articles 10 and 16 of the Covenant, which protected the existing order, as well as Article 19, which spoke in guarded terms of revision. Any questions particularly concerning them which might be left outstanding by the Disarmament Conference they would discuss together. The reference to colonial questions disappeared altogether. The revised text could hurt nobody. It was so harmless that, at the last moment, Germany almost refused to accept it.

But in the end it was safely initialled in Rome by representatives of the four Powers on June 7th, 1933.

The Little Entente had declared itself satisfied with the innocence of the final text. But an unpleasant feeling remained in Little Entente circles that Italy had attacked their vital interests and that France had been unduly lukewarm in their defence. Polish *amour-propre* was more gravely wounded. Poland, the greatest of the lesser Powers, bitterly resented the success of Italy, the least of the Great Powers, in excluding her from the select company of the leaders of European policy. Her anger vented itself on France, who had sacrificed Polish dignity to the vanity of Mussolini. The Four-Power Pact, though it never came into force (both France and Germany failed to ratify it), did therefore achieve one of its objects by sowing resentment between France and her allies and loosening the bonds between them. In so doing, it paved the way for that new alignment of Powers which was to result from the new direction of German policy.

PART IV

THE RE-EMERGENCE OF GERMANY:
THE END OF THE TREATIES

(1933–1939)

On January 30th, 1933, Hitler became German Chancellor in a government composed of three Nazis
and eight Nationalists ; and the Reichstag was dissolved for a fresh general election. At the election
of the previous July, the Nazi party, with 230 seats,
had become the largest single party in the Reichstag.
It now hoped to secure an absolute majority. On
February 27th, while the election was pending, the
Reichstag building was burned down in mysterious
circumstances ; and this act was made the pretext for
a general round-up of alleged communists and communist sympathisers, conducted partly by the police,
but mainly by irregular forces wearing the brown Nazi
uniform. The election increased the number of Nazi
deputies by 92 ; and from this point all pretence of
respect for legality and constitutional form vanished.
Jews, Social-Democrats and Communists were, in
effect, outlawed. Large numbers of them were driven
from their homes, confined in concentration camps or
subjected to great physical brutality. Many assassina-
tions took place without any attempt being made to
bring the perpetrators to justice. Similar treatment
was meted out to members of other parties who resisted
or criticised the new dictatorship ; and by the middle
of 1933 all non-Nazi parties and party organisations had

been forcibly dissolved. The Reichstag had henceforth no function but to meet at rare intervals for the
purpose of applauding the Chancellor's declarations
of policy. When Hindenburg died in August 1934,
Hitler was elected by an overwhelming vote to the
Presidency, combining this office with the Chancellorship.

In the sphere of foreign policy, the first pronouncements of the new régime were reassuringly pacific.
Hitler emphatically disclaimed any desire to revise the
treaty settlement by force. But it was not forgotten
that his spiritual autobiography, *Mein Kampf*, which
had been written in 1924, and which now circulated in
millions of copies, denounced France as Germany's
irreconcilable foe, claimed to incorporate in Germany
all the scattered German minorities living beyond her
present borders, and treated Eastern Europe as a suitable field for German colonisation. Moreover, the
secret rearmament of Germany, which had been going
on for some years, now proceeded at an accelerated
pace, and less care was taken to conceal it, an air
force being openly established in defiance of the
treaty prohibition. In one respect only Hitler showed
consistent self-restraint. Conscious of the fundamental error of German policy which had made Great
Britain the enemy of Germany, he firmly opposed any
repetition of the attempt to compete with British naval
power.

The Nazi revolution made a deep impression
throughout the civilised world. The impression was
of two kinds. In some countries, the predominant
feeling was one of moral indignation at the cruelties and

excesses of the dictatorship ; in others, a not less profound anxiety at this open challenge to the peace settlement of 1919. The second kind of reaction seemed
more effective than the first. In Great Britain and the
United States, where the prevailing emotion was one of
indignation, not of fear, there was no marked change
of policy towards Germany. In Italy and the Soviet
Union, whose governments had themselves risen to
power by violence, there was less room for moral
censure. But these countries, moved by keen apprehension of the international consequences of
Hitler's assumption of power, executed an abrupt
reversal of policy. The present chapter will deal with
the striking changes brought about by the Nazi revolution in the political orientation of several of the more
important European Powers.

POLAND AND THE SOVIET UNION

The first of these changes was a surprising reconciliation. Nowhere in Europe since 1919 had animosity
been more bitter than between Germany and Poland.
The Polish corridor to the sea, separating East Prussia
from the rest of Germany, had supplied Germans with
their most dramatic grievance against the Versailles
Treaty. No minority had been more persistent in
appeals to the League of Nations against the injustice of
its treatment than the German minority in Poland. No
question had been more frequently on the agenda of the
Council than disputes between Poland and Danzig. On
the morrow of the Nazi revolution, one of the most
serious of these disputes occurred when 200 Polish

soldiers were landed without authorisation at a point in the port of Danzig. Yet within a few months of this incident the first step towards a *rapprochement* had been taken; and in January 1934, on the eve of the first anniversary of Hitler's Chancellorship, a German-Polish pact was signed which completely transformed Polish foreign policy and the diplomatic configuration of Eastern Europe. Among the most conspicuous consequences of the pact were the cessation of the campaign of mutual vituperation conducted by the German and Polish press for the past fifteen years, and the disappearance from the agenda of the League of complaints of the German minority in Poland and disputes about Danzig.

The motives which led on both sides to the signature of this pact require some explanation. Hitler had shocked and antagonised Western Europe; and in view of his persecution of the communists he could not, like his predecessors at Rapallo (see p. 75), call in the Soviet Union to redress the balance. He was in danger of complete isolation. Moreover, he had come to the conclusion—a conclusion which may have been influenced by his own Austrian origin—that Germany's first advance should be southwards. Everything pointed to a truce with his eastern neighbour. He purchased Polish friendship by an undertaking to refrain from any action against Poland, whether by propaganda or otherwise, for a period of ten years.

The motives of Poland were equally cogent. For fifteen years she had lived uncomfortably between two hostile Powers. Her one ally, France, was far away. France had already shown, in the Locarno Treaty, an inclination to subordinate Polish interests to her own security ; and she had recently wounded Poland to the quick by signing the Four-Power Pact (see p. 193). The revival of Germany as a Great Power made French help in time of trouble more uncertain than ever. Poland could no longer afford to incur the enmity of both her big neighbours. She must choose between them ; and she chose the one which she judged to be the stronger and more reliable. It was true that the German-Polish pact only promised her a ten years' respite. But situations which can be stabilised for ten years have a way of lasting. It was worth making the experiment.

A more detailed account must be given of reactions in the Soviet Union. By 1927 official relations had been established by the Soviet Government with all the principal Powers except the United States, and in that year Soviet delegates appeared for the first time at Geneva (see p. 103). The same year saw the triumph of Stalin's policy of " socialism in a single state " (see p. 77). The adoption of the first Five-Year Plan, which came into operation on October 1st, 1928, meant the initiation of a vast process of industrialisation in which the practical interests of the state must take precedence over the theoretical prin-ciples of revolution. The re-establishment of official relations between the Soviet Union and Great Britain in 1929 was a further step towards normal conditions. It only remained for the Soviet authorities to come to terms with the United States and with the League of Nations.

No further progress was made for three years. But

in the autumn of 1932, the Soviet Union concluded non-aggression pacts with Italy and France ; and in the first quarter of the following year two events occurred which gave an entirely new turn to Soviet policy. Hitler came to power in Germany, and Japan, condemned by the Assembly, left the League. These events produced their appropriate reactions in Moscow. The summer of 1933 witnessed a rapid *rapprochement*, based on common fear of Germany, between the Soviet Union and France ; and a series of pronouncements against treaty revision appeared in the Soviet press. Simultaneously, the two Powers which had most to fear from Japan—the Soviet Union and the United States —drew closer together. In November 1933, Litvinov visited Washington, and gave suitable pledges on behalf of the Soviet Government to refrain from propaganda in the United States, and to accord religious freedom to American residents in the Soviet Union ; and the American Government officially recognised the Soviet Government. Soviet diplomacy had thus secured two potential allies—on the one side against Germany and on the other against Japan.

One further retractation of its ancient prejudices was required of the Soviet Government ; its entry into the League of Nations. France insisted on this step. A Franco-Soviet alliance would have savoured too much of pre-war diplomacy, and might have been disagreeable to Great Britain. Common interest in defence against German aggression must be expressed by common membership of the League. In July 1934 France induced Great Britain and Italy to join with her in canvassing the other members of the League for the admission of the Soviet Union ; and at the Assembly in September, the admission duly took place, only three states—Switzerland, Holland and Portugal—voting against it. Poland took two precautions. She obtained a private undertaking from the Soviet Government that the latter would not promote or support any petitions to the League by the Russian minority in Poland, and she publicly declared at the Assembly that she no longer recognised the right of the League to concern itself with Polish minority questions—a virtual denunciation of the minorities treaty.

The security afforded by membership of the League was inadequate to allay Soviet apprehensions of Hitler ; and the Soviet Government continued to press for a direct agreement with France. France was unwilling to reject the request. She ascertained that Great Britain would not object to a guarantee pact between France and the Soviet Union, provided Germany were invited to join it, and the guarantee made applicable, on the Locarno precedent, in both directions. The French and Soviet Governments accordingly prepared the draft of an Eastern Pact, under which France and the Soviet Union would not only guarantee each other against aggression by Germany, but would each guarantee Germany against aggression by the other. The plan seemed somewhat artificial ; for it was difficult to imagine any circumstances in which Germany would obtain the help of France against the Soviet Union or of the Soviet Union against France. The draft was, however, approved by the British Government in February 1935 and submitted, with other proposals which will be mentioned later, to the

German Government. Germany raised objections which were tantamount to a refusal. This was the result which the French and Soviet Governments had expected and perhaps desired. They took advantage of it to sign, in May 1935, a Franco-Soviet Pact under which each undertook to come to the assistance of the other if attacked by any European Power. The result of the Nazi revolution had been to reconstitute the pre-war Franco-Russian Alliance.

AUSTRIA AND ITALY

Hitler's decision to make Austria the first object of his foreign policy proved in many respects unfortunate. Never from 1919 to 1933 had there been any doubt that the vast majority of the Austrian people desired union with Germany ; and no article of the treaties could be more legitimately criticised than the veto on this union. But the Nazi revolution had alienated large sections of Austrian opinion. Neither the Social-Democrats, who were the largest party in the Austrian Parliament, nor the Jews, who were numerous and influential in Vienna, wished to share the fate of their comrades in Nazi Germany; and the Catholic Church, which played a considerable role in Austrian politics, had been antagonised by its treatment at the hands of the German Nazis. Besides these particular causes of mistrust, the traditionally easy-going Austrian looked askance at the brutal and ruthless efficiency of the new régime in Germany. It is probable that, at any time since Hitler's accession to power, a free vote in Austria would still have given a majority for union with Germany. But the majority would have been by no means as overwhelming and incontestable as prior to January 1933.

The first Austrian reaction to the Nazi revolution was, however, one of imitation. In March 1933, Dollfuss, the Austrian Chancellor, overruled Social-Democrat opposition in the Chamber by suspending the constitution. Henceforth, the Austrian Government relied largely on the support of a private military organisation, the Heimwehr, which had come into being some years earlier as a make-weight to the armed forces of the Social-Democrats. The German Government then entered the field. Broadcasts attacking the Austrian Government became a constant feature of the Munich programme. German aeroplanes dropped Nazi propaganda leaflets on Austrian territory. Money and arms were smuggled across the frontier to Austrian Nazis. A prohibitive visa fee was imposed on intending German visitors to Austria. In June 1933, the Austrian Government replied by suppressing the Austrian Nazi party.

Notwithstanding the resistance of the Heimwehr and of certain sections of the population, Austria might soon have yielded to German pressure but for the intervention of the Great Powers. The general indignation against the excesses of the Nazi régime was now at its height, and was intensified by the German campaign against Austria. British opinion became scarcely less insistent than French opinion on the importance of maintaining Austrian independence. Diplomatic representations were made at Berlin without much effect. In August, Austria obtained a further international loan guaranteed by Great Britain, France, Italy and several smaller Powers.

From this point onwards, Italy became Austria's principal patron. For some years past Italy had been a discontented and "revisionist" power (see p. 191); and recently she had ranged herself on the German side on nearly all important issues. Now, under the stimulus of the Nazi revolution, the foreign policy of Italy changed as dramatically as that of the Soviet Union. Italy might want treaty revision in Africa or in Eastern Europe. But if Germany were allowed to acquire Austria, she might be a dangerous neighbour for a Power which had annexed the German-Austrian province of South Tyrol. During the winter of 1933–34 the Italian Government began to pay secret subsidies to the Heimwehr, which it regarded as the bulwark of Austrian independence. As the price of these subsidies, Mussolini demanded the overthrow of the Austrian Social-Democrats, who still controlled the municipality of Vienna, and the establishment in Austria of a régime on Fascist lines. This demand was complied with in February 1934. There was no serious resistance. Several hundred leading Social-Democrats were imprisoned, and all socialist institutions suppressed. Austrian policy, both domestic and foreign, passed under the control of Italy.

The result of these proceedings was to deprive Austria of much of the sympathy she had hitherto enjoyed in Great Britain, though the British Government continued to declare its interest in Austrian independence. The Nazis were spurred to fresh effort. On July 25th, 1934, a band of Austrian Nazis occupied the Federal Chancery and fatally wounded Dollfuss as he tried to escape. The rebels failed, however, to win over the troops or the bulk of the population ; and by the end of the day the government was once more in control of Vienna. Elsewhere there were only sporadic outbreaks. It was generally felt that the rebellion could not have been organised without German support ; and many regarded Hitler as morally responsible for the death of Dollfuss. Italian reinforcements were hurried to the frontier. There was much speculation whether they would have marched into Austria if the insurrection had succeeded.

The events of July 1934 proved to be another turning-point in Austrian affairs. Hitler became seriously impressed with the discredit which his Austrian policy had brought on him, and was perhaps afraid of Italian military reprisals if it were pursued. Germany changed her tactics. No further encouragement was given to Austrian Nazis to commit acts of violence ; and German attacks on the Austrian Government were virtually suspended. Hitler more than once disclaimed any intention of threatening the independence of Austria or interfering in her domestic affairs. This policy was maintained for two years. In July 1936, when Italy's Abyssinian venture had weakened her hold on Central Europe, Austria concluded a pact of reconciliation with Germany ; and shortly afterwards the Heimwehr, which Italy could no longer afford to subsidise, was disbanded. The result of these events was to establish a sort of German-Italian *condominium* over Austria. But as this was accompanied by an improvement of relations between Germany and Italy, no

occasion arose for some time to test which was the predominant partner.

FRANCE, ITALY AND THE LITTLE ENTENTE

The alienation of Italy from Germany in the winter
of 1933–34, and the establishment of an Italian quasi-
protectorate over Austria, had important repercussions
in Central and Southern Europe.

The first of these was a rapid improvement in relations between France and Italy. Franco-Italian rivalry
had flared up soon after the war as the result of French
support of Yugoslav claims. Since then, it had spread
to many other spheres. In Africa, France had failed to
satisfy Italy's claim under the London Treaty of 1915
(see p. 70), and there was constant friction over the
status of Italians in the French dependency of Tunis.
In naval matters, Italy was mortified by France's refusal
to concede her claim to parity (see p. 181). In general
European questions, Italy consistently supported the
grievances of the ex-enemy Powers and maintained her
hostility to France's ally, Yugoslavia. Relations continued to deteriorate down to 1933. But Hitler's designs on Austria were a menace to which France and
Italy were equally sensible. Common interest in
Austrian independence drew them quickly together;
and in September 1934, the possibility was canvassed
of an official visit by Barthou, the French Foreign
Minister, to Rome for the purpose of settling outstanding difficulties.

But the solution was less simple than it appeared.
Both parties had their clients in Central Europe.

Czechoslovakia, Yugoslavia and Roumania were France's allies. Italy had long supported Hungary; and in March 1934 a series of agreements of a semi-political, semi-economic character had been signed at Rome between Italy, Austria and Hungary. Unless, therefore, either France or Italy was prepared to abandon her clients, it was necessary to effect a reconciliation between the rival groups in Central Europe before the Franco-Italian *rapprochement* would be consummated. Italy was in a position to put pressure on Austria and Hungary. It remained to be seen what France could do with the Little Entente.

The Little Entente had resented, though less keenly than Poland, French participation in the Four-Power Pact; and the present French move towards Italy was also regarded with suspicion. But the suspicion was not shared equally by all three members of the Entente. In fact, Hitler's threat to Austria had caused the first serious rift in the partnership. Czechoslovakia would be dangerously encircled if Germany annexed Austria; and she welcomed any steps which Italy and France might take to ward off that event. Yugoslavia had little to fear from the absorption of Austria by Germany. But if Italy were mistress of Austria, Yugoslavia would feel herself encircled by Italy; and she disliked a reconciliation between France and Italy which was evidently designed to strengthen the latter's hold over Austria. Roumania was too far off to be directly affected, and was concerned only to preserve the solidarity of the Little Entente against Hungary. In short, all three members of the Little Entente could do lip-service to the maintenance of

Austria's independence. But once that independence had ceased to be real, and Austria passed under the directing influence of some other Power, Czechoslovakia preferred that that Power should be Italy, and Yugoslavia that it should be Germany.

In October 1934, while the issue hung in the balance, King Alexander of Yugoslavia paid an official visit to France to lay his views before the French Government. He was met at Marseilles by Barthou ; and as they drove away together from the ship, both men were killed by the revolver of a Croat terrorist. It was notorious that both Italy and Hungary had harboured, and even subsidised, disaffected Yugoslavs, who might some day be useful in fomenting a rebellion. It was difficult to establish direct Italian or Hungarian complicity in the Marseilles crime. But Yugoslavia decided to protest to the League of Nations ; and the situation might have been dangerous but for the firm resolve of the two Great Powers concerned—France and Italy— not to allow this tragedy to impede the incipient *rapprochement* between them. A tacit bargain was struck. Yugoslavia was persuaded to direct her charges exclusively against Hungary, and to make no mention of Italy in her protest at Geneva. In return, Italy would induce Hungary, who was helpless without Italian support, to accept such measure of censure as could suffice to appease Yugoslav indignation. The proceedings at Geneva were conducted on this plan ; and after arduous negotiations, the Council was able to declare unanimously that " certain Hungarian authorities may have assumed, at any rate through negligence, certain responsibilities relative to acts having a connexion with the preparation of the crime of Marseilles ", and that it was the duty of the Hungarian Government to punish any of its officials whose guilt might be established.

The assassination of King Alexander on French soil had three main consequences. It increased Yugoslav suspicions of Italy ; it produced a certain coolness between Yugoslavia and France ; and it hastened the reconciliation between France and Italy. In the first days of January 1935 Laval, Barthou's successor, visited Rome, and signed with Mussolini a series of agreements which marked the end of the long Franco-Italian feud. As regards Germany, the two Powers agreed to " concert upon the attitude to be adopted " in the event of Germany pursuing a policy of rearmament. As regards Central Europe, they agreed to recommend to Austria and all her neighbours (other than Switzerland) to enter into a pact undertaking not to intervene in one another's affairs and not to support attempts to destroy the independence, or overthrow the " political or social régime ", of their respective countries. (No attempt was, in fact, ever made to negotiate the proposed pact.) In the meanwhile, they undertook to consult together with Austria, and with such of her neighbours as might be willing, in the event of a threat to Austria's independence. As regards Africa, France ceded to Italy, in settlement of her claim under the London Treaty, a strip of French Equatorial Africa adjacent to the Italian province of Libya, and a small triangle of French Somaliland adjoining Eritrea ; the status of Italians in Tunis was regulated ; and Laval gave Mussolini to understand that France disinterested herself in any concessions which Italy might obtain in Abyssinia. It was afterwards stated from the French side that this understanding, the terms of which were kept secret, related only to economic concessions.

The reconciliation between France and Italy was the last important diplomatic *volte-face* directly inspired by Hitler's advent to power ; and the results of the whole process may now be briefly summarised. Poland had drawn away from France (though the Franco-Polish alliance was not formally denounced), and entered into a close association with Germany. The Soviet Union had abandoned its traditional revisionist attitude, and whole-heartedly embraced the French policy of upholding the Versailles settlement. Italy had also joined the anti-German front, though she continued to use Austria and Hungary as her outposts in Central Europe. In the Little Entente, Czechoslovakia shared the Franco-Italian position, and had drawn nearer to Austria (though not to Hungary, whose revisionist claims had not been dropped) ; Yugoslavia, on the other hand, moving in the opposite direction to Italy, had drawn away from France and was coming rapidly nearer to Germany. In May 1935 this regrouping of the Powers was completed by the conclusion of a pact between Czechoslovakia and the Soviet Union in the same terms as the Franco-Soviet Pact signed a fortnight earlier. This pact emphasised the growing rift in the ranks of the Little Entente ; for Roumania declined an invitation to conclude a similar agreement, and Yugoslavia was one of the few European states which still refused even to recognise the Soviet Government.

THE BALKAN ENTENTE

The year 1934 also witnessed new groupings in the Balkans, though here the Nazi revolution was not a determining factor. Just as Czechoslovakia, Yugoslavia and Roumania had been drawn together after the war by common fear of Hungary, so Yugoslavia, Roumania and Greece were united by common hostility to Bulgaria. Turkey, the fourth beneficiary of the partition of Bulgaria after the Balkan War of 1913, had herself been a defeated Power in 1918 ; and for many years she remained aloof from her former Balkan partners, cultivating close relations only with the Soviet Union. But in 1930 she buried the hatchet with Greece, her most implacable foe. In 1932, she joined the League of Nations. In 1934, Turkey, Yugoslavia, Roumania and Greece signed a pact mutually guaranteeing one another's Balkan frontiers. Bulgaria refused to accede to a pact confirming frontiers against whose injustice she had never ceased to protest. Albania, in whose affairs Italy continued to play a dominant role (see p. 70), was not invited to join.

But the " Balkan Entente " established by this pact proved a fragile structure. For Yugoslavia the principal object of the pact was to secure her against Italian interference in Balkan affairs. Greece, on the other hand, unable to risk a conflict with the Italian navy, accompanied her ratification of the Pact with a declaration that she recognised no obligation to engage in hostilities with a non-Balkan Power ; and this led to a coolness between Greece and Yugoslavia. Meanwhile, relations between Yugoslavia and Bulgaria took a turn for the better. A new Bulgarian Government with Yugoslav sympathies freed itself from the Italian influence which had hitherto been paramount at Sofia and, for the first time since the war, dealt firmly with the Macedonian terrorists who infested the Yugoslav frontier (see p. 12). The situation in the Balkans remained thereafter fluid and undefined. The Balkan Entente survived. But Yugoslavia stood closer to Bulgaria, who was outside it, than to Greece, who was a member of it. A civil war in Greece in March 1935, followed by a restoration of the monarchy, did not disturb the general tranquillity.

In June 1936, at a conference at Montreux, the principal signatories of the Treaty of Lausanne agreed, at Turkey's request, to alter the articles of the treaty providing for the demilitarisation of the Straits (see p. 15). Turkey obtained freedom to fortify the Straits and regulations were laid down for the passage of war-ships through the Straits in time of peace and war.

CHAPTER 11 : THE REPUDIATION OF TREATIES

THE story unfolded in the last chapter shows how promptly the world at large realised that the Nazi revolution meant the return of Germany, after an eclipse of fifteen years, to the ranks of the Great Powers. The short but dramatic period of fifteen months which began in March 1935 was marked by the open violation, on a scale yet unknown in post-war history, of international engagements. Hitherto provisions of the peace treaties had been set aside by mutual agreement, by tacit consent, or by silent evasion. Now Germany was strong enough to adopt the method of formal repudiation, and extended this repudiation not only to the dictated peace of Versailles, but to the freely negotiated Locarno Treaty. Meanwhile, another European Great Power, with an absence of excuse which distinguished this operation even from the Japanese action of 1931, invaded and annexed the territory of another member of the League of Nations. Staggering blows were thus dealt simultaneously from two quarters both at the peace settlement itself and at the Covenant which formed part of it. These fifteen months demonstrated that the statesmen of 1919 had seriously overestimated the possibility of imposing penal restrictions for a prolonged period on a defeated Power, and of constructing a new world order on the basis of common action in defence of the *status quo*.

THE GERMAN REPUDIATION

Before launching his attack on the Versailles Treaty, Hitler had to wait for the settlement of one outstanding question. Fifteen years after the coming into force of the treaty the fate of the Saar was to be decided by a plebiscite (see p. 6) ; and the fifteen years elapsed in January 1935. The plebiscite was duly held, an international force under British command being stationed in the area to maintain order and guarantee a free vote. The inhabitants were invited to choose between return to Germany, union with France and the continuance of the League administration. Of the 500,000 votes cast, 90 per cent were for Germany and just under 9 per cent for League administration. The return of the territory to Germany took place on March 1st. Germany had now, as Hitler more than once declared, no further territorial ambitions in the West. Germany had also nothing further to hope for from the Versailles Treaty.

At the beginning of February, British and French ministers met in London and issued a statement of policy for the information of the German Government and the other governments concerned. They expressed the hope that the German Government would co-operate in the proposed Eastern and Central European Pacts (see pp. 203 and 211) ; and they suggested that the Locarno Treaty should be supplemented by an Air Pact, under which the Locarno Powers would agree to give the assistance of their air forces to any one of their number which was attacked by another from the air. The principal novelty of this suggestion was that Great Britain would not appear, as in the Locarno Treaty, only as guarantor, but would be guaranteed by France and Belgium against air attack by Germany, and by Germany against France and Belgium.

The German Government welcomed the Air Pact, promised non-committally to examine the other proposals, and suggested a meeting with the British Government to discuss the whole matter. Somewhat to the alarm of the French Government, the British Government fell in with this suggestion; and Simon, the Foreign Secretary, and Eden, the Minister for League of Nations affairs, accepted an invitation to visit Berlin. But before the visit could take place, much happened. The British Government had occasion to issue a memorandum explaining to Parliament the reasons for their rearmament programme; and in this memorandum stress was laid, to the complete exclusion of other factors, on the threat of German armaments. Great indignation was expressed in Germany at this attack. Hitler, on the plea of a minor indisposition, cancelled the date fixed for the British ministers' visit. The French Chamber was at the same time debating an increase in the French army. Hitler decided on a dramatic counter-stroke. On March 16th, 1935 he announced that Germany no longer considered herself bound by the military clauses of the Versailles Treaty, that the peace strength of her army would be fixed in future at thirty-six divisions or 550,000 men, and that it would be raised by conscription.

This announcement caused considerable consternation in France. In Great Britain, public opinion had long discounted German rearmament as the inevitable result of the failure of the Disarmament Conference. Hitler now renewed his invitation to Simon and Eden ; and the British Government saw no reason to refuse it. The anxiety caused by this decision in French, Italian and Soviet circles was barely allayed by the fact that Eden was also to visit Warsaw, Moscow and Prague. The visit to Berlin duly took place on March 25th. But its practical results were small. Hitler reiterated his welcome of the Air Pact and his dislike of the Eastern and, in a lesser degree, of the Central European Pacts. He reaffirmed his pacific intentions. The size of the German army was irrevocably fixed. But Germany would consent, on land, to any limitation of material accepted by the other Powers. In the air, she claimed parity with France, though the rapid growth of the Soviet air force might oblige her to reconsider this. On the sea, she would be content with 35 per cent of British naval strength in all categories of ships.

In the meanwhile, France had demanded a special session of the League Council in April to consider Germany's action ; and by way of preparation for this session, British, French and Italian statesmen met in conference at Stresa. The Stresa Conference reaffirmed its approval of the proposed Eastern and Central European Pacts. It had an inconclusive discussion on the question whether the lesser ex-enemy states should now be given formal permission to rearm, Italy (prompted by Austria and Hungary) being in favour of this step, and France (inspired by the Little

Entente) against it. But the principal business of the conference was to draft a resolution for submission to the League Council condemning Germany's repudiation of her obligations under the Versailles Treaty. The resolution was duly presented to the Council by the three Powers and carried unanimously, only Denmark recording, by her abstention from the vote, her opinion that Germany was entitled to share the blame for what had happened with her accusers. The resolution was an empty gesture, since no action followed or was intended to follow. But it provoked great anger in Germany. In particular, Germany was puzzled that Great Britain, having appeared to condone the German action by sending the Foreign Secretary to Berlin, should now have taken the lead at Geneva in proposing an unqualified vote of censure.

But a still greater surprise was in store. Scarcely had the League Council dispersed when an intimation was sent to Berlin that the British Government was prepared to accept Hitler's offer to limit German naval strength in all categories of ships to 35 per cent of British strength, and would welcome an agreement on this basis. German delegates duly came to London, and in June an Anglo-German naval agreement was signed. Thus the British Government, having condemned in strong terms Germany's repudiation of the disarmament provisions of Versailles, now explicitly recognised her right to ignore (up to 35 per cent of British strength) the naval restrictions imposed by the treaty and to possess categories of ships, including submarines, altogether prohibited by it. The agreement in itself seemed a tribute to British common sense.

For while France, by refusing every compromise, had provoked unlimited German rearmament on land, Great Britain, by her readiness to come to terms, had secured an important limitation of German naval strength. But the agreement seemed so inconsistent with what had gone before that it caused in France, Italy and the Soviet Union a bewilderment even greater than that provoked in Germany by British sponsorship of the Geneva resolution.

The vacillations of British policy towards Germany in the first half of 1935 were indeed so conspicuous as to call for comment. The explanation seems to have been that two conflicting policies were at work. During the first two years after the Nazi revolution, British opinion as a whole was too deeply moved by Nazi excesses to feel much sympathy for German grievances and aspirations ; and the British Government, though unwilling itself to undertake any commitments, had encouraged the French, the Italian and the Soviet Governments in their efforts to build up a system of defensive alliances for the maintenance of the *status quo*, particularly in Central Europe where it seemed most directly menaced. But by January 1935, when this system of alliances had been virtually completed by the Franco-Italian reconciliation, indignation in Great Britain against the Nazi régime began to subside. A growing body of opinion came round to the view that the only effect of the French understandings with Italy and the Soviet Union was to isolate and encircle Germany and to perpetuate the inequalities of the Versailles Treaty—in short, to maintain those very conditions which had been largely responsible for the Nazi revolution. Those who held this opinion, while not denying that Germany might be a danger to peace, believed that French, Italian and Soviet policy merely aggravated that danger, and that the British Government's first aim should be to break the ring round Germany, to engage in friendly discussion of her grievances, and to bring her back to the League of Nations. Simon's visit to Berlin was a concession to this trend of thought. But the other opinion, *i.e.* that the right way for Great Britain to meet the German danger was to give all possible support to other Powers which felt themselves threatened, was still strongly held in many quarters ; and this opinion prevailed in the attitude of the British Delegations at Stresa and Geneva. Then the policy of coming to terms with Germany again came uppermost with the conclusion of the Anglo-German naval agreement. The resulting uncertainty not only made France and her associates gravely suspicious of British intentions, but encouraged Germany to hope for a reversal of British policy which did not materialise.

THE ITALIAN REPUDIATION

The final settlement of Italy's claims under the London Treaty left her with still unsatisfied colonial ambitions. Nothing more was to be expected from Great Britain or France. But Mussolini had for some time contemplated the possibility of Italy fending for herself. He had hitherto always reckoned on the jealousy and opposition of France. Indeed his policy of encouraging and assisting Germany may have been partly inspired by the desire that France should have too many anxieties in Europe to be an obstacle to Italian designs elsewhere.   But events turned out otherwise. By the beginning of 1935, France stood so much in need of Italian friendship in Europe that she was prepared to make almost any concession in Africa.   Mussolini was quick to seize the opportunity and, at the Rome meeting, secured Laval's acquiescence in a forward Italian policy (the scope of which was perhaps not precisely defined at this stage) in Abyssinia.

The choice of Abyssinia was dictated by several considerations.   Abyssinia was the only independent native state left in Africa, except Liberia.   It lay between the existing Italian colonies of Somaliland and Eritrea ; and it was reputed to possess mineral wealth in the hitherto undeveloped interior.   Moreover, a recent incident, which may or may not have been due to deliberate Italian provocation, gave a pretext for Italian action in that quarter.   In December 1934, a clash occurred between Abyssinian forces and a detachment of troops from Italian Somaliland near the village of Walwal.   A few Italians were killed in the skirmish ; and the Italian Government demanded an apology and a substantial indemnity from Abyssinia.   Abyssinia appealed to the League of Nations, and requested that the dispute should be placed on the agenda of the Council under Article 11 of the Covenant.

Apart from the Covenant and the Pact of Paris, two other treaties stood in the way of warlike action by Italy.   In 1906 Great Britain, France and Italy had concluded an agreement in which they declared it to be in their common interest to " maintain intact the integrity of Abyssinia " ; and in 1928 Italy concluded a treaty with Abyssinia in which the two parties promised each other " constant peace and perpetual friendship ", at the same time mutually undertaking to submit all disputes to a " procedure of conciliation and arbitration ". Italy had also been one of the principal supporters of the admission of Abyssinia to membership of the League in 1923. When, therefore, the Abyssinian appeal came before the Council in January 1935, the Italian Delegate deprecated discussion of the Walwal incident under Article 11 of the Covenant, since he " did not regard it as likely to affect the peaceful relations between the two countries ", and professed willingness to settle the dispute by conciliation and arbitration under the 1928 Treaty. On this understanding, the Council adjourned the question.

For the next three months the Italian Government delayed the appointment of arbitrators ; and large reinforcements of men and material from Italy to the troops in Eritrea and Italian Somaliland showed that serious military operations were in contemplation. On March 16th, the Abyssinian Government invoked Article 15 of the Covenant. Three weeks later, British, French and Italian ministers met at Stresa (see p. 218). In spite, however, of the gravity of the African situation, no allusion was made to it by any of the delegates. The " final declaration " of the Conference recorded their opposition to " any unilateral repudiation of treaties which may endanger the peace of Europe " ; and the addition of the last two words was, so far at any rate as Mussolini was concerned, hardly accidental. The British delegates, preoccupied with Europe, were doubtless unwilling to sound a discordant note by mentioning the unwelcome Abyssinian problem. But their silence in face of undisguised Italian preparations for war was interpreted by Mussolini to mean that Great Britain, like France, was content to regard his African venture with a benevolent, or at least an indifferent, eye.

At the session which followed the Stresa Conference, the Council of the League was once more deterred from examining the Abyssinian appeal by a further assurance from the Italian Government of its readiness to proceed to arbitration on the Walwal incident. This time the arbitrators were, in fact, appointed; and at length, on September 3rd, the arbitrators reached a unanimous conclusion. It was to the effect that neither government could be held responsible for the incident at Walwal. The incident was, in fact, of no intrinsic importance. It had served its purpose by providing the pretext for an extensive concentration of Italian troops, and it could now be dismissed.

In the meanwhile, attempts had been made elsewhere to discuss the real issue, *i.e.* Italy's military threat to Abyssinia. In June 1935 Eden visited Rome, and made a proposal that Great Britain should cede to Abyssinia the port of Zeila in British Somaliland, and that Abyssinia should in exchange cede her southern province of Ogaden to Italy. Mussolini rejected this offer on the double ground that the proposed cession to Italy was totally inadequate, and that Abyssinia would be strengthened by obtaining access to the sea. In August, delegates of Great Britain, France and Italy, in their capacity as parties to the 1906 agreement, met in Paris. The result of the meeting was a Franco-

British proposal that Abyssinia should be invited to apply to the League for collaboration in promoting the " economic development and administrative reorganisation of the country ", and that, in according such collaboration, the League should take " particular account " of the " special interests of Italy ". This, too, was rejected by the Italian Government. When, therefore, on September 4th—the day after the Walwal arbitrators issued their report—the Council of the League at last began to examine the Abyssinian appeal of March 16th, things had gone too far for any proceedings at Geneva to affect the issue. The new British Foreign Secretary, Sir Samuel Hoare, made at the Assembly an unexpectedly emphatic declaration of the British Government's intention to carry out its obligations under the Covenant. A Council committee drew up proposals, which were endorsed by the Council, for a " scheme of assistance " for Abyssinia and " territorial readjustments " between Abyssinia and Italy. On October 2nd the Italian invasion of Abyssinia began.

The Foreign Secretary's Assembly speech, and the enthusiastic reception given to it by the smaller states at Geneva and by public opinion in Great Britain, made it plain that Mussolini had been wrong in anticipating that the League would remain quiescent. The prompt action of the Council, once hostilities had begun, contrasted with its previous evasion of the real issue and with its reluctance to pass an adverse verdict on Japan in the Manchurian case. On October 7th a committee of the Council drafted a report pronouncing that Italy had " resorted to war in disregard of its covenants under Article 12 of the Covenant "; and next day this report was adopted by the members of the Council, Italy alone dissenting from it. Two days later, the Assembly, having reminded members of the League of their obligations under Article 16, recommended them to set up a committee for the purpose of co-ordinating the measures to be taken by them. By October 19th the co-ordinating committee had invited all members of the League (1) to prohibit all loans or credits from their respective countries to Italy, (2) to place an embargo on exports to Italy of war material of every kind and of certain commodities especially necessary for war purposes, and (3) to place an embargo on all imports from Italy. These measures were approved by all European members of the League except Austria, Hungary and Albania and, with insignificant exceptions, by members of the League outside Europe. France was in the unhappy position of having to employ sanctions against the new ally whom she had gained less than a year ago. But she had so long protested her loyalty to the League and her desire to make Article 16 a reality that she could not now resist. On November 18th, 1935, for the first time in the history of the League, sanctions—though only of an economic character, and these far from complete—came into operation.

The first three months of the war went less well than had been expected for Italy. Italian forces penetrated far into Abyssinia and, supported by bombing aeroplanes, broke Abyssinian resistance wherever it was encountered. But the main Abyssinian armies remained intact; and military experts doubted whether the two Italian forces advancing from Eritrea and

Italian Somaliland respectively could reach the one railway in Abyssinia (the line from Addis Ababa to the coast), and effect a junction there, before the rainy season came on in June.

In December France became apprehensive that an Italian failure in Abyssinia might react on the situation in Central Europe. The British Government seems to have shared this fear and, furthermore, to have been afraid lest Mussolini, in a moment of desperation, should launch an attack on Great Britain as the principal author of sanctions. Hoare visited Laval in Paris ; and terms of peace were worked out between them for submission to the Italian and Abyssinian Governments. The negotiators were principally concerned to make the terms sufficiently attractive to Mussolini to induce him to abandon the campaign. It was proposed to cede to Italy considerably more Abyssinian territory than had yet been invaded by Italian troops, the pill being gilded for Abyssinia by the offer of a corridor to the sea through British Somaliland. The disclosure of these proposals caused a storm of indignation in Great Britain. Public opinion believed that the plan had been designed to help Italy to extract herself with credit from a hazardous position ; and it was felt to be no part of the duty of Great Britain, as a member of the League, to help an aggressor reap the fruits of his aggression. Hoare resigned, and was succeeded by Eden ; and no more was heard of " the Hoare-Laval Plan ".

It was not until March 1936 that the Italian advance in Abyssinia became perceptibly more rapid. Before the end of April the Eritrean army was within striking distance of the railway and the capital. Internal order broke down ; and on May 1st the Emperor of Abyssinia left the country. His flight meant the end of organised resistance. Addis Ababa was occupied a few days later by Italian troops. On May 9th, the King of Italy was proclaimed Emperor, and the whole country officially annexed to Italy.

The Italian victory was a grave blow to the League and an acute embarrassment for Great Britain. Although economic sanctions had paralysed Italy's trade and caused a drain on her gold reserve, they had not sufficed to hamper her military operations. It was clear that nothing short of war would compel her to release her prize ; and Great Britain was not less firm than France in her resolve not to be drawn into war with Italy. At a special meeting of the League Assembly in July, the British Government proposed the withdrawal of sanctions. In spite of a personal appeal by the Emperor, this was unanimously agreed to ; and a resolution was passed inviting members of the League to submit to the next Assembly their views on the best means of " improving the application of the principles of the Covenant ".

THE END OF LOCARNO

The apparently pusillanimous attitude of the other Great Powers towards Italy was partly explained by another German repudiation which coincided with the later stages of the Abyssinian war. The Franco-Soviet Pact of May 1935 (see p. 204) had from the first been regarded by Germany as a military alliance directed exclusively against her and therefore incompatible with the Locarno Treaty—a view not shared by the French and British Governments. Germany protested against it with increased vehemence ; and when, early in 1936, it was presented to the French Chamber for ratification, Hitler once more decided on a bold counter-stroke.

Under the Versailles Treaty, Germany was prohibited from maintaining armed forces or constructing fortifications in the Rhineland ; and under the Locarno Treaty, the signatories " collectively and severally guaranteed " the observance of these provisions. In March 1935, Hitler had repudiated the dictated Versailles Treaty, but had reaffirmed his loyalty to the freely negotiated Treaty of Locarno. On March 7th, 1936, the German Government informed the British, French and Belgian Governments that the Franco-Soviet Pact, involving as it did obligations incompatible with those undertaken by France under the Locarno Treaty, had deprived that treaty of its " inner meaning ". Germany, therefore, no longer considered herself bound by it, and was, on that very day, re-occupying the Rhineland with German troops. The memorandum conveying this information also contained a number of proposals. Germany offered to agree to the establishment of a new demilitarised zone extending for an equal distance on both sides of the frontier (since France and Belgium were known to be unwilling to demilitarise any part of their territory, this was a debating-point rather than a proposal) ; to negotiate a new pact on the same lines as the Locarno Treaty, but omitting the clauses relating to the Rhineland ; to conclude non-aggression pacts with her eastern neighbours (and, as Hitler subsequently added, with Austria and Czechoslovakia) ; and to return to the League of Nations.

In France, although alarm was expressed, no serious proposals were made for sanctions or reprisals. In Great Britain public opinion was shocked by this repudiation of a freely negotiated treaty, but was, on the whole, more interested in considering Hitler's proposals for the future than in condemning his past action. Negotiations between the British, French and Belgian Governments took place in March. The Council of the League, specially summoned in London, pronounced that Germany had violated the Versailles Treaty " by causing . . . military forces to enter and establish themselves in the demilitarised zone ". In order to allay French and Belgian anxieties, the British Government consented to conversations between the General Staffs on the steps to be taken in the event of a German attack on France and Belgium. Germany and France drew up " peace plans ". But both these documents were so vague and so comprehensive that they were of little practical use. Early in May, after consultation with the French Government, the British Government addressed a questionnaire to the German Government in the hope of further elucidating its proposals. The tone of this communication seems to have displeased Hitler, who left it unanswered. Throughout the summer the political world was preoccupied with the Abyssinian _débâcle_ to the exclusion of the Locarno negotiations ; and when, in September, an attempt was made to reopen these negotiations, the difficulties seemed insuperable. Germany, while ready to conclude a fresh guarantee pact for the west, would enter into no agreement with the Soviet Union. A Western Pact, unaccompanied by some kind of Eastern Pact, was unacceptable to France.

Meanwhile, there was a fresh complication. Belgium, like most of the smaller Powers, was deeply impressed by the failure of collective security and the growth of Germany's power. She felt that her commitments to France under the Franco-Belgian alliance (see p. 30) and under the Locarno Treaty might be more of a danger than a safeguard, particularly if France were involved in a war with Germany as a result of the Franco-Soviet Pact. On October 14th, 1936, a declaration was issued stating that Belgium would in future pursue an exclusively Belgian policy, would enter no alliances and would, like Switzerland and Holland, adopt an attitude of complete neutrality in the disputes of her neighbours. The renewal of Locarno in the old form was therefore precluded. Belgium was ready to receive, but would no longer give, guarantees. In November, Eden publicly stated that " Belgium could count on our help were she ever the victim of unprovoked aggression ", and a few days later he gave a similar assurance to France. The French Minister for Foreign Affairs replied by stating in the French Chamber that France would, in the same circumstances, come to the assistance of either Great Britain or Belgium. These declarations could be regarded as taking the place of the now unrealisable Western Pact.

CHAPTER 12 : THE NON-EUROPEAN WORLD

By the end of 1936 it was clear that the general settlement imposed after the first world war had no longer any accepted basis ; and we shall have to consider how the repudiation of treaties was followed by startling action to upset the order which the treaties were designed to establish. But since this book, like almost every other book on the subject, devotes what may seem a disproportionate amount of attention to European affairs, the present chapter may help to redress the balance, before we come back to what is still the focal centre ; for in international politics more than in any other sphere the leadership remained for good or evil in European hands. Some of the countries now to be discussed have not yet received more than a passing mention in these pages. Others have already been dealt with at greater length ; and in the case of these, it will only be necessary to bring the story up to date.

THE MIDDLE EAST

The complex of countries stretching from the Eastern Mediterranean to the north-west frontier of India, and conveniently known as " the Middle East ", became after 1919 the scene of constant effervescence and some striking changes. Of these countries, Turkey deliberately discarded the religion and tradition of Islam and, by separating herself from the

THE MIDDLE EAST

Moslem world, realised her ambition of becoming a Near Eastern and European instead of a Middle Eastern and Asiatic Power. Iran, fortunate in possessing one of the richest oil deposits in the eastern

233

hemisphere, prospered under the rule of her masterful Shah, Riza Khan, who usurped the throne in 1925. Afghanistan, devoid of natural wealth and sandwiched in between Soviet Central Asia and British India, enjoyed a somewhat precarious independence, which was, however, strengthened by her admission to the League of Nations in 1934.

The other Middle Eastern countries were the former Arab provinces of the Turkish Empire, whose fate has already been described (see p. 17). In all these countries Arab nationalism was the principal problem of the years between the wars. The division of the principal Arab territories between British and French mandates was a keen disappointment to those Arab leaders who had looked forward to the establishment of a united Arab kingdom. The British Government did something to mitigate this disappointment. One of the sons of King Hussein of the Hedjaz became King of Iraq, and another Emir of Transjordania. But the problem was complicated by the wide divergence in tradition and development between different sections of the Arabs who ranged from civilised town-dwellers to primitive nomads. Arab political unity was still a dream of the future. But Arab nationalism, deliberately fostered by the Allies during the war for the discomfiture of the Turk, on many occasions after the war brought the Arab peoples into conflict both with the Mandatory Powers and with non-Arab minorities living in their midst.

The status of the first British mandated territory, Iraq, was from the outset anomalous. No formal mandate was ever granted, its place being taken by a treaty between Great Britain and Iraq, which was approved by the League, and under which Great Britain promised to afford Iraq " such advice and assistance as may be required . . . without prejudice to her national sovereignty ". The importance of Iraq to Great Britain resided partly in her rich oil-wells and partly in her favourable position on the direct air-route between Europe and India. A considerable section of British opinion was, however, opposed to an indefinite prolongation of British rule over an almost land-locked territory in Asia ; and Iraq was encouraged to look forward to the time when she would be, in the words of the Covenant, " able to stand alone ". This result was achieved in 1932. The mandate was terminated, and Iraq, having concluded a treaty of alliance with Great Britain for twenty-five years, became a member of the League of Nations. The most difficult problem raised by Iraq's independence was that of her non-Arab minorities, of whom the Kurds and Assyrians were the most important. Unhappily, within a year of Iraq's admission to the League, disturbances occurred among the Assyrians, which resulted in the massacre of five hundred of them by Iraqi troops. The continued stability of this new recruit to the family of independent states—the first Arab member of the League—appeared to depend in large measure on the retention of the experienced British advisers who continued to assist the Iraqi Government in many branches of the administration.

The second British mandated territory in Asia was divided, geographically and administratively, by the River Jordan, Palestine lying to the west of that river and Transjordania to the east. Transjordania was a purely Arab state; and its international history was limited to occasional frontier disputes with its neighbours. Palestine, on the other hand, presented a graver problem than that raised by any other mandate.

The terms of the Palestine mandate (which were the fulfilment of a promise made by the British Government to the Jews in 1917) laid on the Mandatory Power the obligation to "place the country under such political, administrative and economic conditions as will secure the establishment of the Jewish national home, while at the same time safeguarding the civil and religious rights of all the inhabitants of Palestine ". This obligation might have been difficult to carry out even if the Allied Governments had not during the war encouraged Arab aspirations for national independence. But the contradiction between the promise given to the Jews and the vaguer undertaking given to the Arabs (which was, rightly or wrongly, assumed to include Palestine) laid up serious trouble for the future. In 1919 the population of Palestine was almost entirely Arab, and was estimated at something under 700,000. The establishment of the mandate made Palestine the official centre of world Jewry, and opened the country to Jewish immigration. The influx of Jews, comparatively modest during the first years, increased rapidly when the economic crisis broke over Europe, and still more when the exodus of Jews from Germany began after the Nazi revolution. By the end of 1934 the number of Jews in Palestine had reached 300,000, and would have been greater if immigration had not been rigorously limited by the authorities. The Jewish immigrants brought Western civilisation to a backward Oriental land. The cultivation of citrus-fruit became a flourishing large-scale industry organised on modern lines ; and Palestine bade fair to become the commercial centre of the Middle East. The creation of the Jewish city of Tel-Aviv and the development of the port of Haifa were among the wonders of the modern world. Palestine was the one country whose trade, both domestic and foreign, increased by leaps and bounds during the whole course of the economic crisis.

In this wave of prosperity the non-Jewish population also shared. Between 1919 and 1934 its numbers rose to 900,000, so that the Jews were still outnumbered by three to one. But the Arab cultivator, untrained, improvident and devoid of capital, was no match for the Jew, and found himself reduced, in his own country, to a position of galling inferiority. Leaving aside minor incidents, grave disturbances of the peace, costing several hundred lives, occurred in 1921, in 1929, and in 1936, the Arabs in each case attacking first the Jews, and then the British police and troops engaged in maintaining order. The most serious fact about these disturbances was that they were directed, not against incidental hardships inflicted on Arab interests by Jewish immigration, but against the whole principle of the Jewish national home in Palestine.

At the end of 1936 a Royal Commission was set up to investigate the causes for the Arab outbreak and to make recommendations. Their Report, issued in July 1937, proposed a tripartite division of the country, under which the Holy Places were to remain permanently under British control, while Galilee and the coastal plains were to form a Jewish sovereign state, the remainder being joined to Transjordania in an Arab state. The scheme was attacked from all quarters, and found no favour with the Mandates Commission of the League, to which it was submitted. Meanwhile outrages continued; not only Jews and British but Arabs were murdered, if they were thought to be in favour of compromise. A further Commission was appointed to enquire into the practicability of the scheme; but this in the course of 1938 reported so decisively against partition that the project was abandoned, and a Conference was summoned to meet in London. Representative Jews and Arabs were invited to state their case separately to the British Government; later, if it seemed possible, a settlement should be worked out in a joint assembly. But no agreement was reached, and the British Government decided to impose its own solution, which laid the foundations of a compromise by providing Jewish immigration should be limited to 10,000 annually for five years. Meanwhile more vigorous military control was successful in restoring order; and the Moslem world in general was to some extent conciliated. To them, Palestine was essentially part of the Arab fatherland. Yet many in the western world, and specially in the Protestant English-speaking nations, familiar with Old Testament and New Testament history, but little informed on the course of events in Asia Minor since the days of Pontius Pilate, were equally sure that Palestine naturally belonged to the Jews. Further, the fierce and increasing persecution of that race seemed to make some place of refuge for them an international necessity.

The French mandated territory was divided by the mandate itself into two : Syria and the Lebanon. In the Lebanon, a coastal strip on the confines of Syria and Palestine, a group of Arab Christians formed the majority of the population ; and this territory enjoyed a republican form of government which, supported by periodical interventions of the Mandatory Power, continued to function. The Lebanese Christians, estranged by their religion from the Arab national movement, seemed content, in spite of minor grievances, with the security assured to them by French protection.

In Syria, on the other hand, Arab nationalism proved as potent a force as in Iraq and Palestine. In Iraq, Great Britain created a unified state at the expense of the minorities. In Syria, France pursued the opposite policy, and excluded from Syria proper three areas inhabited mainly by non-Arabs. Two of these— Latakia on the coast, and the Jebel Druse territory in the south—were placed under direct French administration. The third—the Turkish district of Alexandretta in the north—became an autonomous province under the nominal suzerainty of the Syrian Government; and in June 1939, as a part of its general Mediterranean policy, France signed an agreement by which the greater part of this district, the Sandjak of Alexandretta, was ceded to Turkey, on condition that the Turks should abandon all other claims on Syria and cease from propaganda in the country. This policy of dismemberment was strongly resented by the

Syrian Arabs. Serious rebellions occurred from time to time, notably in 1925, when Damascus was bombarded by French troops ; and from 1933 the Syrian constitution was completely suspended. During 1936 fresh negotiations took place between the French Government and the Syrian leaders, and resulted in November in the signature of a treaty on the model of the Anglo-Iraqi Treaty. Ratification of this was to be followed by Syria's application with French support for admission to the League of Nations. But ratification was delayed so long that in the beginning of 1939 nationalist disturbances broke out at Damascus, and the High Commissioner decreed the dissolution of the Syrian parliament and placed the executive power in the hands of a Council of five Directors—military defence being controlled from France.

In Arabia, the most striking event of the period was the rise of Ibn Saud, formerly the Sultan of Nejd. During the first world war, Ibn Saud assisted the Allies against Turkey, and was subsidised by them. He was not recognised in the peace settlement. But in this region of nomadic populations and undefined frontiers, he extended his domain by a process of gradual encroachment and vigorous administration ; and in 1926, having defeated and expelled King Hussein of the Hedjaz, he annexed the territory and proclaimed himself King of the Hedjaz and Nejd, the title of the whole country being subsequently changed to Saudi Arabia. Ibn Saud clearly established his claim to be regarded as the most powerful independent Arab ruler. Saudi Arabia did not apply for admission to the League of Nations. But during 1936 she consolidated her international situation by concluding treaties with Iraq, with Transjordania and with Egypt. These demonstrations of Arab solidarity appear to have been inspired in part by fear of Italian ambitions following Italy's success in Abyssinia ; and the same circumstance increased the cordiality of relations between Great Britain and the Arab states.

Egypt, though not usually included in the term " Middle East ", requires mention in this brief survey of Arab-speaking countries. The construction of the Suez Canal made Egypt a vital point in British Imperial communications ; and for thirty years before the war Egypt, though nominally under Turkish suzerainty, was in British occupation. When Turkey entered the war in December 1914, Turkish suzerainty was abrogated and a British protectorate proclaimed. After the war the rising tide of nationalism made it difficult to maintain the protectorate ; and in 1922, after a vain effort to reach an agreement with the Egyptian nationalist leaders, Great Britain issued a declaration recognising the independence of Egypt, but reserving to herself the defence of the country, the protection of foreigners and of the minorities, and joint sovereignty with Egypt over the Sudan. This declaration was followed by a communication to foreign Powers intimating that interference in the affairs of Egypt by any foreign Power would be regarded by Great Britain as a menace to her own security.

The anomalous situation resulting from the declaration was full of embarrassments for both sides. On more than one occasion attempts were made to regularise the position by a treaty. But not until 1936, when the Italian success in Abyssinia inspired both Great Britain and Egypt with a strong desire to improve their mutual relations, were these attempts successful. Under the treaty signed in August 1936, Great Britain undertook, under certain conditions, to withdraw British troops from the interior of the country, maintaining them only in the Canal zone ; to help Egypt to secure the abolition of the Capitulations, *i.e.* the extra-territorial rights enjoyed by nationals of the principal foreign Powers in the country ; to support Egypt's claim to membership of the League ; and to give Egyptian officials a share in the administration of the Sudan.

These promises were fulfilled when, at a Convention held at Montreux on May 8th, 1937, the interested Powers renounced their rights under the Capitulations ; and on May 26th Egypt was admitted as a sovereign state to the League of Nations. In 1938 an agreement with Great Britain was negotiated concerning the accommodation of British troops which under previous agreements were stationed to protect the Suez Canal ; and Egypt, while upholding her independent position, remained fully loyal to her obligations to Great Britain.

THE FAR EAST

Japan's withdrawal from the League in March 1933 created in the Far East a situation of growing tension. Japan soon consolidated her conquest of Manchuria and asserted her position as the dominant power in East Asia. The first important declaration of her policy was contained in a statement issued to the press by the Japanese Foreign Office in April 1934. This state-

ment, after referring to Japan's " special responsibilities in East Asia ", declared explicitly that " there is no
country but China which is in a position to share with
Japan the responsibility for the maintenance of peace
in East Asia ", and that Japan " objected " to any
operations undertaken singly or jointly by foreign
Powers to assist China. The objection applied to
operations undertaken " in the name of technical or
financial assistance " (such as had recently been
accorded to China by the League of Nations) as well as
to military assistance in the form of the supply of war
material or the loan of instructors or advisers. This
declaration, which came to be known as " Japan's
Monroe Doctrine ", was repeated on several subsequent occasions. In the summer of 1935 an
attempt to separate from the rest of China several of her
northern provinces broke down in face of the passive
resistance of the Chinese. But in the strip of Chinese
territory adjacent to Manchuria, the local Japanese
military authorities succeeded in setting up a puppet
administration under the name of the East Hopei
Autonomous Government ; further they subsequently,
by deliberate interference with the operations of the
Chinese customs authorities, encouraged an extensive
smuggling traffic through this important area—a clever
manœuvre designed to put illicit profits into the pockets
of Japanese traders and to sap the resources and the
prestige of the Chinese administration. During 1936
sporadic murders of Japanese in several parts of China
bore testimony to the bitter feelings which had been
aroused.

In China itself, fear of Japan acted as a unifying

force, though its effects were slower and more partial than might have been hoped. In Central China
numerous local Soviets continued, long after Borodin's
departure, to be a thorn in the side of the Nanking
Government, and extensive areas remained under the
control of a so-called Chinese Soviet Government.
After 1933 most of these areas were reabsorbed by the
Nanking Government. Organised Chinese communist
forces still existed in North-West China; but in
accordance with the policy laid down at the 1935 congress of the Communist International, these forces now
sought, not to overthrow the Nanking Government, but
to stiffen and support its resistance to Japan in North
China. In South China, a military rebellion against
the Nanking Government in the summer of 1936 met
with no support, and ended in the suppression of the
semi-independent Canton Government. Co-operation
between Nanking and Canton appeared to be closer
than at any time in recent years. Thus, at the end of
1936, the Chinese Government at Nanking, ably led by
General Chiang Kai-shek, was slowly strengthening
its hold in Central and South China, and tenaciously
maintaining its influence in North China against
Japan. In December there was a short-lived rebellion on the north-western frontier; and Chiang
Kai-shek himself was held prisoner for several days by
mutinous troops. The submission of his captors, however, strengthened his position, and China appeared
on the way to be united, and united in resistance to
Japanese aggression.

But in July 1937 a clash between Japanese and
Chinese troops not far from Peking led to further

incidents; and, without declaration of war, war began. Peking was evacuated and the Chinese, still resisting, were gradually driven back to the line of the Yellow River, while naval and air forces attacked Shanghai. By the end of the year the Japanese had captured not only this city but the capital, Nanking. Aerial bombardment inflicted great slaughter on defenceless multitudes, and, incidentally, whether by accident or mistaken zeal, wounded the British Ambassador to China and damaged an American and a British vessel on the Upper Yangtse. But the course of events in Europe forced Great Britain to limit resentment to diplomatic protest, while the United States accepted an apology. Meanwhile the League of Nations, before which the facts were laid by Chinese representatives, formally condemned Japan's action as an unjustifiable breach of treaty obligations, and members of the League were invited to consider how far they could individually help the victim of aggression.

China's spirit of resistance remained unbroken, though the Japanese armies, superior both in equipment and discipline, everywhere succeeded in forcing their way. First Hankow with its satellite cities, which had become the temporary capital, fell in July 1938, and in October Canton was taken with unexpected ease. Gradually Japan mastered all the ports and left the Chinese armies dependent for supplies on what they could obtain overland from the Soviet Union, or import by rail from French Indo-China, or, by a newly created motor road, from British sources in Burma. Towards the end of 1939 the Japanese cut the rail to Indo-China; the motor road was overburdened; and

Soviet aid could no longer be counted on. But China continued to resist.

On the Soviet side, Japan's conquest of Manchukuo had caused serious apprehension and provoked various counter-measures. These were of several kinds. In the first place, the Soviet Government sought and obtained the official recognition of the United States Government (see p. 202). Secondly, it sought to lessen the occasions of friction by selling to Japan (or, nominally, to Manchukuo) the Russian interest in the Chinese Eastern Railway which crosses Manchuria. Thirdly, it extended Soviet influence in Central Asia. The westernmost province of China, Sinkiang or Chinese Turkestan, inhabited by a mixed population of many races, had for long been virtually independent of the Nanking Government, and had been the scene of periodical civil wars between rival authorities. In 1933 Soviet troops and aeroplanes intervened in one of these local struggles, and enabled the local Chinese Governor recognised by the Nanking Government to restore order and re-establish his authority. For some time, Soviet influence, political and economic, became paramount in Sinkiang. In March 1936 Outer Mongolia which, though nominally under Chinese sovereignty, had been in effect a Soviet republic since 1921, concluded with the Soviet Union a treaty of alliance under which each party promised to come to the other's assistance in the event of foreign aggression ; and about the same time Stalin pointedly informed an American journalist that any Japanese interference in Outer Mongolia would mean war with the Soviet Union. Thus the Soviet Union possessed in Sinkiang and in

Outer Mongolia outposts similar to that established by Japan in Manchukuo, though Soviet control of the local administrations was less direct than that of Japan in Manchukuo.

AMERICA AND WORLD POLITICS

In many countries the economic crisis of 1930–33 produced more disastrous results than in the United States. But nowhere did it cause a more direct and radical change in the prevalent conception of the functions of the state. Before the crisis, the United States had maintained almost undiluted, except for the single item of tariff protection, the principles of *laissez-faire* and unrestricted individual enterprise. State interference in industry and commerce was still widely regarded as something undesirable, un-American and even immoral. The crisis showed up in glaring colours the fallacy of this view. When the whole structure of industry and finance tottered, and one-tenth of the population were unemployed, both capital and labour looked to the state for salvation ; and the history of President Roosevelt's administration was one long effort to rebuild American economic life on a new basis. When recovery began, the forces of reaction tried to reassert themselves against what had come to be known as the " New Deal ". The American Constitution gave Congress power " to regulate Commerce with foreign Nations and among the several States ". It was only by a somewhat strained interpretation that this could be made to cover such matters as price-control and the fixing of labour conditions. Some of the administration's more radical measures for the control of industry and agriculture and the protection of labour were ruled by the Supreme Court to be unconstitutional, and had to be withdrawn. But the overwhelming majority by which President Roosevelt was re-elected in November 1936 showed how whole-heartedly the mass of the American people had accepted the new principle of state regulation.

This peaceful domestic revolution engrossed the main energies of the American Government during the years after 1933, and foreign affairs took second place. The first effect of Japan's Manchurian venture had been to stimulate American co-operation with the League (see p. 165). In the summer of 1932 both Republican and Democratic parties declared themselves in favour of consultation between the American Government and other governments in the event of a breach, or threatened breach, of the Pact of Paris; and in May 1933 the American delegate at the Disarmament Conference stated that, if a disarmament convention were concluded, the American Government would agree, in future emergencies, to consult with other governments and not to obstruct any action which might be decided on by them. But when the Conference broke down, and the situation in Europe and in the Pacific grew darker and more menacing, American opinion moved rapidly in the direction of isolation. In December 1935 a naval conference met in London to consider the situation which would arise when the London naval treaty (see p. 182) lapsed at the end of the year. At the end of 1934, Japan had given the prescribed two years' notice to terminate the Washington Five-Power Treaty of 1921 ; and it proved impossible to secure Japan's continued acceptance of the Washington ratio, or of any other ratio which limited her fleet at a lower level than the British and American fleets. The only result of the London conference was an agreement between Great Britain, the United States and France to give one another advance information regarding ships of war constructed or acquired by them, and to limit the maximum tonnage of different categories of war vessel. In other respects, all parties regained their liberty at the end of 1936.

Since the beginning of 1935 the principal aim of the American Government in international affairs had been to avoid any possibility of becoming involved in war. In that year, in pursuance of the policy of reducing its commitments, it decided to withdraw from the Philippines, the only American base in the western Pacific, and to grant full independence to the islands after a probationary period of ten years. Equally significant was the passage in the summer of 1935 of a Neutrality Act which authorised the President, in the event of an outbreak of war, to place an embargo on the export of war material and key products to both belligerents. This authority was exercised by the President in the Italo-Abyssinian War ; and an amendment to the Act in February 1936 made such an embargo not merely optional, but obligatory, in future wars. It added an embargo on loans to belligerents and, significantly, exempted the American republics from the operation of the Act.

This attempt on the part of the United States to isolate themselves from the political troubles of Europe and the Far East was accompanied by an equally marked desire to draw nearer to the other American countries. There had been for many years a traditional mistrust of the United States among the countries of Central and South America. The Monroe Doctrine was widely interpreted as implying that the United States had the right and duty to intervene in Central and South America where necessary in order to maintain order and protect foreign lives and property. Thus the treaty between Cuba and the United States of 1903 explicitly gave the latter the right of intervention for these purposes. United States marines had been stationed in Nicaragua, with one short interval, ever since 1912, and in Haiti since 1915; and there had been less permanent interventions in other countries. Periodical Pan-American congresses, of which the first met in 1889, did not remove the ill-will produced by what was freely described as the policy of the " Big Stick " and of " Dollar Imperialism ".

About 1930, partly as a result of the economic crisis, American opinion began to set away from a policy of intervention in Central and South America. At the beginning of 1933, the United States marines were withdrawn from Nicaragua ; and when, in his inaugural address in March of that year, President Roosevelt " dedicated this Nation to the policy of the Good Neighbour ", the words were thought to herald a definite reversal of the traditional attitude. In the same year, the Argentine Republic promoted a fresh pact providing for the renunciation of aggressive war and the non-recognition of situations created by the use of force. This was welcomed by the United States and signed by many American, as well as by some European, states. The Seventh Pan-American Congress at Montevideo at the end of 1933 was the occasion of a conciliatory utterance by the United States Secretary of State. The next year saw the final withdrawal from Haiti and the abrogation of the 1903 treaty with Cuba. In December 1936, immediately after his re-election, President Roosevelt paid Latin America the signal compliment of attending in person the opening meeting of the Eighth Pan-American Congress at Buenos Aires; and the Congress adopted a treaty providing that, in the event of a threat to the peace of any of the American republics, the signatories would " consult among themselves for the adoption of measures of peaceful co-operation ". In spite of the two wars which disfigured South America during the nineteen-thirties (see p. 174), international relations within the American continents became more sincerely friendly than at any previous time.

In the meanwhile, the double tendency to draw the American republics into closer accord and to prevent their involvement in the wars of other nations continued under the leadership of the United States, where legislation designed to preserve neutrality had been further developed. The provisions of the Act of 1935 and its later amendments were adopted only for two years; and in 1937 a fresh Neutrality Act was passed. It renewed the embargo on export of arms and on loans. It forbade American merchantmen to be armed, and American citizens to travel on the vessels of any belligerent—since injury to them might involve the United States. It gave the

President discretion to prohibit the export of goods in American vessels to belligerent States, leaving it to be conducted, on the " cash and carry " principle, by nationals of such States as could transport the materials after paying for them. He was also authorised to permit the transport of goods to " lands bordering on the United States "—in other words, to Canada—since no cause of conflict could arise from interruption *en route*.

Determination to avoid political commitments in Europe did not, however, involve complete isolation. American opinion gave almost unanimous assent to a policy of economic collaboration with Europe as with other continents. Secretary Cordell Hull took full advantage of the Reciprocal Trade Agreement Act, first passed in 1934, renewed for a further three years in 1937, to negotiate with twenty-two countries, covering the larger part of America's foreign trade, trade agreements on the most-favoured-nation basis involving reciprocal reduction of tariffs and limitation of other restrictions upon trade. He believed that economic nationalism had been a major factor in the development of the political crisis which led ultimately to war, and that the restoration of multi-lateral trade, on the freest possible basis compatible with reasonable tariff protection, would do more to prevent a recurrence of dictatorship, aggression and wars, than mere political and territorial rearrangements.

In the Far East, moreover, the United States showed signs of a reaction against the 1934-37 policy of reduced commitments. The President deliberately refrained from recognising that the Japanese operations in China constituted a state of war, since such recognition would have brought into operation the provisions of the Neutrality Act and cut off American aid to China. Marked preference was displayed for the Chinese in their struggle, and loans were made available to them through the Import-Export Bank. The United States Government resolutely refused to surrender any of its traditional rights in China, and maintained fully its naval and military forces in Chinese treaty ports and waters. In July 1939 it issued notice of denunciation of the Japanese-American commercial treaty, which therefore was finally terminated in January 1940. Commercial relations between the United States and Japan continued on a day-to-day basis and the threat of an embargo or of discriminatory duties on Japanese imports, strongly urged by powerful groups in Congress and in the country, remained as a deterrent to further Japanese encroachment upon American rights. There was also a growing movement in the Philippine Islands and in the United States against the complete independence legally due to take effect in 1946. The period during which preferential advantages for Philippine trade will continue was extended, and amendment of the Act calling for political and military withdrawal was frequently mooted.

THE BRITISH COMMONWEALTH OF NATIONS

Relations between Great Britain and the self-governing Dominions are not international relations in the full sense of the term, and fall outside the scope of this book. But since the Dominions are members of the League of Nations (as is also India) and have independent foreign policies, some mention must be made here of their position.

The first appearance of Canada, Australia, New Zealand, South Africa and India as members of the international community was in 1919, when they signed the Versailles Treaty in their own right. The fact that they did not figure in their proper alphabetical place among the other signatories, but were grouped together under the rubric of the "British Empire", showed that they were not regarded as independent sovereign states ; and Article 1 of the Covenant, which throws the League open to " any fully self-governing State, Dominion or Colony " was evidently designed to take account of their special status. When the Irish Free State applied for membership in 1923, its application was approved by the Assembly on the ground that " the Irish Free State is a Dominion forming part of the British Empire upon the same conditions as the other Dominions which are already members of the League ". No further attempt was made to elucidate the status of the Dominions till 1926. In that year the Imperial Conference defined Great Britain and the self-governing Dominions as " autonomous communities within the British Empire, equal in status . . . though united by a common allegiance to the Crown, and freely associated as members of the British Commonwealth of Nations "; and in 1931 the Statute of Westminster, in which this status was given a legal and constitutional basis, was voted by the British Parliament and accepted by the Dominions.

The international situation resulting from this definition was not free from ambiguities. The British Government (whose official title, after 1926, was " His Majesty's Government in the United Kingdom of Great Britain and Northern Ireland ") always maintained that neither the Covenant itself nor any international agreement concluded between members of the League of Nations was applicable to the relations of members of the British Commonwealth with one another. This view was, however, consistently attacked by Irish politicians ; and the other Dominions for the most part avoided any pronouncement on the question of principle. The divergence was clearly marked when, in 1929, all the members of the British Commonwealth signed the Optional Clause of the Statute of the Permanent Court (see p. 112). Great Britain, followed by Australia and New Zealand, made a reservation excluding from its acceptance disputes between members of the British Commonwealth. Canada and South Africa made the same reservation, but accompanied it with statements implying that they did not subscribe to the view that such disputes were *ipso facto* outside the competence of the Court. The Irish delegate made no reservation of such disputes at all. Another aspect of the same problem was the question (happily destined to remain academic) whether, in the event of a member of the British Commonwealth resorting to war in violation of the Covenant, the other members of the Commonwealth would be bound by the obligations of Article 16.

While these theoretical difficulties existed, there were few important divergencies of opinion on fundamental issues. The fears of those foreigners who thought that the constitution of the League gave the British Government six votes had, indeed, not been justified ; for on points of detail—the only points which were decided at Geneva by a majority vote—the members of the British Commonwealth were rarely all to be found on the same side. In financial and economic matters, the Dominions and India fully asserted their national interests even against those of Great Britain. In the political sphere India was precluded from independent action ; and differences between other members of the British Commonwealth proved to be differences of emphasis rather than of substance. Canada, secure herself and influenced by the proximity of the United States, displayed a strong desire to restrict to a minimum the obligation to defend the security of other members of the League. Australia and New Zealand seemed too remote to take a sustained interest in international affairs. But they from time to time were apprehensive of Japan, and they were always sensitive to any criticism of their policy of excluding coloured immigrants. South Africa exhibited perhaps a keener interest in the problems of security, and was one of the few countries which expressed disapproval of the withdrawal of sanctions against Italy in July 1936 (see p. 228). The Irish seemed more concerned to establish the principle of their independence than to pursue an international policy of their own. Three Dominions—Australia, New Zealand and South Africa —administered mandated territories (see p. 18) on which they reported annually to the League. After 1927 a non-permanent seat on the Council was always held by one of the Dominions.

The outbreak of war in 1939 finally showed that the Dominions did not feel themselves bound automatically to follow the lead of Great Britain and that each of them acted in its own right, in obedience to a sense of its own prestige and interest.

CHAPTER 13: RELAPSE INTO WAR

It has been seen that by the end of 1936 the states which were discontented with the settlement of 1919 had asserted their freedom from obligations under it; they were now asserting claims to satisfaction, with war implied as the alternative. Under this menace, the British Government finally abandoned their attempt to produce disarmament by example. In March 1937 Neville Chamberlain, as Chancellor of the Exchequer, announced that expenditure on defence would no longer be financed solely by taxation. He proposed a loan of four hundred millions for the purpose, and projected a total outlay of one thousand five hundred millions in a space of five years. Baldwin, the Prime Minister, defended these proposals by saying that their purpose was to deter aggression, and that the country, after some years of limited expenditure, could now finance defence without affecting the standard of living or the social services. Both he and Eden, the Foreign Secretary, declined to admit that Great Britain had abandoned the League of Nations. But while Baldwin expressed a hope that its action might be supplemented by " regional pacts ", offering a guarantee from certain Powers for certain spheres, Eden had to allow that little progress was made in this direction; and he defended

British armament as the best guarantee of peace.

At the moment, the threat of war was indefinite; Germany's energies were fully occupied in constructing defences opposite the French Maginot Line. This " Siegfried Line ", when completed, would enable her to hold the western front with a united force and concentrate her effort to the East. But Europe at large, and more specially France and Great Britain, felt uncertain what might come out of a new theatre of war.

THE SPANISH CIVIL WAR

By far the most important event of the latter half of 1936 occurred in a country which had, for many years past, played an inconsiderable rôle in international affairs. The dictatorship set up in Spain in 1923 (see p. 71) was overthrown in 1930. In the next year, King Alfonso XIII abdicated, and a democratic republic was established. But the democratic tradition has never been strong in Spain ; and from 1931 to 1936 democracy maintained itself by a somewhat precarious balance between royalists and other reactionaries on the Right, and anarchists and communists on the Left. State finances were chaotic, and public order was frequently threatened. In July 1936, General Franco, the commander of the troops in Spanish Morocco, proclaimed a military rebellion, and crossed into Spain with an army composed largely of Moorish troops. He overran without much opposition the extreme south and gradually conquered the whole of western Spain. In the middle of November the insurgents were in the suburbs of Madrid, the government withdrew to Valencia, and the fall of the capital seemed imminent. From that point, the resistance of the government forces stiffened ; and at the end of the year, the three possible issues—a victory of the Left, a victory of the Right, or a stalemate between them—seemed almost equally likely.

The Spanish Civil War might not, in other circumstances, have been an international event. The causes which made it one were of two kinds. In the first place Italy, fresh from her Abyssinian victory, which had thrown into relief the strategic importance of the Mediterranean, welcomed an opportunity to strengthen her position in western Mediterranean waters. Secondly, the notion had grown up since the first world war that a country whose internal organisation was based on a certain political theory was expected to encourage and assist the triumph of that theory in other countries. This policy was pursued by the Soviet Union prior to 1927, and was adopted later by other countries. In 1933–34 Germany supplied the Austrian Nazis with money and arms ; and Italy, more successfully, insisted on the establishment of a Fascist régime in Austria (see p. 206). In 1936 Italy and Germany treated the Spanish Civil War, on somewhat unconvincing grounds, as a struggle between Communism and Fascism, and thought it appropriate that they should support the insurgents. In nearly all such cases, it seems difficult to distinguish between the supposed interests of a political theory and the national interests of the intervening country.

There can be little doubt that Italy, at any rate, was

privy to General Franco's rebellion ; for the help of Italian aeroplanes was forthcoming at the very outset to transport his troops from Morocco. Within a few weeks, the Spanish Civil War threatened to divide all Europe into two camps, Italy, Germany and Portugal openly sympathising with the insurgents, and the Soviet Union with the government. On August 15th the British Government, anxious at all costs to remain neutral, placed an embargo on the shipment of war material from Great Britain to Spain, and France followed the British example. These two countries then invited all European countries to enter into an agreement not to supply war material to either side, and to form a non-intervention committee in London to supervise the working of the agreement. After some delay, mainly due to Portugal's reluctance, the agreement was concluded. For a few weeks it seems to have checked the supply of arms to Spain. But soon the Spanish and Soviet Governments began to denounce violations of the agreement by Italy, Germany and Portugal ; and these charges were answered by accusations, which soon became equally well-founded, against the Soviet Government. From October onwards, Italy and Germany were more or less openly sending arms to the insurgents, and the Soviet Union to the government ; and in November, when the fall of Madrid seemed imminent, Italy and Germany officially recognised the government set up by General Franco. Considerable numbers of Italian and German troops were fighting in the insurgent ranks, and contingents of Russians, anti-Fascist Italians and anti-Nazi Germans, as well as volunteers from other countries, on the side

of the government.   The Spanish Civil War assumed
many of the aspects of a European civil war fought on
Spanish territory.

RIVAL GROUPING OF THE POWERS

The second most striking event of the last months
of 1936 was an agreement between Germany and Japan.
Politically, this agreement was the consequence and
the counterpart of the Franco-Soviet Pact ; and
the only cause for surprise is that it should not have
been reached sooner.   But it was characteristic of the
period that the understanding should take the form, not
of a pact of alliance, but of an agreement for mutual
support in combating Communism.

The end of 1936 saw therefore a considerable part of
the world divided into two groups, one led by Germany,
Italy and Japan, the other by France and the Soviet
Union.   The first group were sometimes called the
Fascist Powers, though the term was of doubtful
application to Japan.   The second group cannot be
so easily labelled.   For though the Soviet Union in
1936 adopted a constitution in which some of the external forms of democracy were observed, it remained
in essence as alien to western democracy as France
to communism.   The current habit of classifying countries by the type of political theory professed by their
government became misleading.   The rival groups were
linked not so much by a common political faith as by
the fact that the first group was, for varying reasons,
dissatisfied with the territorial settlement of the world
made in 1919—a settlement which the second group

desired to maintain. The fundamental division was between those who were in the main satisfied with the existing international distribution of the world's goods and those who were not.

For the moment, the British Government refused to commit itself to either group and maintained an attitude of cautious neutrality, until forced out of it by the disquieting action of other Powers. Early in 1937 anxiety was caused by a rumoured concentration of Germans in Spanish Morocco; the fear was that General Franco might bargain away this territory as the price of help. The French Government recalled publicly the agreement of 1922 by which Spain, after receiving French assistance in the Riff war, debarred itself from alienating this strategically important territory. Germany, however, denied any such ambition; and General Franco declared that he was determined on maintaining the integrity of Spanish territory. As the year advanced, Germany left the main rôle in Spain to Italy; her contribution was chiefly confined to material and technicians, while Italian troops operated as separate and distinctive units, whose achievements were acclaimed in Rome as victories. On the Government's side, the International Brigade was less clearly identified with any country; but the material, much of it probably furnished from Russia, came largely through France.

The general European situation was still profoundly affected by a political crisis in France which had become acute in June 1936, when a government representing the *Front Populaire*—an alliance of Radicals, Socialists and Communists—came into office under

Léon Blum, and rapidly carried into law changes in the relation between workers and employers which were regarded by the wealthier classes as revolutionary. In these circles Blum, a wealthy and cultivated Jew, was denounced as an agent of Moscow. In Spain, victory went to the side favoured by the so-called Fascist Powers, very largely because Germany and Italy, while officially members of the International Committee pledged to see that there should be no intervention, supplied material and reinforcements up to the point which they thought necessary to turn the scale. France might have been in a position to supply a counter-weight. But Blum, whatever his feelings on the Spanish question, thought, like all Frenchmen, that the vital interest of France was to keep step with Great Britain; and the British Government made every effort, if not to keep non-intervention a reality, at least to prevent intervention from bringing about general European war. The tension persisted till the spring of 1939, when, after the Republican stronghold of Catalonia had been reduced, Madrid was finally occupied by General Franco's troops. His government was then formally recognised both by France and Great Britain.

But the world situation did not grow less dangerous. While the Spanish war was in full progress, Japan embarked on her operations in China (see p. 245), which were none the less an aggressive invasion because there was no declaration of war. In November 1937 Italy joined the "Anti-Comintern pact" concluded between Germany and Japan; and as a sequel to this she announced on December 11th her withdrawal from the

League of Nations. Her solidarity with Germany had been emphasised by a ceremonial official visit paid by Mussolini in person to Hitler at Munich. It was returned in 1938, when Hitler was received with great ceremony at Rome; nothing was omitted that could affirm the strength of the Berlin-Rome axis—to which, at least in theory, Japan was attached. Action to gain satisfaction for the unsatisfied Powers grew imminent; already the German elements in Czechoslovakia announced their discontent, and their desire to be included in the Reich. Henlein, leader of the Sudeten Germans, became a European figure, and paid a propaganda visit to Britain.

Meanwhile in the Soviet Union a remarkable purge was in progress. During 1936 the Soviet Government had brought to trial many of the politicians who had been most prominent in Lenin's band of revolutionaries; now, in 1937, a group of the best-known generals were similarly liquidated. It became matter of speculation whether the military value of the Franco-Soviet alliance was not gravely lessened. There was also increasing doubt whether Italy would maintain that interest in the independence of Austria, which she had demonstrated in 1934 by the appearance of her troops on the Brenner (see p. 207).

But on the whole, 1937 was only a year of preparation for undisclosed events; and the threat of war seemed most immediate in the Mediterranean where Italy loudly asserted her dissatisfaction with the existing division of power. She claimed that her new acquisition in Abyssinia entitled her to a share in control of the Suez Canal, which led to it, and also that the preponderating Italian element in the population of Tunis marked this colony as properly belonging to Italy. Violent Italian propaganda was directed against Great Britain, whose massive rearmament was regarded as indicating a new policy of positive resistance both to Germany and to Italy. British military preparation was described on January 16th, 1938, before the Council of the League of Nations at Geneva by Eden, the British Foreign Secretary, as a support for those principles of co-operation to promote international security on which the League was based. But debates in the British Parliament indicated a division of opinion in the British Cabinet, and on February 20th Eden's resignation was made known. He had been repeatedly denounced both by German and Italian organs of publicity as an obstacle to the legitimate claims of these countries, and in explaining his resignation to the House of Commons he made clear his opposition to opening any negotiations with Italy until she had made good her pledges to cease from hostile propaganda and to withdraw her troops from Spain. Neville Chamberlain, who had succeeded Baldwin as Prime Minister, declared his intention to open negotiations with Italy, in concert with Lord Halifax, who replaced Eden ; and on February 22nd he remarked that it would be wrong to encourage small countries in the belief that they would be protected against aggression by the League of Nations. Since Baldwin, a couple of years earlier, had declared the League to be the sheet anchor of British policy, there was plainly a change of front ; and Chamberlain admitted that he had previously believed such protection to be possible, but had altered his opinion. In return for assurances that British plans for the withdrawal of foreign troops from Spain were accepted, Great Britain pledged itself to advocate to the League of Nations the recognition of Italy's conquest of Abyssinia.

GERMANY BEGINS AGGRESSION

Meanwhile a new threat to international security developed. Under an agreement signed at Stresa in 1935, Britain had declared her interest in the independence and integrity of Austria, in concert with France and Italy. This independence was now gravely challenged by the first of Nazi Germany's aggressions on other States.

Early in 1938 Hitler had assumed supreme command of all the armed forces of the Reich, thus asserting his will against such officers as questioned his general line of action ; and Ribbentrop, who had been Ambassador to Great Britain, replaced Neurath as Minister for Foreign Affairs. Then aggressive action began. After turbulent demonstrations organised by the Austrian Nazis, Schuschnigg, the Austrian Chancellor, was summoned to interview Hitler at Berchtesgaden, and accepted some kind of ultimatum under which Nazi representatives were included in his government. This did not, however, save him. On March 12th, German troops marched in and occupied Vienna. A detachment of them immediately presented itself on the Brenner Pass and exchanged salutations with the Italian posts ; Italy's attitude had changed radically since 1934. There was no resistance in Austria and probably inclusion with the Reich was welcome to a majority of the population. But it was evident that aggression might follow in another country where it would be passionately opposed. The effect on Czechoslovakia was that German power now faced her on a greatly extended frontier. Part of this, facing Germany along the Carpathians, was strongly fortified: the rest, opposite Austria, lay open. Her total population was less than fifteen millions: of these nearly three millions and a half were Sudeten Germans, settled in compact groups along the frontier. To the south towards the Danube were close on a million Magyars, demanding reunion with Hungary: on the east Poland claimed the important mining district of Teschen which the Czechs had acquired in 1920 through a compromise imposed by the Allies (see p. 33).

In this condition of things, Germany made preparations to hold manœuvres on a grand scale along the Czech border. The Czech Government called up some of their reserves and meanwhile made anxious attempts to reach a settlement with the Sudetens. But they were not only able to maintain internal order but also ready to resist invasion by force; and France and the Soviet Union were pledged to assist them if they were attacked. Britain was under no direct obligation to act. But on March 24th Chamberlain had said in the House of Commons that, if her ally France became involved in war for this cause, the inexorable pressure of facts might well prove more powerful than formal pronouncements. This utterance was construed as conveying a pledge that Britain would stand by Czechoslovakia if France did the same.

Nevertheless, fears of European war were still mainly connected with the struggle in Spain, where British vessels, while delivering cargo in ports held by the Republican Government, were repeatedly bombed by insurgent aeroplanes, said to be manned by German or Italian aviators; but a scheme for withdrawal of foreign troops from both sides promoted by Great Britain was under discussion. In order to allay the growing signs of trouble in Central Europe, Lord Runciman was despatched to Prague (nominally at the request of the Czech Government) to act as conciliator and adviser. But the Sudeten claims, put forward in consultation with the German Government, grew more and more insistent; and though fresh concessions were offered, on September 12th Hitler, before a great gathering at Nuremberg, advised the Sudetens to insist on their return to the Reich and promised them the support of the German army. Since France and the Soviet Union were pledged to support the Czechs, this threatened war. Chamberlain, on behalf of Great Britain, now took the initiative. On September 14th he proposed to go in person to Germany in pursuit of a peaceful solution, and on the 15th he went by air to Munich and was conducted to a meeting with Hitler at Berchtesgaden. Thence he returned next day to London, again by air, and on September 18th was joined by Daladier, the French Prime Minister, and his Foreign Minister Bonnet. At the same period the League Assembly was in session; and Litvinov publicly repeated the pledge which he had given to the Czech Government and to the French—that if France intervened on behalf of Czechoslovakia, the Soviet

Union would use all its resources to help the Czechs. But there was no consultation as to military co-operation. Throughout this year, as throughout the last, Stalin's purge was still operating, and inspired widespread mistrust of the efficiency of the Soviet military machine.

Chamberlain and Daladier had agreed upon a plan which they should jointly propose to the Czecho-slovak Government. This involved cession of a con-siderable area inhabited by the Sudeten Germans, which Chamberlain described later as a drastic but necessary surgical operation. The Czechoslovak Government an-nounced that, under irresistible pressure from Britain and France, they had been forced to acquiesce; and Chamberlain flew back to Germany for a second interview at Godesberg on the Rhine. On this occasion the Führer formulated demands so startling that Chamberlain refused to do more than transmit a memorandum of them to Prague. It was decided that, if Hitler carried out his threat of an immedi-ate march on Czech territory, France and Britain should support the Czechs in their resistance: the British navy was mobilised and hasty measures against an air raid were taken in London. But Chamber-lain, still contending that the concessions already made had left no differences outstanding which were worth a war, appealed to Mussolini to bring about a new con-ference; and this appeal succeeded. On September 29th a meeting of Hitler, Mussolini, Chamberlain and Daladier settled the terms which were to be imposed upon the Czechs. No representative of the Czechs, nor of the Soviet Union, was present at the discussion; and the Czechoslovak Government, having submitted to the terms, resigned their offices, unable to face an angry people. General Syrovy, who had been a distinguished leader in the Czech Legion, assumed the charge of government. A few days later Benes, who had held the presidency since Masaryk's death, also resigned and left the country. For the moment it appeared that Chamberlain had triumphed. Flying back, he was received with immense enthusiasm and proudly displayed a document, signed by Hitler and himself, which proclaimed the ardent desire of both their countries to avoid all possible sources of difference and to contribute to the peace of Europe. Daladier, though without the addition of a similar document, was equally well received in France.

It was made known later that Hitler had assured Chamberlain that the acquisition of the Sudeten territories was the last of his territorial ambitions in Europe, and that he had no wish to include in the Reich people of other races than the German. He himself, speaking on September 26th, 1938, at the Sport Palast in Berlin, said, " I have assured Mr. Chamberlain, and I emphasise it now, that when this problem is solved Germany has no more territorial problems in Europe. I shall not be interested in the Czech State any more, and I can guarantee it. We don't want any Czechs any more."

The Czechoslovak State had undergone drastic reduction. On the east, Poland demanded, under threat of armed action, the Teschen area with its important coal mines, and the demand was conceded. On the south, Hungary claimed a large tract of territory in which were nearly a million Magyars, and this also was ceded perforce. Slovakia, always an uneasy and discontented partner in a Czechoslovak State, demanded autonomy. It was by comparison a backward region, and the administration had been chiefly conducted by Czech officials ; jealousies resulted, which German agents had industriously fomented. Slovakia became increasingly separated from the Czech regions, which were now gravely disorganised. According to the terms imposed at Munich, an international commission on which Britain, France, Italy and Czechoslovakia should be represented along with Germany, was to decide the line separating the Sudeten districts from Czech territory. But in practice the German army, moving in, occupied what it chose, including several towns where the population was preponderantly Czech. There was no attempt to secure a workable unit of administration for the Czech State ; and meanwhile Poles and Hungarians sought to make good claims by military occupation, which Czech troops resisted. In particular, the backward province of Ruthenia at the extreme eastern projection of the long narrow Czechoslovakian territory was in dispute. Hungary desired it because possession would give her a common frontier with Poland ; but Germany preferred that this wedge, stretching to the Roumanian border, should remain nominally subject to Slovakia, which was increasingly under German control. Thus the settlement imposed by the Great Powers at Munich had indeed avoided the outbreak of war, but had settled nothing, except that three million Germans, and the control of the great arms factory at Skoda, should be permanently attached to the Reich. Great Britain and France, recognising that a major diplomatic defeat had been inflicted on them, took energetically in hand the task of their own rearmament; while the embarrassed statesmen who succeeded one another as heads of the Czech Government expressed on all occasions their desire to conform to German policy.

But submission was not enough. Hitler professed anxiety for the security of the Germans, numbering about a quarter of a million, who still remained under Czech rule, and on March 15th, 1939, having summoned to him Hacha, who had succeeded Benes as President of the State, he forced him, under threat of violent military action, to agree that the old provinces of Bohemia and Moravia should come under the protection of the Reich, and be occupied by German troops. These indeed were already at that moment on their march across the frontier and occupying certain Czech towns. Slovakia was left with a nominal independence; but six and a half million Czechs were now brought once more under German rule—a rule very different from that which they had experienced as part of the Austrian Empire.

THE OUTBREAK OF WAR

Immediately after making his entry into Prague as a conqueror, Hitler presented an ultimatum to the Government of Lithuania, demanding the cession of Memel and the surrounding district. It was occupied on March 21st and the re-militarisation of this

Baltic port began at once. About the same time Ribbentrop peremptorily dictated to the Polish Ambassador terms which Germany proposed to impose on the Polish Government. These were that Danzig, commanding the mouth of the Vistula, should return to the Reich, and that Germany should be given a strip of territory connecting East Prussia across the Corridor with the rest of Germany. The Polish reply was a refusal to accept any dictated terms.

Since it was plain that Hitler's personal undertaking to Chamberlain had no value, and that the same manœuvres were beginning in regard to Poland as had been adopted towards Czechoslovakia, the British Government now took the decisive step of declaring that " in the event of any action which clearly threatened Polish independence and which the Polish Government accordingly considered it vital to resist with their national forces ", Great Britain would lend all support that was in its power. France was already allied to Poland ; but Chamberlain was authorised to say that he spoke for France as well.

Only a few days later Italy, not to be outdone, occupied the Albanian ports by a swift raid, and made herself mistress of a country, the task of protecting whose independence had, by an odd irony, been specially delegated to her (see p. 70). Aggression had thus declared itself in a fresh region ; and Great Britain extended her new departure so far as to join France in a guarantee of support for Greece and for Roumania, similar to that given to Poland, though Poland, with a sense of her importance, made the guarantee reciprocal and pledged assistance to

France and Britain, should they be attacked. Yugoslavia, which might have seemed no less threatened than Greece, declared that she felt in no need of assistance. Her commercial relations with both Germany and Italy were developing; and with the example of Czechoslovakia present to the mind, it was not easy to feel such a guarantee a very adequate protection. Greece, however, with her harbours, could be reached by British assistance; and Roumania, which held territory that had belonged to Russia in Bessarabia, territory that had belonged to Bulgaria in the Dobrudja, and territory that had been Hungarian in Transylvania, had reason to accept any offer of support. Further, at this time the British Government succeeded in securing a treaty with Turkey in which each Power was pledged to support the other in case of any threat to its interests in the Mediterranean area. A similar pact between Turkey and France was concluded when Turkey's claims on the Sandjak of Alexandretta (see p. 239) had been fully met.

These preparations were reinforced in Great Britain by the introduction on April 20th of a Bill making all men of military age liable to compulsory military training; and on its passing, one class of men between nineteen and twenty was at once called up. This formation of a conscript army on the Continental model in time of peace was regarded as the strongest proof of Great Britain's determination to use all her power to resist further aggression. The German Government construed these actions of the British as evidence " that the British no longer regard war by Britain as an impossibility, but on the contrary as a capital problem of British policy "; and on April 27th they denounced the Anglo-German naval agreement of 1935, under which Germany had agreed to limit its naval forces to thirty-five per cent of the British. Hitler complained that Great Britain was disregarding the agreement signed by him and Chamberlain after the Munich Conference, " symbolical of the desire of both people never again to wage war on one another ", and that Britain had returned to the policy of encirclement.

This policy was indeed being actively pursued, and with good reason ; for it was plain that if Germany should attack Poland, neither Britain nor France could give any direct assistance. Their guarantee had only the value of a possible deterrent. It was equally clear that, if the Soviet Union joined with the two western democracies, an army of immense numbers with a very large air force would be arrayed within striking distance of the aggressor. France was still allied to the Soviet Union, and from March onward, negotiations for joint action were in progress at Moscow, and a favourable issue was confidently expected, especially after it was announced that military representatives of France and Great Britain had been sent out to join in the discussion. But there were perplexing delays ; and it became known that the Soviet Union was unwilling to enter into any pact unless it included a Soviet guarantee of the integrity of the Baltic States, Lithuania, Latvia, Estonia and Finland. These countries, however, declared that they had no desire for such a guarantee, which might seem to lessen their independence ; they proposed to conclude non-aggression pacts with

Germany, and did so. Poland also refused to contemplate under any conditions the entry of Soviet troops into Polish territory. None the less, since the main purpose of Hitler's policy was always declared to be a violent opposition to all that the Soviet Union stood for, it seemed natural to expect Soviet support for any action taken to repress the growing power of the Third Reich. Then suddenly it became known that Ribbentrop had arrived at Moscow to negotiate a non-aggression pact between Germany and Russia. It was signed on August 23rd. This not only limited to Poland's own resources the opposition which Germany might meet in the East, but promised her a source of supply which would greatly lessen the menace of a maritime blockade.

Expectation that this announcement would determine Great Britain to withdraw from her commitment in Poland was known to be so strong that Chamberlain wrote personally to the German Chancellor warning him that "if the case should arise, the British Government would employ without delay all the forces at their command ". He added that in his judgment no question was at issue between Germany and Poland which " could not and should not be resolved without the use of force ".

The immediate dispute concerned Danzig and the so-called Corridor, which had been separated from Germany by the Versailles Treaty (see p. 8). Division of East Prussia from the rest of the Reich had been always resented : on the other hand, Hitler himself had admitted repeatedly that Poland needed access to the sea. But Poland, by creating in the fishing village of Gdynia a new harbour in its own territory, had not only interfered with Danzig's monopoly as the port for trade along the Vistula but had actually outstripped it in efficiency. Commercial rivalry as well as political idealism entered into the matter. But the desire to include Danzig in the Reich marked an ambition to establish such a centre of military power as would enable the Power holding it to cut off Poland's communications with the sea. The further claim for an extra-territorial belt across the Corridor was repelled by Poland as the first step to a much wider annexation. On these grounds the Poles refused to give way; and it was left for Germany to open hostilities by a concerted invasion of Polish territory on three separate fronts. This took place on September 1st. On September 3rd war was declared by Great Britain, and a few hours later by France.

APPENDIX I

THE MONROE DOCTRINE

(Extracts from President Monroe's Declaration of
December 2nd, 1823)

. . . The occasion has been judged proper for asserting, as a principle in which the rights and interests of the United States are involved, that the American continents, by the free and independent condition which they have assumed and maintain, are henceforth not to be considered as subjects for future colonization by any European powers.

. . . It is only when our rights are invaded or seriously menaced that we resent injuries or make preparation for our defense. With the movements in this hemisphere we are of necessity more immediately connected, and by causes which must be obvious to all enlightened and impartial observers. The political system of the allied powers[1] is essentially different in this respect from that of America. This difference proceeds from that which exists in their respective governments; and to the defense of our own, which has been achieved by the loss of so much blood and treasure, and matured by the wisdom of their most enlightened citizens, and under which we have enjoyed unexampled felicity, this whole nation is devoted. We owe it, therefore, to candor and to the amicable relations existing between the United States and those powers to ˙declare that we should consider any attempt on their part to

[1] *I.e.* Austria, France, Prussia and Russia.

extend their system to any portion of this hemisphere as dangerous to our peace and safety. With the existing colonies or dependencies of any European power we have not interfered and shall not interfere. But with the Governments who have declared their independence and maintained it, and whose independence we have, on great consideration and on just principles, acknowledged, we could not view any interposition for the purpose of oppressing them, or controlling in any other manner their destiny, by any European power in any other light than as the manifestation of an unfriendly disposition toward the United States.

WILSON'S FOURTEEN POINTS

(*Extract from President Wilson's Address to Congress of
January 8th, 1918*)

I. Open covenants of peace, openly arrived at, after which there shall be no private international understandings of any kind, but diplomacy shall proceed always frankly and in the public view.

II. Absolute freedom of navigation upon the seas, outside territorial waters, alike in peace and in war, except as the seas may be closed in whole or part by international action for the enforcement of international covenants.

III. The removal, so far as possible, of all economic barriers and the establishment of an equality of trade conditions among the nations consenting to the peace and associating themselves for its maintenance.

IV. Adequate guarantees given and taken that national armaments will be reduced to the lowest point consistent with domestic safety.

V. A free, open-minded, and absolutely impartial adjustment of all colonial claims, based upon a strict observance of the principle that in determining all such questions of sovereignty the interests of the populations concerned must have equal weight with the equitable claims of the government whose title is to be determined.

VI. The evacuation of all Russian territory and such a settlement of all questions affecting Russia as will secure the best and freest co-operation of the other nations of the world in obtaining for her an unhampered and unembarrassed opportunity for the independent determination of her own political development and national policy and assure her of a sincere welcome into the society of free nations under institutions of her own choosing ; and more than a welcome, assistance of every kind that she may need and may herself desire. The treatment accorded Russia by her sister nations in the months to come will be the acid test of their goodwill, of their comprehension of her needs as distinguished from their own interests, and of their intelligent and unselfish sympathy.

VII. Belgium, the whole world will agree, must be evacuated and restored, without any attempt to limit the sovereignty which she enjoys in common with all other free nations. No other single act will serve as this will serve to restore confidence among the nations in the laws which they themselves have set and determined for the government of their relations with one another. Without this healing act the whole structure and validity of international law is for ever impaired.

VIII. All French territory should be freed and the invaded portions restored, and the wrong done to France by Prussia in 1871 in the matter of Alsace-Lorraine, which has unsettled the peace of the world for nearly fifty years, should be righted, in order that peace may once more be made secure in the interest of all.

IX. A readjustment of the frontiers of Italy should be effected along clearly recognizable lines of nationality.

X. The peoples of Austria-Hungary, whose place among the nations we wish to see safeguarded and assured, should be accorded the freest opportunity of autonomous development.

XI. Rumania, Serbia and Montenegro should be

evacuated ; occupied territories restored ; Serbia accorded free and secure access to the sea ; and the relations of the several Balkan states to one another determined by friendly counsel along historically established lines of allegiance and nationality ; and international guarantees of the political and economic independence and territorial integrity of the several Balkan states should be entered into.

XII. The Turkish portions of the present Ottoman Empire should be assured a secure sovereignty, but the other nationalities which are now under Turkish rule should be assured an undoubted security of life and an absolutely unmolested opportunity of autonomous development, and the Dardanelles should be permanently opened as a free passage to the ships and commerce of all nations under international guarantees.

XIII. An independent Polish state should be erected which should include the territories inhabited by indisputably Polish populations, which should be assured a free and secure access to the sea, and whose political and economic independence and territorial integrity should be guaranteed by international covenant.

XIV. A general association of nations must be formed under specific covenants for the purpose of affording mutual guarantees of political independence and territorial integrity to great and small states alike.

EXTRACTS FROM THE COVENANT OF THE LEAGUE OF NATIONS

(including all the clauses referred to in the text)

Article 1

. . . Any fully self-governing State, Dominion or Colony not named in the Annex may become a Member of the League if its admission is agreed to by two-thirds of the Assembly, provided that it shall give effective guarantees of its sincere intention to observe its international obligations, and shall accept such regulations as may be prescribed by the League in regard to its military, naval and air forces and armaments. . . .

Article 4

. . . Any Member of the League not represented on the Council shall be invited to send a Representative to sit as a Member at any meeting of the Council during the consideration of matters specially affecting the interests of that Member of the League. . . .

Article 5

Except where otherwise expressly provided in this Covenant or by the terms of the present Treaty, decisions at any meeting of the Assembly or of the Council shall require the agreement of all the Members of the League represented at the meeting.

All matters of procedure at meetings of the Assembly or of the Council, including the appointment of Committees to investigate particular matters, shall be regulated by the Assembly or by the Council and may be decided by a majority of the Members of the League represented at the meeting. . . .

Article 8

The Members of the League recognise that the maintenance of peace requires the reduction of national armaments to the lowest point consistent with national safety and the enforcement by common action of international obligations. . . .

Article 10

The Members of the League undertake to respect and preserve as against external aggression the territorial integrity and existing political independence of all Members of the League. In case of any such aggression or in cases of any threat or danger of such aggression the Council shall advise upon the means by which this obligation shall be fulfilled.

Article 11

Any war or threat of war, whether immediately affecting any of the Members of the League or not, is hereby declared a matter of concern to the whole League, and the League shall take any action that may be deemed wise and effectual to safeguard the peace of nations. In case any such emergency should arise the Secretary-General shall on the request of any Member of the League forthwith summon a meeting of the Council.

It is also declared to be the friendly right of each

Member of the League to bring to the attention of the Assembly or of the Council any circumstance whatever affecting international relations which threatens to disturb international peace or the good understanding between nations upon which peace depends.

Article 12

The Members of the League agree that, if there should arise between them any dispute likely to lead to a rupture, they will submit the matter either to arbitration or judicial settlement or to inquiry by the Council and they agree in no case to resort to war until three months after the award by the arbitrators or the judicial decision, or the report by the Council. . . .

Article 14

The Council shall formulate and submit to the Members of the League for adoption plans for the establishment of a Permanent Court of International Justice. The Court shall be competent to hear and determine any dispute of an international character which the parties thereto submit to it. The Court may also give an advisory opinion upon any dispute or question referred to it by the Council or by the Assembly.

Article 15

If there should arise between Members of the League any dispute likely to lead to a rupture, which is not submitted to arbitration or judicial settlement in accordance with Article 13, the Members of the League agree that they will submit the matter to the Council. Any party to the dispute may effect such submission by giving notice of the existence of the dispute to the Secretary-General, who will make all necessary arrangements for a full investigation and consideration thereof. . . .

The Council shall endeavour to effect a settlement of the dispute, and if such efforts are successful, a statement shall be made public giving such facts and explanations regarding the dispute and the terms of settlement thereof as the Council may deem appropriate.

If the dispute is not thus settled, the Council either unanimously or by a majority vote shall make and publish a report containing a statement of the facts of the dispute and the recommendations which are deemed just and proper in regard thereto. . . .

If a report by the Council is unanimously agreed to by the members thereof other than the Representatives of one or more of the parties to the dispute, the Members of the League agree that they will not go to war with any party to the dispute which complies with the recommendations of the report.

If the Council fails to reach a report which is unanimously agreed to by the members thereof, other than the Representatives of one or more of the parties to the dispute, the Members of the League reserve to themselves the right to take such action as they shall consider necessary for the maintenance of right and justice.

If the dispute between the parties is claimed by one of them, and is found by the Council to arise out of a matter which by international law is solely within the domestic jurisdiction of that party, the Council shall so report, and shall make no recommendation as to its settlement.

The Council may in any case under this Article refer the dispute to the Assembly. The dispute shall be so referred at the request of either party to the dispute, provided that such request be made within fourteen days after the submission of the dispute to the Council. . . .

APPENDICES

Article 16

Should any Member of the League resort to war in disregard of its covenants under Article 12, 13, or 15, it shall *ipso facto* be deemed to have committed an act of war against all other Members of the League, which hereby undertake immediately to subject it to the severance of all trade or financial relations, the prohibition of all intercourse between their nationals and the nationals of the covenant-breaking State, and the prevention of all financial, commercial or personal intercourse between the nationals of the covenant-breaking State and the nationals of any other State, whether a Member of the League or not.

It shall be the duty of the Council in such case to recommend to the several Governments concerned what effective military, naval or air force the Members of the League shall severally contribute to the armed forces to be used to protect the Covenants of the League. . . .

Article 17

In the event of a dispute between a Member of the League and a State which is not a Member of the League, or between States not Members of the League, the State or States not Members of the League shall be invited to accept the obligations of Membership in the League for the purposes of such dispute, upon such conditions as the Council may deem just. . . .

Article 19

The Assembly may from time to time advise the reconsideration by Members of the League of treaties which have become inapplicable and the consideration of international conditions whose continuance might endanger the peace of the world.

Article 21

Nothing in the Covenant shall be deemed to affect the validity of international engagements, such as treaties of arbitration or regional understandings like the Monroe doctrine, for securing the maintenance of peace.

Article 22

To those colonies and territories which as a consequence of the late war have ceased to be under the sovereignty of the States which formerly governed them and which are inhabited by peoples not yet able to stand by themselves under the strenuous conditions of the modern world, there should be applied the principle that the well-being and development of such peoples form a sacred trust of civilisation and that securities for the performance of this trust should be embodied in this Covenant.

The best method of giving practical effect to this principle is that the tutelage of such peoples should be entrusted to advanced nations who by reason of their resources, their experience or their geographical position can best undertake this responsibility, and who are willing to accept it, and that this tutelage should be exercised by them as Mandatories on behalf of the League.

The character of the mandate must differ according to the stage of the development of the people, the geographical situation of the territory, its economic conditions and other similar circumstances.

Certain communities formerly belonging to the Turkish Empire have reached a stage of development where their existence as independent nations can be provisionally recognised subject to the rendering of administrative advice and assistance by a Mandatory until such time as they are able to stand alone. The wishes of these communities must be a principal consideration in the selection of the Mandatory.

Other peoples, especially those of Central Africa, are at such a stage that the Mandatory must be responsible for the administration of the territory under conditions which will guarantee freedom of conscience and religion, subject only to the maintenance of public order and morals, the prohibition of abuses such as the slave trade, the arms traffic and the liquor traffic, and the prevention of the establishment of fortifications or military and naval bases and of military training of the natives for other than police purposes and the defence of territory, and will also secure equal opportunities for the trade and commerce of other Members of the League.

There are territories, such as South-West Africa and certain of the South Pacific Islands, which, owing to the sparseness of their population, or their small size, or their remoteness from the centres of civilisation, or their geographical contiguity to the territory of the Mandatory, and other circumstances, can be best administered under the laws of the Mandatory as integral portions of its territory, subject to the safeguards above mentioned in the interests of the indigenous population.

In every case of mandate, the Mandatory shall render to the Council an annual report, in reference to the territory committed to its charge.

The degree of authority, control, or administration to be exercised by the Mandatory shall, if not previously agreed upon by the Members of the League, be explicitly defined in each case by the Council.

A permanent Commission shall be constituted to receive and examine the annual reports of the Mandatories and to advise the Council on all matters relating to the observance of the mandates.

CHRONOLOGICAL TABLE OF IMPORTANT
EVENTS

1918
Jan. 18   President Wilson's Fourteen Points
Nov. 11   Armistice granted to Germany

1919
June 28   Treaty of Versailles with Germany
Sept. 10   Treaty of Saint-Germain with Austria
Nov. 27   Treaty of Neuilly with Bulgaria

1920
Jan. 10   Exchange of Ratifications of Versailles Treaty:
            League of Nations comes into existence
June 4   Treaty of Trianon with Hungary

1921
March 16   Trade agreement between Great Britain and
            Soviet Russia
    „ 18   Treaty of Riga between Poland and Soviet
            Russia
Dec. 13   Four-Power Pacific Treaty signed at Washington

1922
Feb. 6   Naval Treaty and Nine-Power Treaty concern-
            ing China signed at Washington
    „ 28   Recognition by Great Britain of independence
            of Egypt
April 16   Treaty of Rapallo between Germany and Soviet
            Russia

1923
Jan. 11   Occupation of the Ruhr by French and Belgian
            troops
July 24   Treaty of Lausanne with Turkey

1924

Feb. 1	Recognition of Soviet Government by Great Britain
Aug. 30	Dawes Agreements signed in London
Oct. 2	Geneva Protocol adopted by League Assembly

1925

March 10	Rejection of Geneva Protocol by Great Britain
Dec. 1	Locarno Treaties signed in London

1926

Sept. 10	Admission of Germany to the League of Nations

1927

Jan. 1	Establishment of Chinese Nationalist Government at Hankow
Dec. 18	Expulsion of Trotsky from Russian Communist Party

1928

Aug. 27	Pact of Paris (Briand-Kellogg Pact) signed

1929

Aug. 31	Approval of Young Plan by the Hague Conference

1930

April 22	Naval Treaty signed in London
June 30	Evacuation of the Rhineland by Allied troops

1931

March 21	Customs Union Agreement between Germany and Austria
June 20	President Hoover proposes a Moratorium
Sept. 19	Japan begins military operations in Manchuria
,, 21	Abandonment of gold standard by Great Britain

CHRONOLOGICAL TABLE OF IMPORTANT EVENTS

1932

Feb. 2	Opening of Disarmament Conference
July 9	Reparation Agreement signed at Lausanne
Aug. 20	Trade Agreements between Great Britain and Dominions signed at Ottawa
Oct. 3	Termination of British mandate over Iraq

1933

Jan. 30	Herr Hitler becomes German Chancellor
Feb. 24	League Assembly Resolution on Manchuria ; Japanese Delegation withdraws
June 12	Opening of World Economic Conference
Oct. 14	Germany announces withdrawal from Disarmament Conference and League of Nations

1934

Jan. 26	German-Polish Agreement signed
Sept. 18	Soviet Union admitted to the League of Nations
Oct. 9	King Alexander of Yugoslavia assassinated at Marseilles

1935

Jan. 7	Franco-Italian Agreements signed by Signor Mussolini and M. Laval in Rome
March 16	Germany repudiates military clauses of Versailles Treaty
May 2	Franco-Soviet Pact signed
Oct. 2	Italian troops enter Abyssinia
Nov. 18	Economic Sanctions applied against Italy

1936

March 7	Germany reoccupies the demilitarised zone
May 9	Annexation of Abyssinia by Italy
July 4	Withdrawal of Sanctions against Italy
„ 18	Outbreak of Spanish Civil War

1937

July 8	Japan begins undeclared war in China

CHRONOLOGICAL TABLE OF IMPORTANT EVENTS

1938

March 12   Annexation of Austria by Germany

Sept. 29   Munich Agreement regarding Czechoslovakia

1939

March 15   German occupation of Bohemia and Moravia

April 1   End of Spanish Civil War

„ 7   Italian occupation of Albania

May 26   Conscription adopted in Great Britain

Aug. 23   German-Soviet Pact signed

Sept. 1   German invasion of Poland

„ 3   War declared on Germany by Great Britain and France

INDEX

Abyssinia, 102, 207, 212, 222-8, 230, 241
Addis Ababa, 227-8
Adriatic Sea, 69
Aegean Sea, 12, 41
Afghanistan, 74, 234
Albania, 69-71, 213, 226, 274
Alexander, King (of Greece), 14
Alexander, King (of Yugoslavia), 210
Alexandretta, 239, 275
Alfonso XIII, King, 259
Allenstein, 8
Alsace, 6
Ambassadors' Conference, 69, 71-2
America, United States of, 18-22, 27-8, 38, 45-7, 49, 51, 59, 72, 77, 83-7, 92-4, 99, 102-4, 111-12, 118-20, 126, 129, 133, 138, 140-41, 143, 147-53, 162, 165-7, 170-71, 173-4, 178-82, 184-6, 199, 201-2, 247-53
Angora, 16
Arabs, 15-17, 234-41 ; see also Saudi Arabia
Arbitration and Security, Committee on, 115-16, 123, 181
Arcos raid, 93
Argentine, 102, 119, 140, 151, 250
Armenia, 74
Assyrians, 235
Australia, Commonwealth of, 18, 92, 140, 254-6
Austria, 3, 6, 8-10, 13, 19, 30-31, 8-9, 61-3, 65-6, 68, 83, 136-40, 200, 204-12, 226, 260, 267-8
Azerbaijan, 74

Baldwin, Stanley, 93, 258, 266
Balkan Entente, 213-14
Balkan War, First, 11
— —, Second, 11, 213
Bank of International Settlements, 127
Bartliou, Louis, 208, 210-11
Bavaria, 51
Bela Kun, 64
Belgium, 6, 18, 20, 30, 45, 49, 52, 54, 56-7, 59, 83, 94, 96, 117-18, 146, 152, 229-31
Benes, Dr. Eduard, 271, 273
Berchtesgaden, 267, 269
Berlin, 59, 188, 205, 217, 219
Bessarabia, 40, 275
Black Sea, 34, 61
Blum, Léon, 264
Bohemia, 10, 38-9, 278
Bolivia, 119, 174
Borodin, 154, 157-60, 244
Brazil, 100-102, 111, 119, 140
Briand, Aristide, 100, 118, 123, 128-9, 165
Briand-Kellogg Pact, see Pact of Paris
British Empire, see Great Britain
Brüning, Heinrich, 135, 139, 147, 183
Brussels Financial Conference 110
Budapest, 64

295

INDEX

70 71 72 73   12 11 10 9 8 7 6 5 4 3

Revised January, 1970

hARPER ⚡ ϽORϽhBOOKS

---

† The New American Nation Series, edited by Henry Steele Commager and Richard B. Morris.
‡ American Perspectives series, edited by Bernard Wishy and William E. Leuchtenburg.
a History of Europe series, edited by J. H. Plumb.
§ The Library of Religion and Culture, edited by Benjamin Nelson.
|| Researches in the Social, Cultural, and Behavioral Sciences, edited by Benjamin Nelson.
Σ Harper Modern Science Series, edited by James A. Newman.
° Not for sale in Canada.
+ Documentary History of the United States series, edited by Richard B. Morris.
# Documentary History of Western Civilization series, edited by Eugene C. Black and Leonard W. Levy.
Λ The Economic History of the United States series, edited by Henry David et al.
¶ European Perspectives series, edited by Eugene C. Black.
** Contemporary Essays series, edited by Leonard W. Levy.
* The Stratum Series, edited by John Hale.

2

ARNOLD M. PAUL: Conservative Crisis and the Rule of Law: *Attitudes of Bar and Bench, 1887-1895. New Introduction by Author*
TB/1415

JAMES S. PIKE: The Prostrate State: *South Carolina under Negro Government.* ‡ *Intro. by Robert F. Durden*
TB/3085

WHITELAW REID: After the War: *A Tour of the Southern States, 1865-1866.* ‡ *Edited by C. Vann Woodward*
TB/3066

FRED A. SHANNON: The Farmer's Last Frontier: ....*Agriculture, 1860-1897*
TB/1348

VERNON LANE WHARTON: The Negro in Mississippi, 1865-1890
TB/1178

American Studies: The Twentieth Century

RICHARD M. ABRAMS, Ed.: The Issues of the Populist and Progressive Eras, 1892-1912 +
HR/1428

RAY STANNARD BAKER: Following the Color Line: *American Negro Citizenship in Progressive Era.* ‡ *Edited by Dewey W. Grantham, Jr. Illus.*
TB/3053

RANDOLPH S. BOURNE: War and the Intellectuals: *Collected Essays, 1915-1919.* ‡ *Edited by Carl Resek*
TB/3043

A. RUSSELL BUCHANAN: The United States and World War II. † *Illus.*
Vol. I TB/3044; Vol. II TB/3045

THOMAS C. COCHRAN: The American Business System: *A Historical Perspective, 1900-1955*
TB/1080

FOSTER RHEA DULLES: America's Rise to World Power: 1898-1954. † *Illus.*
TB/3021

JEAN-BAPTISTE DUROSELLE: From Wilson to Roosevelt: *Foreign Policy of the United States, 1913-1945. Trans. by Nancy Lyman Roelker*
TB/1370

HAROLD U. FAULKNER: The Decline of Laissez Faire, 1897-1917
TB/1397

JOHN D. HICKS: Republican Ascendancy: 1921-1933. † *Illus.*
TB/3041

ROBERT HUNTER: Poverty: *Social Conscience in the Progressive Era.* ‡ *Edited by Peter d'A. Jones*
TB/3065

WILLIAM E. LEUCHTENBURG: Franklin D. Roosevelt and the New Deal: 1932-1940. † *Illus.*
TB/3025

WILLIAM E. LEUCHTENBURG, Ed.: The New Deal: *A Documentary History* +
HR/1354

ARTHUR S. LINK: Woodrow Wilson and the Progressive Era: 1910-1917. † *Illus.* TB/3023

BROADUS MITCHELL: Depression Decade: *From New Era through New Deal, 1929-1941* ∧
TB/1439

GEORGE E. MOWRY: The Era of Theodore Roosevelt and the Birth of Modern America: 1900-1912. † *Illus.*
TB/3022

WILLIAM PRESTON, JR.: Aliens and Dissenters: *Federal Suppression of Radicals, 1903-1933*
TB/1287

WALTER RAUSCHENBUSCH: Christianity and the Social Crisis. ‡ *Edited by Robert D. Cross*
TB/3059

GEORGE SOULE: Prosperity Decade: *From War to Depression, 1917-1929* ∧
TB/1349

GEORGE B. TINDALL, Ed.: A Populist Reader: *Selections from the Works of American Populist Leaders*
TB/3069

TWELVE SOUTHERNERS: I'll Take My Stand: *The South and the Agrarian Tradition. Intro. by Louis D. Rubin, Jr.; Biographical Essays by Virginia Rock*
TB/1072

Art, Art History, Aesthetics

CREIGHTON GILBERT, Ed.: Renaissance Art **
Illus.
TB/1465

EMILE MALE: The Gothic Image: *Religious Art in France of the Thirteenth Century.* § *190 illus.*
TB/344

MILLARD MEISS: Painting in Florence and Siena After the Black Death: *The Arts, Religion and Society in the Mid-Fourteenth Century. 169 illus.*
TB/1148

ERWIN PANOFSKY: Renaissance and Renascences in Western Art. *Illus.*
TB/1447

ERWIN PANOFSKY: Studies in Iconology: *Humanistic Themes in the Art of the Renaissance. 180 illus.*
TB/1077

JEAN SEZNEC: The Survival of the Pagan Gods: *The Mythological Tradition and Its Place in Renaissance Humanism and Art. 108 illus.*
TB/2004

OTTO VON SIMSON: The Gothic Cathedral: *Origins of Gothic Architecture and the Medieval Concept of Order. 58 illus.*
TB/2018

HEINRICH ZIMMER: Myths and Symbols in Indian Art and Civilization. *70 illus.* TB/2005

Asian Studies

WOLFGANG FRANKE: China and the West: *The Cultural Encounter, 13th to 20th Centuries. Trans. by R. A. Wilson*
TB/1326

L. CARRINGTON GOODRICH: A Short History of the Chinese People. *Illus.*
TB/3015

DAN N. JACOBS, Ed.: The New Communist Manifesto and Related Documents. *3rd revised edn.*
TB/1078

DAN N. JACOBS & HANS H. BAERWALD, Eds.: Chinese Communism: *Selected Documents*
TB/3031

BENJAMIN I. SCHWARTZ: Chinese Communism and the Rise of Mao
TB/1308

BENJAMIN I. SCHWARTZ: In Search of Wealth and Power: *Yen Fu and the West* TB/1422

Economics & Economic History

C. E. BLACK: The Dynamics of Modernization: *A Study in Comparative History* TB/1321

STUART BRUCHEY: The Roots of American Economic Growth, 1607-1861: *An Essay in Social Causation. New Introduction by the Author.*
TB/1350

GILBERT BURCK & EDITORS OF *Fortune*: The Computer Age: *And its Potential for Management*
TB/1179

JOHN ELLIOTT CAIRNES: The Slave Power. ‡ *Edited with Introduction by Harold D. Woodman*
TB/1433

SHEPARD B. CLOUGH, THOMAS MOODIE & CAROL MOODIE, Eds.: Economic History of Europe: *Twentieth Century* #
HR/1388

THOMAS C.COCHRAN: The American Business System: *A Historical Perspective, 1900-1955*
TB/1180

ROBERT A. DAHL & CHARLES E. LINDBLOM: Politics, Economics, and Welfare: *Planning and Politico-Economic Systems Resolved into Basic Social Processes*
TB/3037

PETER F. DRUCKER: The New Society: *The Anatomy of Industrial Order* TB/1082

HAROLD U. FAULKNER: The Decline of Laissez Faire, 1897-1917 ∧
TB/1397

PAUL W. GATES: The Farmer's Age: *Agriculture, 1815-1860* ∧
TB/1398

WILLIAM GREENLEAF, Ed.: American Economic Development Since 1860 +
HR/1353

J. L. & BARBARA HAMMOND: The Rise of Modern Industry. || *Introduction by R. M. Hartwell*
TB/1417

ROBERT L. HEILBRONER: The Future as History: *The Historic Currents of Our Time and the Direction in Which They Are Taking America* TB/1386

ROBERT L. HEILBRONER: The Great Ascent: *The Struggle for Economic Development in Our Time* TB/3030

FRANK H. KNIGHT: The Economic Organization TB/1214

DAVID S. LANDES: Bankers and Pashas: *International Finance and Economic Imperialism in Egypt. New Preface by the Author* TB/1412

ROBERT LATOUCHE: The Birth of Western Economy: *Economic Aspects of the Dark Ages* TB/1290

ABBA P. LERNER: Everybody's Business: *A Reexamination of Current Assumptions in Economics and Public Policy* TB/3051

W. ARTHUR LEWIS: Economic Survey, 1919-1939 TB/1446

W. ARTHUR LEWIS: The Principles of Economic Planning. *New Introduction by the Author°* TB/1436

ROBERT GREEN MC CLOSKEY: American Conservatism in the Age of Enterprise TB/1137

PAUL MANTOUX: The Industrial Revolution in the Eighteenth Century: *An Outline of the Beginnings of the Modern Factory System in England°* TB/1079

WILLIAM MILLER, Ed.: Men in Business: *Essays on the Historical Role of the Entrepreneur* TB/1081

GUNNAR MYRDAL: An International Economy. *New Introduction by the Author* TB/1445

HERBERT A. SIMON: The Shape of Automation: *For Men and Management* TB/1245

PERRIN STRYER: The Character of the Executive: *Eleven Studies in Managerial Qualities* TB/1041

RICHARD S. WECKSTEIN, Ed.: Expansion of World Trade and the Growth of National Economies ** TB/1373

Education

JACQUES BARZUN: The House of Intellect TB/1051

RICHARD M. JONES, Ed.: Contemporary Educational Psychology: *Selected Readings *** TB/1292

CLARK KERR: The Uses of the University TB/1264

Historiography and History of Ideas

HERSCHEL BAKER: The Image of Man: *A Study of the Idea of Human Dignity in Classical Antiquity, the Middle Ages, and the Renaissance* TB/1047

J. BRONOWSKI & BRUCE MAZLISH: The Western Intellectual Tradition: *From Leonardo to Hegel* TB/3001

EDMUND BURKE: On Revolution. Ed. by Robert A. Smith TB/1401

WILHELM DILTHEY: Pattern and Meaning in History: *Thoughts on History and Society.° Edited with an Intro. by H. P. Rickman* TB/1075

ALEXANDER GRAY: The Socialist Tradition: *Moses to Lenin°* TB/1375

J. H. HEXTER: More's Utopia: *The Biography of an Idea. Epilogue by the Author* TB/1195

H. STUART HUGHES: History as Art and as Science: *Twin Vistas on the Past* TB/1207

ARTHUR O. LOVEJOY: The Great Chain of Being: *A Study of the History of an Idea* TB/1009

JOSE ORTEGA Y GASSET: The Modern Theme. *Introduction by Jose Ferrater Mora* TB/1038

RICHARD H. POPKIN: The History of Scepticism from Erasmus to Descartes. *Revised Edition* TB/1391

G. J. RENIER: History: *Its Purpose and Method* TB/1209

MASSIMO SALVADORI, Ed.: Modern Socialism # TB/1374

GEORG SIMMEL et al.: Essays on Sociology, Philosophy and Aesthetics. *Edited by Kurt H. Wolff* TB/1234

BRUNO SNELL: The Discovery of the Mind: *The Greek Origins of European Thought* TB/1018

W. WARREN WAGER, ed.: European Intellectual History Since Darwin and Marx TB/1297

W. H. WALSH: Philosophy of History: In Introduction TB/1020

History: General

HANS KOHN: The Age of Nationalism: *The First Era of Global History* TB/1380

BERNARD LEWIS: The Arabs in History TB/1029

BERNARD LEWIS: The Middle East and the West ° TB/1274

History: Ancient

A. ANDREWS: The Greek Tyrants TB/1103

ERNST LUDWIG EHRLICH: A Concise History of Israel: *From the Earliest Times to the Destruction of the Temple in A.D. 70 °* TB/128

ADOLF ERMAN, Ed.: The Ancient Egyptians: *A Sourcebook of their Writings. New Introduction by William Kelly Simpson* TB/1233

THEODOR H. GASTER: Thespis: *Ritual Myth and Drama in the Ancient Near East* TB/1281

MICHAEL GRANT: Ancient History ° TB/1190

A. H. M. JONES, Ed.: A History of Rome through the Fifgth Century # *Vol. I: The Republic* HR/1364

Vol. II The Empire: HR/1460

SAMUEL NOAH KRAMER: Sumerian Mythology TB/1055

NAPHTALI LEWIS & MEYER REINHOLD, Eds.: Roman Civilization *Vol. I: The Republic* TB/1231

Vol. II: The Empire TB/1232

History: Medieval

MARSHALL W. BALDWIN, Ed.: Christianity Through the 13th Century # HR/1468

MARC BLOCH: Land and Work in Medieval Europe. *Translated by J. E. Anderson* TB/1452

HELEN CAM: England Before Elizabeth TB/1026

NORMAN COHN: The Pursuit of the Millennium: *Revolutionary Messianism in Medieval and Reformation Europe* TB/1037

G. G. COULTON: Medieval Village, Manor, and Monastery HR/1022

HEINRICH FICHTENAU: The Carolingian Empire: *The Age of Charlemagne. Translated with an Introduction by Peter Munz* TB/1142

GALBERT OF BRUGES: The Murder of Charles the Good: *A Contemporary Record of Revolutionary Change in 12th Century Flanders. Translated with an Introduction by James Bruce Ross* TB/1311

F. L. GANSHOF: Feudalism TB/1058

F. L. GANSHOF: The Middle Ages: *A History of International Relations. Translated by Rémy Hall* TB/1411

W. O. HASSALL, Ed.: Medieval England: *As Viewed by Contemporaries* TB/1205

DENYS HAY: The Medieval Centuries ° TB/1192

DAVID HERLIHY, Ed.: Medieval Culture and Socitey # HR/1340

4

J. M. HUSSEY: The Byzantine World   TB/1057
ROBERT LATOUCHE: The Birth of Western Economy: *Economic Aspects of the Dark Ages* °
TB/1290
HENRY CHARLES LEA: The Inquisition of the Middle Ages. || *Introduction by Walter Ullmann*   TB/1456
FERDINAND LOT: The End of the Ancient World and the Beginnings of the Middle Ages. *Introduction by Glanville Downey*   TB/1044
H. R. LOYN: The Norman Conquest   TB/1457
ACHILLE LUCHAIRE: Social France at the time of Philip Augustus. *Intro. by John W. Baldwin*
TB/1314
GUIBERT DE NOGENT: Self and Society in Medieval France: *The Memoirs of Guibert de Nogent*. || Edited by John F. Benton TB/1471
MARSILIUS OF PADUA: The Defender of Peace. *The Defensor Pacis. Translated with an Introduction by Alan Gewirth*   TB/1310
CHARLES PETET-DUTAILLIS: The Feudal Monarchy in France and England: *From the Tenth to the Thirteenth Century* °   TB/1165
STEVEN RUNCIMAN: A History of the Crusades Vol. I: *The First Crusade and the Foundation of the Kingdom of Jerusalem. Illus.*
TB/1143
Vol. II: *The Kingdom of Jerusalem and the Frankish East 1100-1187. Illus.*   TB/1243
Vol. III: *The Kingdom of Acre and the Later Crusades. Illus.*   TB/1298
J. M. WALLACE-HADRILL: The Barbarian West: *The Early Middle Ages, A.D. 400-1000*
TB/1061

History: Renaissance & Reformation

JACOB BURCKHARDT: The Civilization of the Renaissance in Italy. *Introduction by Benjamin Nelson and Charles Trinkaus. Illus.*
Vol. I TB/40;   Vol. II TB/41
JOHN CALVIN & JACOPO SADOLETO: A Reformation Debate. *Edited by John C. Olin*   TB/1239
FEDERICO CHABOD: Machiavelli and the Renaissance   TB/1193
THOMAS CROMWELL: Thomas Cromwell on Church and Commonwealth,: *Selected Letters 1523-1540. ¶ Ed. with an Intro. by Arthur J. Slavin*   TB/1462
R. TREVOR DAVIES: The Golden Century of Spain, 1501-1621 °   TB/1194
J. H. ELLIOTT: Europe Divided, 1559-1598 *a* °
TB/1414
G. R. ELTON: Reformation Europe, 1517-1559 ° *a*
TB/1270
DESIDERIUS ERASMUS: Christian Humanism and the Reformation: *Selected Writings. Edited and Translated by John C. Olin*   TB/1166
DESIDERIUS ERASMUS: Erasmus and His Age: *Selected Letters. Edited with an Introduction by Hans J. Hillerbrand. Translated by Marcus A. Haworth*   TB/1461
WALLACE K. FERGUSON et al.: Facets of the Renaissance   TB/1098
WALLACE K. FERGUSON et al.: The Renaissance: *Six Essays. Illus.*   TB/1084
FRANCESCO GUICCIARDINI: History of Florence. *Translated with an Introduction and Notes by Mario Domandi*   TB/1470
WERNER L. GUNDERSHEIMER, Ed.: French Humanism, 1470-1600. * *Illus.*   TB/1473
MARIE BOAS HALL, Ed.: Nature and Nature's Laws: *Documents of the Scientific Revolution* #   HR/1420
HANS J. HILLERBRAND, Ed., The Protestant Reformation #   HR/1342
JOHAN HUIZINGA: Erasmus and the Age of Reformation. *Illus.*   TB/19

JOEL HURSTFIELD: The Elizabethan Nation
TB/1312
JOEL HURSTFIELD, Ed.: The Reformation Crisis
TB/1267
PAUL OSKAR KRISTELLER: Renaissance Thought: *The Classic, Scholastic, and Humanist Strains*
TB/1048
PAUL OSKAR KRISTELLER: Renaissance Thought II: *Papers on Humanism and the Arts*
TB/1163
PAUL O. KRISTELLER & PHILIP P. WIENER, Eds.: Renaissance Essays   TB/1392
DAVID LITTLE: Religion, Order and Law: *A Study in Pre-Revolutionary England. § Preface by R. Bellah*   TB/1418
NICCOLO MACHIAVELLI: History of Florence and of the Affairs of Italy: *From the Earliest Times to the Death of Lorenzo the Magnificent. Introduction by Felix Gilbert*   TB/1027
ALFRED VON MARTIN: Sociology of the Renaissance. ° *Introduction by W. K. Ferguson*
TB/1099
GARRETT MATTINGLY et al.: Renaissance Profiles. *Edited by J. H. Plumb*   TB/1162
J. E. NEALE: The Age of Catherine de Medici °
TB/1085
J. H. PARRY: The Establishment of the European Hegemony: 1415-1715: *Trade and Exploration in the Age of the Renaissance*   TB/1045
J. H. PARRY, Ed.: The European Reconnaissance: *Selected Documents* #   HR/1345
BUONACCORSO PITTI & GREGORIO DATI: Two Memoirs of Renaissance Florence: *The Diaries of Buonaccorso Pitti and Gregorio Dati. Edited with Intro. by Gene Brucker. Trans. by Julia Martines*   TB/1333
J. H. PLUMB: The Italian Renaissance: *A Concise Survey of Its History and Culture*
TB/1161
A. F. POLLARD: Henry VIII. *Introduction by A. G. Dickens.* °   TB/1249
RICHARD H. POPKIN: The History of Scepticism from Erasmus to Descartes   TB/139
PAOLO ROSSI: Philosophy, Technology, and the Arts, in the Early Modern Era 1400-1700. || *Edited by Benjamin Nelson. Translated by Salvator Attanasio*   TB/1458
FERDINAND SCHEVILL: The Medici. *Illus.* TB/1010
FERDINAND SCHEVILL: Medieval and Renaissance Florence. *Illus.* Vol. I: *Medieval Florence*
TB/1090
Vol. II: *The Coming of Humanism and the Age of the Medici*   TB/1091
R. H. TAWNEY: The Agrarian Problem in the Sixteenth Century. *Intro. by Lawrence Stone*
TB/1315
H. R. TREVOR-ROPER: The European Witch-craze of the Sixteenth and Seventeenth Centuries and Other Essays °   TB/1416
VESPASIANO: Rennaissance Princes, Popes, and *XVth Century: The Vespasiano Memoirs. Introduction by Myron P. Gilmore. Illus.*
TB/1111

History: Modern European

RENE ALBRECHT-CARRIE, Ed.: The Concert of Europe #   HR/1341
MAX BELOFF: The Age of Absolutism, 1660-1815
TB/1062
OTTO VON BISMARCK: Reflections and Reminiscences. *Ed. with Intro. by Theodore S. Hamerow* ¶   TB/1357
EUGENE C. BLACK, Ed.: British Politics in the Nineteenth Century #   HR/1427

EUGENE C. BLACK, Ed.: European Political History, 1815-1870: *Aspects of Liberalism* ¶ TB/1331

ASA BRIGGS: The Making of Modern England, 1783-1867: *The Age of Improvement* ° TB/1203

D. W. BROGAN: The Development of Modern France ° Vol. I: *From the Fall of the Empire to the Dreyfus Affair* TB/1184 Vol. II: *The Shadow of War, World War I, Between the Two Wars* TB/1185

ALAN BULLOCK: Hitler, A Study in Tyranny. ° *Revised Edition. Illus.* TB/1123

EDMUND BURKE: On Revolution. *Ed. by Robert A. Smith* TB/1401

E. R. CARR: International Relations Between the Two World Wars. 1919-1939 ° TB/1279

E. H. CARR: The Twenty Years' Crisis, 1919-1939: *An Introduction to the Study of International Relations* ° TB/1122

GORDON A. CRAIG: From Bismarck to Adenauer: *Aspects of German Statecraft. Revised Edition* TB/1171

LESTER G. CROCKER, Ed.: The Age of Enlightenment # HR/1423

DENIS DIDEROT: The Encyclopedia: *Selections. Edited and Translated with Introduction by Stephen Gendzier* TB/1299

JACQUES DROZ: Europe between Revolutions, 1815-1848. ° *a Trans. by Robert Baldick* TB/1346

JOHANN GOTTLIEB FICHTE: Addresses to the German Nation. *Ed. with Intro. by George A. Kelly* ¶ TB/1366

FRANKLIN L. FORD: Robe and Sword: *The Re-Louis XIV* TB/1217

ROBERT & ELBORG FORSTER, Eds.: European Society in the Eighteenth Century # HR/1404

C. C. GILLISPIE: Genesis and Geology: *The Decades before Darwin* § TB/51

ALBERT GOODWIN, Ed.: The European Nobility in the Enghteenth Century TB/1313

ALBERT GOODWIN: The French Revolution TB/1064

ALBERT GUERARD: France in the Classical Age: *The Life and Death of an Ideal* TB/1183

JOHN B. HALSTED, Ed.: Romanticism # HR/1387

J. H. HEXTER: Reappraisals in History: *New Views on History and Society in Early Modern Europe* ° TB/1100

STANLEY HOFFMANN et al.: In Search of France: *The Economy, Society and Political System In the Twentieth Century* TB/1219

H. STUART HUGHES: The Obstructed Path: *French Social Thought in the Years of Desperation* TB/1451

JOHAN HUIZINGA: Dutch Civilisation in the 17th Century and Other Essays TB/1453

LIONAL KOCHAN: The Struggle for Germany: *1914-45* TB/1304

HANS KOHN: The Mind of Germany: *The Education of a Nation* TB/1204

HANS KOHN, Ed.: The Mind of Modern Russia: *Historical and Political Thought of Russia's Great Age* TB/1065

WALTER LAQUEUR & GEORGE L. MOSSE, Eds.: Education and Social Structure in the 20th Century. ° *Volume 6 of the Journal of Contemporary History* TB/1339

WALTER LAQUEUR & GEORGE L. MOSSE, Ed.: International Fascism, 1920-1945. ° *Volume 1 of the Journal of Contemporary History* TB/1276

WALTER LAQUEUR & GEORGE L. MOSSE, Eds.: Literature and Politics in the 20th Century. ° *Volume 5 of the Journal of Contemporary History.* TB/1328

WALTER LAQUEUR & GEORGE L. MOSSE, Eds.: The New History: *Trends in Historical Research and Writing Since World War II.* ° *Volume 4 of the Journal of Contemporary History* TB/1327

WALTER LAQUEUR & GEORGE L. MOSSE, Eds.: 1914: *The Coming of the First World War.* ° *Volume3 of the Journal of Contemporary History* TB/1306

C. A. MACARTNEY, Ed.: The Habsburg and Hohenzollern Dynasties in the Seventeenth and Eighteenth Centuries # HR/1400

JOHN MCMANNERS: European History, 1789-1914: *Men, Machines and Freedom* TB/1419

PAUL MANTOUX: The Industrial Revolution in the Eighteenth Century: *An Outline of the Beginnings of the Modern Factory System in England* TB/1079

FRANK E. MANUEL: The Prophets of Paris: *Turgot, Condorcet, Saint-Simon, Fourier, and Comte* TB/1218

KINGSLEY MARTIN: French Liberal Thought in the Eighteenth Century: *A Study of Political Ideas from Bayle to Condorcet* TB/1114

NAPOLEON III: Napoleonic Ideas: *Des Idées Napoléoniennes, par le Prince Napoléon-Louis Bonaparte. Ed. by Brison D. Gooch* ¶ TB/1336

FRANZ NEUMANN: Behemoth: *The Structure and Practice of National Socialism, 1933-1944* TB/1289

DAVID OGG: Europe of the Ancien Régime, 1715-1783 ° *a* TB/1271

GEORGE RUDE: Revolutionary Europe, 1783-1815 ° *a* TB/1272

MASSIMO SALVADORI, Ed.: Modern Socialism # TB/1374

HUGH SETON-WATSON: Eastern Europe Between the Wars, 1918-1941 TB/1330

DENIS MACK SMITH, Ed.: The Making of Italy, 1796-1870 # HR/1356

ALBERT SOREL: Europe Under the Old Regime. *Translated by Francis H. Herrick* TB/1121

ROLAND N. STROMBERG, Ed.: Realism, Naturalism, and Symbolism: *Modes of Thought and Expression in Europe, 1848-1914* # HR/1355

A. J. P. TAYLOR: From Napoleon to Lenin: *Historical Essays* ° TB/1268

A. J. P. TAYLOR: The Habsburg Monarchy, 1809-1918: *A History of the Austrian Empire and Austria-Hungary* ° TB/1187

J. M. THOMPSON: European History, 1494-1789 TB/1431

DAVID THOMSON, Ed.: France: Empire and Republic, 1850-1940 # HR/1387

ALEXIS DE TOCQUEVILLE & GUSTAVE DE BEAUMONT: Tocqueville and Beaumont on Social Reform. *Ed. and trans. with Intro. by Seymour Drescher* TB/1343

G. M. TREVELYAN: British History in the Nineteenth Century and After: 1792-1919 ° TB/1251

H. R. TREVOR-ROPER: Historical Essays TB/1269

W. WARREN WAGAR, Ed.: Science, Faith, and MAN: *European Thought Since 1914* # HR/1362

MACK WALKER, Ed.: Metternich's Europe, 1813-1848 # HR/1361

ELIZABETH WISKEMANN: Europe of the Dictators, 1919-1945 ° *a* TB/1273

JOHN B. WOLF: France: 1814-1919: *The Rise of a Liberal-Democratic Society* TB/3019

Literature & Literary Criticism

JACQUES BARZUN: The House of Intellect TB/1051

W. J. BATE: From Classic to Romantic: *Premises of Taste in Eighteenth Century England*
TB/1036
VAN WYCK BROOKS: Van Wyck Brooks: The Early Years: *A Selection from his Works, 1908-1921 Ed. with Intro. by Claire Sprague*
TB/3082
ERNST R. CURTIUS: European Literature and the Latin Middle Ages. *Trans. by Willard Trask*
TB/2015
RICHMOND LATTIMORE, Translator: The Odyssey of Homer
TB/1389
JOHN STUART MILL: On Bentham and Coleridge. *Introduction by F. R. Leavis*
TB/1070
SAMUEL PEPYS: The Diary of Samual Pepys. ° *Edited by O. F. Morshead. 60 illus. by Ernest Shepard*
TB/1007
ROBERT PREYER, Ed.: Victorian Literature **
TB/1302
ALBION W. TOURGEE: A Fool's Errand: *A Novel of the South during Reconstruction. Intro. by George Fredrickson*
TB/3074
BASIL WILEY: Nineteenth Century Studies: *Coleridge to Matthew Arnold* °
TB/1261
RAYMOND WILLIAMS: Culture and Society, 1780-1950 °
TB/1252

Philosophy

HENRI BERGSON: Time and Free Will: *An Essay on the Immediate Data of Consciousness* °
TB/1021
LUDWIG BINSWANGER: Being-in-the-World: *Selected Papers. Trans. with Intro. by Jacob Needleman*
TB/1365
H. J. BLACKHAM: Six Existentialist Thinkers: *Kierkegaard, Nietzsche, Jaspers, Marcel, Heidegger, Sartre* °
TB/1002
J. M. BOCHENSKI: The Methods of Contemporary Thought. *Trans. by Peter Caws* TB/1377
CRANE BRINTON: Nietzsche. *Preface, Bibliography, and Epilogue by the Author* TB/1197
ERNST CASSIRER: Rousseau, Kant and Goethe. *Intro. by Peter Gay* TB/1092
FREDERICK COPLESTON, S. J.: Medieval Philosophy
TB/376
F. M. CORNFORD: From Religion to Philosophy: *A Study in the Origins of Western Speculation* §
TB/20
WILFRID DESAN: The Tragic Finale: *An Essay on the Philosophy of Jean-Paul Sartre* TB/1030
MARVIN FARBER: The Aims of Phenomenology: *The Motives, Methods, and Impact of Husserl's Thought*
TB/1291
MARVIN FARBER: Basic Issues of Philosophy: *Experience, Reality, and Human Values*
TB/1344
MARVIN FARBER: Phenomenology and Existence: *Towards a Philosophy within Nature* TB/1295
PAUL FRIEDLANDER: Plato: *An Introduction*
TB/2017
MICHAEL GELVEN: A Commentary on Heidegger's "Being and Time" TB/1464
J. GLENN GRAY: Hegel and Greek Thought
TB/1409
W. K. C. GUTHRIE: The Greek Philosophers: *From Thales to Aristotle* ° TB/1008
G. W. F. HEGEL: On Art, Religion Philosophy: *Introductory Lectures to the Realm of Absolute Spirit. || Edited with an Introduction by J. Glenn Gray* TB/1463
G. W. F. HEGEL: Phenomenology of Mind. ° || *Introduction by George Lichtheim* TB/1303
MARTIN HEIDEGGER: Discourse on Thinking. *Translated with a Preface by John M. Anderson and E. Hans Freund. Introduction by John M. Anderson* TB/1459

F. H. HEINEMANN: Existentialism and the Modern Predicament TB/28
WERER HEISENBERG: Physics and Philosophy: *The Revolution in Modern Science. Intro. by F. S. C. Northrop* TB/549
EDMUND HUSSERL: Phenomenology and the Crisis of Philosophy. § *Translated with an Introduction by Quentin Lauer* TB/1170
IMMANUEL KANT: Groundwork of the Metaphysic of Morals. *Translated and Analyzed by H. J. Paton* TB/1159
IMMANUEL KANT: Lectures on Ethics. § *Introduction by Lewis White Beck* TB/105
WALTER KAUFMANN, Ed.: Religion From Tolstoy to Camus: *Basic Writings on Religious Truth and Morals* TB/123
QUENTIN LAUER: Phenomenology: *Its Genesis and Prospect. Preface by Aron Gurwitsch*
TB/1169
MAURICE MANDELBAUM: The Problem of Historical Knowledge: *An Answer to Relativism*
TB/1338
GEORGE A. MORGAN: What Nietzsche Means
TB/1198
H. J. PATON: The Categorical Imperative: *A Study in Kant's Moral Philosophy* TB/1325
MICHAEL POLANYI: Personal Knowledge: *Towards a Post-Critical Philosophy* TB/1158
KARL R. POPPER: Conjectures and Refutations: *The Growth of Scientific Knowledge* TB/1376
WILLARD VAN ORMAN QUINE: Elementary Logic *Revised Edition* TB/577
WILLARD VAN ORMAN QUINE: From a Logical Point of View: *Logico-Philosophical Essays*
TB/566
JOHN E. SMITH: Themes in American Philosophy: *Purpose, Experience and Community*
TB/1466
MORTON WHITE: Foundations of Historical Knowledge TB/1440
WILHELM WINDELBAND: A History of Philosophy *Vol. I: Greek, Roman, Medieval* TB/38
Vol. II: Renaissance, Enlightenment, Modern
TB/39
LUDWIG WITTGENSTEIN: The Blue and Brown Books ° TB/1211
LUDWIG WITTGENSTEIN: Notebooks, 1914-1916
TB/1441

Political Science & Government

C. E. BLACK: The Dynamics of Modernization: *A Study in Comparative History* TB/1321
KENNETH E. BOULDING: Conflict and Defense: *A General Theory of Action* TB/3024
DENIS W. BROGAN: Politics in America. *New Introduction by the Author* TB/1469
CRANE BRINTON: English Political Thought in the Nineteenth Century TB/1071
ROBERT CONQUEST: Power and Policy in the USSR: *The Study of Soviet Dynastics* °
TB/1307
ROBERT A. DAHL & CHARLES E. LINDBLOM: Politics, Economics, and Welfare: *Planning and Politico-Economic Systems Resolved into Basic Social Processes* TB/1277
HANS KOHN: Political Ideologies of the 20th Century TB/1277
ROY C. MACRIDIS, Ed.: Political Parties: *Contemporary Trends and Ideas* ** TB/1322
ROBERT GREEN MC CLOSKEY: American Conservatism in the Age of Enterprise, 1865-1910
TB/1137
MARSILIUS OF PADUA: The Defender of Peace. *The Defensor Pacis. Translated with an Introduction by Alan Gewirth* TB/1310
KINGSLEY MARTIN: French Liberal Thought in the Eighteenth Century: *A Study of Political Ideas from Bayle to Condorcet* TB/1114

7

Religion: Early Christianity Through Reformation

ANSELM OF CANTERBURY: Truth, Freedom, and Evil: *Three Philosophical Dialogues. Edited and Translated by Jasper Hopkins and Herbert Richardson* TB/317

MARSHALL W. BALDWIN, Ed.: Christianity through the 13th Century # HR/1468

W. D. DAVIES: Paul and Rabbinic Judaism: *Some Rabbinic Elements in Pauline Theology. Revised Edition* ° TB/146

ADOLF DEISSMAN: Paul: *A Study in Social and Religious History* TB/15

JOHANNES ECKHART: Meister Eckhart: *A Modern Translation by R. Blakney* TB/8

EDGAR J. GOODSPEED: A Life of Jesus TB/1

ROBERT M. GRANT: Gnosticism and Early Christianity TB/136

WILLIAM HALLER: The Rise of Puritanism TB/22

GERHART B. LADNER: The Idea of Reform: *Its Impact on the Christian Thought and Action in the Age of the Fathers* TB/149

ARTHUR DARBY NOCK: Early Gentile Christianity and Its Hellenistic Background TB/111

ARTHUR DARBY NOCK: St. Paul ° TR/104

ORIGEN: On First Principles. *Edited by G. W. Butterworth. Introduction by Henri de Lubac* TB/311

GORDON RUPP: Luther's Progress to the Diet of Worms ° TB/120

Religion: The Protestant Tradition

KARL BARTH: Church Dogmatics: *A Selection. Intro. by H. Gollwitzer. Ed. by G. W. Bromiley* TB/95

KARL BARTH: Dogmatics in Outline TB/56

KARL BARTH: The Word of God and the Word of Man TB/13

HERBERT BRAUN, et al.: God and Christ: *Existence and Province. Volume 5 of Journal for Theology and the Church, edited by Robert W. Funk and Gerhard Ebeling* TB/255

WHITNEY R. CROSS: The Burned-Over District: *The Social and Intellectual History of Enthusiastic Religion in Western New York, 1800-1850* TB/1242

NELS F. S. FERRE: Swedish Contributions to Modern Theology. *New Chapter by William A. Johnson* TB/147

WILLIAM R. HUTCHISON, Ed.: American Protestant Thought: *The Liberal Era* ‡ TB/1385

ERNST KASEMANN, et al.: Distinctive Protestant and Catholic Themes Reconsidered. *Volume 3 of Journal for Theology and the Church, edited by Robert W. Funk and Gerhard Ebeling* TB/253

SOREN KIERKEGAARD: On Authority and Revelation: *The Book on Adler, or a Cycle of Ethico-Religious Essays. Introduction by F. Sontag* TB/139

SOREN KIERKEGAARD: Crisis in the Life of an Actress, *and Other Essays on Drama. Translated with an Introduction by Stephen Crites* TB/145

SOREN KIERKEGAARD: Edifying Discourses. *Edited with an Intro. by Paul Holmer* TB/32

SOREN KIERKEGAARD: The Journals of Kierkegaard. ° *Edited with an Intro. by Alexander Dru* TB/52

SOREN KIERKEGAARD: The Point of View for My Work as an Author: *A Report to History. § Preface by Benjamin Nelson* TB/88

SOREN KIERKEGAARD: The Present Age. § *Translated and edited by Alexander Dru. Introduction by Walter Kaufmann* TB/94

SOREN KIERKEGAARD: Purity of Heart. *Trans. by Douglas Steere* TB/4

SOREN KIERKEGAARD: Repetition: *An Essay in Experimental Psychology* § TB/117

SOREN KIERKEGAARD: Works of Love: *Some Christian Reflections in the Form of Discourses* TB/122

WILLIAM G. MCLOUGHLIN, Ed.: The American Evangelicals: 1800-1900: *An Anthology* TB/1382

WOLFHART PANNENBERG, et al.: History and Hermeneutic. *Volume 4 of Journal for Theology and the Church, edited by Robert W. Funk and Gerhard Ebeling* TB/254

JAMES M. ROBINSON, et al.: The Bultmann School of Biblical Interpretation: New Directions? *Volume 1 of Journal for Theology and the Church, edited by Robert W. Funk and Gerhard Ebeling* TB/251

F. SCHLEIERMACHER: The Christian Faith. *Introduction by Richard R. Niebuhr.*
Vol. I TB/108; Vol. II TB/109

F. SCHLEIERMACHER: On Religion: *Speeches to Its Cultured Despisers. Intro. by Rudolf Otto* TB/36

TIMOTHY L. SMITH: Revivalism and Social Reform: *American Protestantism on the Eve of the Civil War* TB/1229

PAUL TILLICH: Dynamics of Faith TB/42

PAUL TILLICH: Morality and Beyond TB/142

EVELYN UNDERHILL: Worship TB/10

Religion: The Roman & Eastern Christian Traditions

A. ROBERT CAPONIGRI, Ed.: Modern Catholic Thinkers II: *The Church and the Political Order* TB/307

G. P. FEDOTOV: The Russian Religious Mind: *Kievan Christianity, the tenth to the thirteenth Centuries* TB/370

GABRIEL MARCEL: Being and Having: *An Existential Diary. Introduction by James Collins* TB/310

GABRIEL MARCEL: Homo Viator: *Introduction to a Metaphysic of Hope* TB/397

Religion: Oriental Religions

TOR ANDRAE: Mohammed: *The Man and His Faith* § TB/62

EDWARD CONZE: Buddhism: *Its Essence and Development.* ° *Foreword by Arthur Waley* TB/58

EDWARD CONZE: Buddhist Meditation TB/1442

EDWARD CONZE et al, Editors: Buddhist Texts through the Ages TB/113

ANANDA COOMARASWAMY: Buddha and the Gospel of Buddhism TB/119

H. G. CREEL: Confucius and the Chinese Way TB/63

FRANKLIN EDGERTON, Trans. & Ed.: The Bhagavad Gita TB/115

SWAMI NIKHILANANDA, Trans. & Ed.: The Upanishads TB/114

D. T. SUZUKI: On Indian Mahayana Buddhism. ° *Ed. with Intro. by Edward Conze.* TB/1403

Religion: Philosophy, Culture, and Society

NICOLAS BERDYAEV: The Destiny of Man TB/61

RUDOLF BULTMANN: History and Eschatology: *The Presence of Eternity* ° TB/91

RUDOLF BULTMANN AND FIVE CRITICS: Kerygma and Myth: *A Theological Debate* TB/80

RUDOLF BULTMANN and KARL KUNDSIN: Form Criticism: *Two Essays on New Testament Research. Trans. by F. C. Grant* TB/96

WILLIAM A. CLEBSCH & CHARLES R. JAEKLE: Pastoral Care in Historical Perspective: *An Essay with Exhibits* TB/148

FREDERICK FERRE: Language, Logic and God. *New Preface by the Author* TB/1407

LUDWIG FEUERBACH: The Essence of Christianity. § *Introduction by Karl Barth. Foreword by H. Richard Niebuhr* TB/11

C. C. GILLISPIE: Genesis and Geology: *The Decades before Darwin* § TB/51

ADOLF HARNACK: What Is Christianity? § *Introduction by Rudolf Bultmann* TB/17

KYLE HASELDEN: The Racial Problem in Christian Perspective TB/116

MARTIN HEIDEGGER: Discourse on Thinking. *Translated with a Preface by John M. Anderson and E. Hans Freund. Introduction by John M. Anderson* TB/1459

IMMANUEL KANT: Religion Within the Limits of Reason Alone. § *Introduction by Theodore M. Greene and John Silber* TB/FG

WALTER KAUFMANN, Ed.: Religion from Tolstoy to Camus: *Basic Writings on Religious Truth and Morals. Enlarged Edition* TB/123

JOHN MACQUARRIE: An Existentialist Theology: *A Comparison of Heidegger and Bultmann. ° Foreword by Rudolf Bultmann* TB/125

H. RICHARD NIERUHR: Christ and Culture TB/3

H. RICHARD NIEBUHR: The Kingdom of God in America TB/49

ANDERS NYGREN: Agape and Eros. *Translated by Philip S. Watson* ° TB/1430

JOHN H. RANDALL, JR.: The Meaning of Religion for Man. *Revised with New Intro. by the Author* TB/1379

WALTER RAUSCHENBUSCHS Christianity and the Social Crisis. ‡ *Edited by Robert D. Cross* TB/3059

JOACHIM WACH: Understanding and Believing. *Ed. with Intro. by Joseph M. Kitagawa* TB/1399

Science and Mathematics

JOHN TYLER BONNER: The Ideas of Biology. Σ *Illus.* TB/570

W. E. LE GROS CLARK: The Antecedents of Man: *An Introduction to the Evolution of the Primates.* ° *Illus.* TB/559

ROBERT E. COKER: Streams, Lakes, Ponds. *Illus.* TB/586

ROBERT E. COKER: This Great and Wide Sea: *An Introduction to Oceanography and Marine Biology. Illus.* TB/551

W. H. DOWDESWELL: Animal Ecology. *61 illus.* TB/543

C. V. DURELL: Readable Relativity. *Foreword by Freeman J. Dyson* TB/530

GEORGE GAMOW: Biography of Physics. Σ *Illus.* TB/567

F. K. HARE: The Restless Atmosphere TB/560

S. KORNER: The Philosophy of Mathematics: *An Introduction* TB/547

J. R. PIERCE: Symbols, Signals and Noise: *The Nature and Process of Communication* Σ TB/574

WILLARD VAN ORMAN QUINE: Mathematical Logic TB/558

Science: History

MARIE BOAS: The Scientific Renaissance, 1450-1630 ° TB/583

W. DAMPIER, Ed.: Readings in the Literature of Science. *Illus.* TB/512

STEPHEN TOULMIN & JUNE GOODFIELD: The Architecture of Matter: *The Physics, Chemistry and Physiology of Matter, Both Animate and Inanimate, as it has Evolved since the Beginnings of Science* TB/584

STEPHEN TOULMIN & JUNE GOODFIELD: The Discovery of Time TB/585

STEPHEN TOULMIN & JUNE GOODFIELD: The Fabric of the Heavens: *The Development of Astronomy and Dynamics* TB/579

Science: Philosophy

J. M. BOCHENSKI: The Methods of Contemporary Thought. *Tr. by Peter Caws* TB/1377

J. BRONOWSKI: Science and Human Values. *Revised and Enlarged. Illus.* TB/505

WERNER HEISENBERG: Physics and Philosophy: *The Revolution in Modern Science. Introduction by F. S. C. Northrop* TB/549

KARL R. POPPER: Conjectures and Refutations: *The Growth of Scientific Knowledge* TB/1376

KARL R. POPPER: The Logic of Scientific Discovery TB/576

STEPHEN TOULMIN: Foresight and Understanding: *An Enquiry into the Aims of Science. Foreword by Jacques Barzun* TB/564

STEPHEN TOULMIN: The Philosophy of Science: *An Introduction* TB/513

Sociology and Anthropology

REINHARD BENDIX: Work and Authority in Industry: *Ideologies of Management in the Course of Industrialization* TB/3035

BERNARD BERELSON, Ed., The Behavioral Sciences Today TB/1127

JOSEPH B. CASAGRANDE, Ed.: In the Company of Man: *Twenty Portraits of Anthropological Informants. Illus.* TB/3047

KENNETH B. CLARK: Dark Ghetto: *Dilemmas of Social Power. Foreword by Gunnar Myrdal* TB/1317

KENNETH CLARK & JEANNETTE HOPKINS: A Relevant War Against Poverty: *A Study of Community Action Programs and Observable Social Change* TB/1480

W. E. LE GROS CLARK: The Antecedents of Man: *An Introduction to the Evolution of the Primates.* ° *Illus.* TB/559

LEWIS COSER, Ed.: Political Sociology TB/1293

ROSE L. COSER, Ed.: Life Cycle and Achievement in America ** TB/1434

ALLISON DAVIS & JOHN DOLLARD: Children of Bondage: *The Personality Development of Negro Youth in the Urban South* ‖ TB/3049

ST. CLAIR DRAKE & HORACE R. CAYTON: Black Metropolis: *A Study of Negro Life in a Northern City. Introduction by Everett C. Hughes. Tables, maps, charts, and graphs* Vol. I TB/1086; Vol. II TB/1087

PETER E. DRUCKER: The New Society: *The Anatomy of Industrial Order* TB/1082

CORA DU BOIS: The People of Alor. *With a Preface by the Author* Vol. I *Illus.* TB/1042; Vol. II TB/1043

EMILE DURKHEIM et al.: Essays on Sociology and Philosophy: *with Appraisals of Durkheim's Life and Thought.* ‖ *Edited by Kurt H. Wolff* TB/1151

LEON FESTINGER, HENRY W. RIECKEN, STANLEY SCHACHTER: When Prophecy Fails: *A Social and Psychological Study of a Modern Group that Predicted the Destruction of the World* ‖ TB/1132

11